I have known Mark for 35 years. He writes out of his personal journey and integrity. "365 Days to Sexual Integrity" is the perfect help for those who travel the path of restoration. This book will love you where you really are. It speaks real truth with real love in real time. It genuinely offers the way out of any ditch. It is the love and life of God. Read it! Share it! Live it!

Rick Ousley
Pastor, GracePoint Church
Birmingham, Alabama

I have made these daily devotions a part of my personal recovery program. They are brief, to the point, practical, and motivational. They start my day on a positive note and are a great addition to my daily recovery.

Ray Thomas
Sarasota, Florida

Every person needs to know they are not alone in their struggle. Mark's latest work brings light to the darkness and illuminates the path to freedom.

Roger Patterson
Pastor, West University Baptist Church
West University, Texas

365 Days

to

Sexual Integrity

Mark Denison, D.Min.

365 Days to Sexual Integrity

Mark Denison D.Min.

Published by Austin Brothers Publishing

Fort Worth, Texas

www.abpbooks.com

ISBN 978-1-7324846-4-1

Copyright © 2019 by Mark Denison

ALL RIGHTS RESERVED: *No part of this book may be reproduced in any form without permission in writing from the publisher, except in the case of brief quotations embodied in critical reviews or articles.*

Printed in the United States of America

2019—First Edition

Praise for *365 Days to Sexual Integrity*

I have known Mark for over 30 years, and I value the insights in this volume. Interesting, insightful, informative, and inspiring. Mark's words bring hope and healing.

Dennis Sims
Pastor, Ellerbe Baptist Church, Shreveport, Louisiana

These daily devotions are uniquely inspiring. They integrate recovery and Christianity. These are not just recovery platitudes; they speak to me in a deep visceral way as a man in recovery and as a Christian seeking to further my walk with Christ.

Gary Johnson
Psychotherapist, Oakland, California

These daily readings have been a key ingredient to my personal recovery. The big difference for me is that Mark is not writing from theory, but from personal experience, and that makes ALL the difference!

Ray Sloan
Brisbane, Queensland (Australia)

"365 Days to Sexual Integrity" may be the most practical devotional a person can read. Each message brings livable solutions to the devastating problem of sexual brokenness. This is not a devotional. It is a do-votional!

Gary Pate
Trial Lawyer and Ordained Minister, Houston, Texas

This is the final piece to the puzzle of my personal recovery and freedom. I read it every day. I highly recommend "365 Days to Sexual Integrity."

Steven Adams
New York City, New York

I begin each day with "365 Days to Sexual Integrity." These readings equip me to remain pure and stay out of the pit. They are the perfect dose of spiritual energy early in the day to set me on the right track as I face the world.

Andrew Wells
Windsor, Ontario (Canada)

"365 Days to Sexual Integrity" is filled with the practical application of sexual sobriety and the life of integrity. Each day will have a better start if you take the time to read and reflect on these devotions as a part of your personal journey.

Kathie Magness
Houston, Texas

"There's Still Hope" has been a part of my daily recovery from the start. Mark's latest book gives me daily insight and hope. I now have faith that I can spend the rest of my life sober and living for the Lord.

Joel Hendricks
Sacramento, California

I dedicate this book to my spiritual fathers.

Dr. Cecil Sewell

*You preach with the mind of Spurgeon
and you love with the heart of Christ.
I am blessed to call you "Pastor."*

Dr. Gene Wofford

*You are the finest professor I know.
But it is what you taught me outside the
classroom that changed my life.*

Contents

FORWARD.. 1

INTRODUCTION... 3

365 DEVOTIONS.. 5

BIBLICAL REFERENCES.. 371

ABOUT THE AUTHOR... 385

ABOUT "THERE'S STILL HOPE"............................. 387

ADDITIONAL RESOURCES.................................... 388

FORWARD

Sexual brokenness is the plague that is costing more marriages, destroying more churches, and attacking more pastors than any other disease in modern times. Meanwhile, at a time when the majority of its men are watching porn, the church remains largely silent – to its own detriment.

Fortunately, God is raising up ministries to address the pandemic of sex and porn addiction. Our ministry, *There's Still Hope*, is at the forefront of this movement. But in addition to practical help, personal coaching, and customized recovery plans, *There's Still Hope* is now offering something rarely found – a daily devotional book for those who suffer from the grip of sexually compulsive behaviors, their spouses, and church leaders.

365 Days to Sexual Integrity is the culmination of the daily *Recovery Minute* devotion that is sent out across America and throughout the world. To sign up for the *Recovery Minute*, simply go to the ministry website at TheresStillHope.org.

INTRODUCTION

The porn industry is now a $12 billion annual business in the United States (NBC News). Porn sites receive more traffic than Netflix, Amazon, and Twitter combined (HuffPost). Forty million Americans view porn sites every day (CBN). Sixty-two percent of evangelical men view pornography at least once a month (Proven Men Ministries). Ninety-five percent of Christian men have viewed porn (Barna). Over 50 percent of church staffs struggle with cybersex (Covenant Eyes). Fifty-four percent of pastors have viewed porn in the last year (Pastors.com). Thirty-seven percent of pastors admit to an ongoing struggle with porn (Christianity Today).

America, we have a problem.
Church, we have a problem.
Pastor, *you have a problem*.

Sadly, the silent response in most churches is deafening. Very few church leaders have a plan in place to address this growing problem. They have few resources to turn to. *365 Days to Sexual Integrity* is such a resource.

This book is the next natural progression of the ministry of *There's Still Hope*. When this addiction recovery ministry was launched in early 2018, a daily devotional became a key component of the ministry. This is a collection of some of those devotionals.

365 Days to Sexual Integrity is one source of recovery. But let's be clear – it is not the only source. And if you suffer from porn or sex addiction, while this is a great start, it will not be enough.

At *There's Still Hope*, we offer a variety of tools for your recovery. Some of these include the following . . .

    One-day couples intensives
    Customized 90-day recovery plans
    Spouse recovery coaching
    Spouse recovery groups
    Recovery maintenance programs
    40-days to porn free living
    Church and school assemblies

We hope you enjoy *365 Days to Sexual Integrity*. More than that, we hope you will pass this on to someone you know who really suffers from the clutch of pornography or sexual addiction.

Notice I keep using that word "hope." That's because we believe in hope. As long as you really want it, there is *hope* for your recovery, *hope* for your marriage, and *hope* for your family. Have you fallen into the depths of sexual behaviors you never imagined possible? I've been there. That's why I can say with certainty – no matter how far you've fallen or how bad it hurts – *There's Still Hope*.

Now, let's get after it. You can experience real hope, real freedom, and real recovery. That journey can begin today . . . and continue tomorrow. Commit just a few minutes each morning to the battle of your life. It is a battle you can – and must win.

It's all here – *365 Days to Sexual Integrity*.

365 DEVOTIONS

It Takes a Team
January 1

Congratulations on your commitment to personal purity! There are two truths you must embrace early on: community and transparency.

Dietrich Bonhoeffer wrote, in *Life Together*, "The final obstacle to true Christian fellowship is the inability to be sinners together."

We must learn to be together, but togetherness is not enough. Sobriety is dependent on connecting with saints who know they are sinners. Then we must become comfortable with being sinners together.

It is impossible to overstate the need for a transparent community in recovery. Alex Lerza, clinical psychologist and Certified Sex Addiction Therapist, says it like this: "The opposite of addiction is not sobriety, but relationship."

The secret sauce for the early church was their interconnectedness. "They devoted themselves to the apostles' teaching and the fellowship" (Acts 2:42). Most churches are big on teaching but weak on fellowship. We need both.

Recovery Step: Find a group with whom you can connect at the deepest levels of life. How will you know you have found the right group? They are comfortable with being sinners together.

So What's Wrong with Porn?
January 2

Josh McDowell says, "Porn presents the greatest threat to the cause of Christ in the history of the world."

So what's wrong with porn? Let me cite just four things.

First, porn rewires the brain. Dr. Norman Doidge of Columbia University explains that "porn creates the perfect conditions and then triggers the release of the right chemicals to making lasting changes in your brain."

Second, porn escalates. Today's "high" will not be enough for tomorrow. Porn leads to fantasy that leads to doing things you never imagined. And it happens fast.

Third, porn drives the user into isolation. It turns sex into a false reality and produces false intimacy, shame, and regret.

Fourth, porn destroys relationships. It drives a wedge between the user and his spouse, his God, and himself. Porn is a drug that destroys lives, marriages, and families.

Paul was kind enough to warn the church, "Put to death therefore what is earthly in you: sexual immorality, impurity, passion, and evil desires" (Colossians 3:5).

Recovery Step: Do you struggle with porn? Every instance of viewing porn makes your fight for purity just a little bit harder. Ask God for the strength to end it today – right now.

Recovery Cycle
January 3

In his groundbreaking work, *Out of the Shadows*, Dr. Patrick Carnes identified the now famous addiction cycle. The four phases of addiction are fantasy, ritual, acting out, and shame. For those active in their addiction, this becomes a predictable, repetitive roller coaster ride from which there appears to be no escape.

But there is an escape. Dr. Mark Laaser has offered a Christian perspective. He has created what he calls the "recovery cycle." It too has four phases: vision, healthy decisions, healthy behavior, and joy.

One of the great leaders in Israel's history was Samuel. Early in life, he discovered the process of growth. "The boy Samuel continued to grow in stature and in favor with the Lord and with people" (1 Samuel 2:26).

Like Samuel, you are growing. You are either growing in your addiction, or you are growing in your recovery.

Comedian Tim Allen calls sobriety "God's greatest gift." But it is a gift that is not unwrapped in a single setting. Sobriety is a growth process that can begin – today.

Recovery Step: Which cycle are you on: addiction or recovery? Get off the crazy train and embrace the gift of sobriety – one day and one choice at a time.

Fantasy
January 4

What we think today is what we do tomorrow. And what we do tomorrow is what we become the next day. It all starts in the head. One of the biggest mistakes people make early in their recovery is to minimize their thought lives.

A leading instrument of relapse is sexual fantasy. An interesting study found that for those in therapy, they spend 42 times more time on their phone apps and social media than in their actual therapy. This, of course, opens the mind to all kinds of intrusive thoughts.

What's so bad about fantasy? We find one answer from Israeli psychologist Dr. Gurit E. Birnbaum. In an article posted in the *Personality and Social Psychology Bulletin*, Birnbaum shares her work. She conducted a case study of 48 married couples. She discovered the reason we fantasize. "Sexual fantasy is a way to avoid intimacy."

Paul spoke to this danger with clarity. "Clothe yourself with the presence of the Lord Jesus Christ. And don't let yourself think about ways to indulge evil desires" (Romans 13:14).

Recovery Step: You have two choices: fantasy or intimacy. And God's word is so clear. The better route for each of us is that we not even *"think about ways to indulge evil desires."* You can have fantasy or you can have intimacy. But you can't have both. Choose wisely.

Titanic Survivor's Tragic Death
January 5

On April 10, 1912, the Titanic left Southampton on her maiden voyage. Five days later the unsinkable did the unthinkable – the Titanic hit an iceberg and sank. A total of 1,503 lives were lost; 705 survived. Let's talk about one of those survivors.

The wealthiest passengers had secured first class tickets. They were given first access to the lifeboats when the ship began to go down. One such family was the Speddens. Frederic and Daisy occupied cabin E-40, along with their only son, six-year-old Douglass, as well as his personal nanny.

Douglass was one of the few children in first class; most of the other 200 children perished in the icy waters. Douglass was a child of privilege. But good fortune yielded to tragedy just three years later. On August 6, 1915, Douglass was killed in the first fatal automobile accident in Maine, near the family's vacation home.

Like Douglass, you may be a survivor. But victory today is no guarantee of survival tomorrow.

Paul told the church, "Even if you think you can stand up to temptation, be careful, lest you fall" (1 Corinthians 10:12, CEV).

On the night of his election as Chicago's first black mayor, Harold Washington told his supporters, "Let's not be overconfident; we still have to count the votes." You may be on the road to early recovery. But not all the votes have yet been counted. Stay in the battle to the very end.

Recovery Step: Don't be overconfident. Thank God for yesterday's victories and today's sobriety. But stay humble and hungry – because tomorrow is another day.

#1 Cause of Relapse
January 6

The Promises Treatment Center has identified seven leading signs of a relapse on sobriety. Topping the list is this – let up on new habits.

There is no silver bullet for recovery. It is all about doing the work, day in and day out.

There's an old joke about the farmer who was struggling to produce a good crop. He prayed, and God wrote two letters across the sky: "PC." The man assumed God was saying, "Preach Christ," so he built a pulpit at his farm and began preaching to all who came his way. When his crop continued to fail, he sought God again. He said, "I preached Christ! What more do you want me to do?" God replied, "By 'PC,' I didn't mean to 'Preach Christ.' I was telling you to 'Plant corn.'"

The man closest to Jesus wrote, "Watch out that you do not lose what you have worked so hard to achieve. Be diligent so you may receive your full reward" (2 John 8).

In one week, I had two friends who both lost their sobriety after three years. They both had one thing in common – they let up on their daily disciplines.

Recovery is hard work, day in and day out. It's about establishing new habits, and then sticking to the plan every day for the rest of your life.

Recovery Step: To maintain sobriety, you must do two things: establish new habits, then stick to the plan.

Green Apples
January 7

Playwright Alice Chapin wrote, "How could I possibly be the apple of God's eye when my behavior is not yet perfect? Because green apples are apples, too. One day I shall be a mature September apple, perfectly formed. But for now, I am still growing."

God's love transcends man's shortcomings. He promises, "I have loved you with an everlasting love; therefore, I have continued my faithfulness to you" (Jeremiah 31:3).

One of the keys to recovery is patience. God is at work in us, whether we see it or not. And he works on his terms and in his timing.

Phillips Brooks, the famous New England pastor of the late 1800s, was once spotted pacing the floor like a caged animal. A friend asked him what was wrong. Brooks responded, "The trouble is I'm in a hurry, but God is not!"

Step four talks about character defects. We all have them, but God is still at work. And if we are faithful to our work, God will be faithful to his. Change will come – if we are patient.

Recovery Step: You are the apple of God's eye, whether you are ripe yet or not. Trust in God's unfinished work in your life, not because you are good, but because he is.

God's Favor
January 8

Mark Twain said, "Heaven goes by favor. If it went by merit, you would stay out, and your dog would get in."

The bridge from addiction to recovery is God's favor. We can't get there any other way. If you don't believe me, find someone with long-term sobriety, and ask them how they did it. They will tell you *they* didn't do it; *God* did it.

This is the promise of Scripture: "By grace, you have been saved through faith. And this is not your own doing; it is the gift of God" (Ephesians 2:8).

When we start taking credit for our recovery, it begins to slip away.

When I was in college, my dear friend was the son of the head of a large oil company. Many times, I was invited to the man's house for dinner or to just hang out. And what a house it was! But not one time did the man call me up and say, "Mark, come on over for dinner." No, I made it into his house for just one reason – I had a relationship with his son.

God wants you to experience the blessings of his kingdom – including lasting sobriety. But there's a price for admission. You must first find favor with the king. And you only do that by having a relationship with his Son.

Recovery Step: Commit yourself to Jesus Christ. This is the key that unlocks the door to God's favor. And in that favor, you can be made well.

Lucky
January 9

I heard about a newspaper advertisement. It read, "Lost – one dog. Very little hair on his body. Right leg broken in auto accident. Bad left hip. Walks with a limp. Right eye missing. Left ear bitten off by another dog. Answers to the name 'Lucky.'"

One of the most common things we say to one another is, "Good luck." I like the way British politician Lain Duncan Smith said it. "Luck is great, but most of life is hard work."

Seneca was right when he said, "Luck is preparation meeting opportunity."

The dog in our story is a lot like us. Crippled by years of our disease, we walk with a limp, but we must keep walking. We can't always see straight, but we keep looking forward.

If your disease has not landed you in jail, consider yourself lucky. If you haven't contracted an STD, you're one of the lucky ones. But luck can only take you so far. At some point, to really be well, you've got to do the hard work.

Solomon said, "All hard work brings a profit, but mere talk leads only to poverty" (Proverbs 14:23).

Recovery Step: Maybe your addiction has not cost you your marriage, job, or health. Consider yourself lucky. But it is only when you put in the work of real recovery that you can call yourself well.

Chaos
January 10

All progress requires change. But what does change look like? Virginia Satir has written about change. In *The Satir Model: Family Therapy and Beyond*, she states the six stages of change: status quo, new information, chaos, new integration, practice, and new status quo.

Let's talk about that third stage – chaos.

Solomon looked at the complexities of life and concluded, "It doesn't make sense" (Ecclesiastes 1:19).

By nature, we run from chaos. We see it as the antithesis of normality. We pray for peace, tranquility, and calm. But we are praying to the God who is often the one behind the chaos in the first place.

We pray for sun and get rain. We pray for smooth and get rough. We pray for healing and get sick. We pray for easy and get hard. We pray for a life free of conflict, pain, and confusion. And what do we get? We get chaos. There's that word again.

So what's the deal? It's really quite simple. Virginia Satir has it right. It is out of chaos that we finally seek change. And only when we change do we get sober.

Recovery Step: Thank God for the chaos. It is his way of setting the table for a feast you can't imagine.

The Best Sermon
January 11

Orel Hershiser was having a bad day. The All-Star pitcher was laboring on the mound when his manager, Tommy Lasorda, left the dugout for a brief visit. Lasorda got in Hershiser's face and proceeded to tell him what he could become as a pitcher. "You're a winner!" Lasorda said. After the manager returned to the dugout, Hershiser struck out the side.

The pitcher looks back on that as a turning point in his career. He credits Lasorda for what he calls the "Sermon on the Mound."

We all need to hear a good sermon from time to time. But the best sermon is not preached in the pulpit as often as it is in the office, on the golf course, or in the mirror.

Yes – in the mirror.

Jerry Bridges, author of *The Pursuit of Happiness,* wisely wrote, "Preach to yourself daily."

The prophet declared, "The righteousness of the righteous shall be upon himself" (Ezekiel 18:20). In other words, we must own our recovery. And we must be our own best encourager.

We all need to hear an encouraging "Sermon on the Mound." If you know someone who is down, visit their mound. But in the meantime, be your own congregation. Remind yourself daily: you're still in the game, God is on your team, and your team will eventually win.

Recovery Step: Be encouraged today, if not by someone else, then by yourself.

Accepting Responsibility
January 12

On an airplane one day, I had forgotten to put my tray table up in the "upright and locked position." When the flight attendant gave me "the look," I immediately put it up. Then I wondered why putting the tray table up really mattered. I mean, I have yet to hear about the man who survived the plane crash because his tray table was up.

I've never understood the need to know where the exits are at 30,000 feet. Or how to use the seat cushion as a flotation device when flying over Nebraska.

But what do I know? I must trust the experts in the field. If the plane goes down and my tray table is in the wrong position, or I miss the exit, or I don't have my seat firmly in hand, the rest is on me. As my mom once said when I was climbing a tree at the age of five, "If you fall out of that tree and break your leg, don't come running to me!"

When our lives crash, we must take responsibility for the damages. One of the biggest hindrances of progress for those of us who struggle with habitual sexual sin is an unwillingness to accept responsibility for our actions. Recovery is hard work, and we are responsible for our own work.

Paul said it like this: "Pay careful attention to your own work" (Galatians 6:4).

Recovery Step: You have issues. That's a fact. Own it. If your life crashes, you will be responsible for the damages.

Lesson from Jimmy Connors
January 13

We cannot get well until we get real. We must admit we have a problem. That is the first step of the 12 steps and the foundation of all recovery.

Say it with me. "I have a problem."

I read an anonymous quote that I have committed to memory. "I would rather go through life sober, believing that I am an alcoholic, than go through life drunk, trying to convince myself that I am not."

You will never know how good things can be until you admit how bad things already are. Your addiction, relapse, and failures can become the launching pad of your success.

Legendary tennis player Jimmy Connors said, "Treat relapse not as a failure, but as a challenge."

Admit your problem to God. Then get ready for the ride of your life. "The God of all grace, who called you to his eternal glory in Christ, after you have suffered a little while, will himself restore you and make you strong, firm, and steadfast" (1 Peter 5:10).

Recovery Step: Suffering comes before restoration. So accept your past. That is the only way to claim a better future.

That's What Friends Are For
January 14

In 1985, Dionne Warwick recorded one of her most popular songs, *That's What Friends Are For.* The closing lines are:

"Keep smiling, keep shining
Knowing you can always count on me, for sure
Cause I tell you, that's what friends are for
Whoa, good times and the bad times
I'll be on your side forever more
That's what friends are for."

Your real friends stick with you, not because you are good but because you are bad. Pick your friends carefully. Why? Because after you make friends, they will make you.

The Bible warns, "Walk with the wise and become wise; associate with fools and get in trouble" (Proverbs 13:20).

Surround yourself, in recovery and in life, with people who will love you on your worst day. For each of us, there are times when we cannot take the next step on our own. And that's okay, because . . . *That's what friends are for.*

Recovery Step: Ask God to bring two or three people into your life with whom you can share your deepest valleys and darkest moments. After all, *that's what friends are for.*

Righteous Pleasures
January 15

God wants to bless you. Really bless you. Now – not just later, in heaven. It's what Blake Williams of Pure Life Alliance calls "righteous pleasures." He says God wants us to enjoy pleasures in this life for three reasons: because he loves us, as a picture of heaven, and to simply give us a break from the difficulties of life.

Jesus would seem to agree. He said, in the Sermon on the Mount, "If you, though you are evil, know how to give good gifts to your children, how much more will your Father in heaven give good gifts to those who ask him!" (Matthew 7:11).

At the risk of sounding like a ladies talk show host, be good to yourself!

Dr. Melanie Greenberg writes, "The biggest struggle in life is the struggle to know, embrace, and accept ourselves, with all of our faults and imperfections."

Yes, you have faults. Of course, you have imperfections. But God loves you as much as if you were perfect. And he wants you to love yourself, too! So do something good for yourself today. Enjoy a few "righteous pleasures."

Recovery Step: Do one thing to bless yourself today. Then, tomorrow, do it again.

Issachar
January 16

Before King David had become king, he surrounded himself with a band of faithful fighting men. Among the group were 200 men from the tribe of Issachar, who met up with David at Hebron. What made these men special? Just one thing. A single verse in the Bible says it all: "They understood the times and they knew what to do" (1 Chronicles 12:32).

With the development of the Internet and the explosion of social media, we live in difficult times with unique challenges in our battle for sexual purity. Our hope is twofold.

We must understand the times and know what to do.

This isn't the 1950s. Gone are the days when porn was hidden away in a closet and could only be purchased over the counter at a place where "decent" people would not go. Gone are the days when everyone went to church, society abhorred the objectification of young women, and living together before marriage was an outrage. Not anymore.

We must understand the times and know what to do.

Today's world calls for Covenant Eyes, real accountability, total transparency, and a willingness to live counter to modern culture.

We must understand the times and know what to do.

Recovery Step: We live in a new age. You don't need to go looking for trouble; it will find you. So be on guard. Be prepared. You must understand the times and know what to do.

More than a Group
January 17

Licensed Mental Health Counselor and noted conference speaker Dr. Jay Stringer has conducted some interesting research on the subject of porn and sex addiction. He has found, among other things, that attending support group/accountability meetings – if not coupled with other recovery activities – yields limited results. Of those who "diligently seek" such a group, 67 percent see no reduction in their porn habit. Only 22 percent see a "significant" change.

The tenth chapter of Ezra paints a painful picture of the moral collapse of God's people. Among their sins were sexual relationships that occurred outside of God's bounds (10:1-2). But then a man named Shekaniah spoke up, offering the words that have become the name of our ministry: "There's still hope" (Ezra 10:2). Now the people had something to celebrate.

But they weren't out of the woods yet. They had gathered together, worshiped together, and prayed together. But recovery required more than a group. Note what came next – a command from God.

"Rise up, for the matter is in your hands" (Ezra 10:4).

God was saying, "It's time to break the huddle and keep the promises you have made, staking out a whole new future." That's the key! To break bad habits, we need to break out of our holy huddles and start doing the things we know to do.

Recovery Step: Rise up. Put your recovery plan in motion. It's time to go to work!

For the Love of Money
January 18

There's an old saying that describes the spending habits of most Americans. We spend money we don't have on things we don't need to impress people we don't like.

In the movie *Wall Street*, Gordon Gekko, played by Michael Douglas, spoke for so many of us. "What's worth doing is worth doing for money."

Americans have a convoluted view of the relationship between money and happiness. As a nation, we owe $793 billion in credit card debt, have only $400 per family in savings, but still spend $70 billion on the lottery.

The time and money spent on porn is even more alarming. Every second, there are 28,000 viewers spending a total of $3,000 on Internet porn. The average American viewed 221 pages of Internet porn in 2015, and porn is an $11 billion industry.

And it gets worse every year because porn – like money – never satisfies. Just ask the man who had the most money – and women – in the world. Solomon said, "Whoever loves money never has enough" (Ecclesiastes 5:10).

It's time to get off the crazy train. Quit chasing money and the things money can buy – because it never satisfies. As we say in 12-step meetings, "There is One who has all power – that One is God. May you find Him now!"

Recovery Step: Money does not satisfy. Porn only makes a bad situation worse. But there is One who has all power. There is One who can satisfy. Seek him and find him now.

Why God Allows Temptation
January 19

J.I. Packer wrote the classic book, *Knowing God*. On the subject of personal hardships in the Christian's life, Packer states, "God exposes us to these things, so as to overwhelm us with a sense of our own inadequacy, and to drive us to cling to him more closely. This is the ultimate reason, from our standpoint, why God fills our lives with troubles and perplexities of one sort or another – it is to ensure that we shall learn to hold him fast."

One of those perplexities is the temptations that keep coming, despite endless moments of remorse, repentance, and recommitments.

You are promised, "No temptation has overtaken you except what is common to mankind. And God is faithful; he will not let you be tempted beyond what you can bear. But when you are tempted, he will also provide a way out so that you can endure it" (1 Corinthians 10:13).

When you face temptation, you have two choices. You can (a) give in, or (b) look up. In our addictions, we need to learn to look up. We must see temptation as a test. Each time we pass the test, we gain new strength for the next time.

Today, when you are tempted, follow Packer's advice. Let that temptation "drive you to cling to him more closely . . . learn to hold him fast."

Recovery Step: When temptation comes, know that you always have a way out.

Prison
January 20

Gary Smalley told the following story, in *Freedom Begins Here.* "A woman wept as she told her story: 'I had sex the first time when I was 14. It felt wonderful and awful at the same time. For some reason, I couldn't get enough, and by the time I was in college, I was roaming bars for pickups. I had sex with two or three men a night. Most of the time, I didn't even know their names. It is the only life I've known since I was a little girl. It feels like a prison, and I can't find a way to escape.'"

Sex inside God's boundaries is a beautiful gift. But outside of God's boundaries, sex takes captive all who dabble. What begins as a curious glance on the Internet escalates to an addiction. Soon, it lands us in the prison of our own soul and throws away the key.

But there is hope. There is always hope. King David knew a little about the prison of sexual pleasures gone astray. He said, "Out of my distress I called on the Lord; the Lord answered me and set me free" (Psalm 118:5).

You may find yourself in real trouble today. For you, sex has become an obsession. You are locked behind the bars of your private cell. But there is hope – if you call on the Lord.

Recovery Step: If you are bound by an addiction to porn, masturbation, or some other form of sexual activity, don't despair. Turn to God today and he can set you free.

Established
January 21

D.L. Moody, famed 19th-century evangelist, told the story of a man who was asked by his young son why he didn't go to church. His dad explained, "I don't need to go to church, son. My faith is established." Later that day, the man drove his horses out of the barn and hitched them to the buggy. As they drove them out of the yard, the horses became mired in a mud hole. The boy said, "Daddy, I don't think the horses are going anywhere. They are established."

"Established" is just another word for "stuck." And that's what happens to our spiritual development when we abandon the fellowship of the local church – we get stuck.

The Bible warns us, "Don't neglect your fellowship together, as has become the habit of some" (Hebrews 10:25).

Recovery is all about breaking old habits and learning new ones. Dr. Susan McQuillan, noted psychologist, says, "We keep doing the wrong thing because it is impossible to unlearn a bad habit on our own."

Recovery never happens in isolation. In fact, it is isolation that gets us in trouble in the first place. You need others along the journey. And you need to be in church. Otherwise, your recovery will stall out. You will become stuck.

Recovery Step: Are you stuck in your recovery? Chances are, you are trying to go it alone. You need others. You need the church. Start this Sunday. Otherwise, get used to the ditch, because your recovery probably isn't going anywhere.

Resentment
January 22

Recovery is incomplete until we deal with our resentments.

In *Wishful Thinking*, Pastor Frederick Buechner wrote about the effects of bitterness on a man harboring resentment. "Of the seven deadly sins, anger is the most fun. To lick your wounds, to smack your lips over grievances long past, to savor to the last morsel both the pain you are given and the pain you are giving back – in many ways is a feast fit for a king. The only drawback is that what you are wolfing down is yourself. The skeleton at the feast is you!"

Jesus was clear. "Whenever you stand praying, forgive, if you have anything against anyone, so that your Father also who is in heaven may forgive you your trespasses" (Mark 11:25).

Against whom do you harbor resentments? Your parents? A pastor? Your spouse? Maybe even God? Regardless of how justified you think you are in your resentments, you must let them go. They are only killing you. And they make a full recovery impossible.

The good news is, forgiveness is actually easier than resentment. M.L. Stedman explains. In her 2012 novel, *The Light Between Oceans*, Stedman writes, "You only have to forgive once. To resent, you have to do it all day, every day."

It's up to you. You can forgive once or resent all day, every day – whichever you think makes the most sense.

Recovery Step: Think of one person against whom you are holding resentment today. Then release them to God by forgiving them for what they have done to you. You will discover that by releasing them, you are really releasing yourself.

Lucy and Ethel
January 23

In life – and recovery – we need friends. Perhaps no television show ever depicted a strong friendship quite like the one between Lucy and Ethel on *I Love Lucy*. In one episode, we discover the essence of friendship.

Ethel: "You always drag me into your crazy schemes!"
Lucy: "Well, this is one time I can do without you."
Ethel: "What's wrong with me all of a sudden?"
Lucy: "Well, alright, Ethel, you can come along if you want to."
Ethel: "No, I don't want to. I just wanted you to ask me."

King David had an unusually close bond with his friend Jonathan. So close was their relationship that the Scriptures tell us that at Jonathan's funeral, David lamented, "I am distressed for you, my brother Jonathan" (2 Samuel 1:26).

Ethel didn't need to be with Lucy all the time. She just needed to be asked. Who have you asked to do life with? You cannot win the victory over temptation, addiction, and isolation alone. As David needed Jonathan and Lucy needed Ethel, you need someone in your life – for encouragement, strength, and accountability.

Recovery Step: Don't try to navigate the road to recovery on your own. You need the encouragement, strength, and accountability of another person.

The Meaning of Surrender
January 24

Oscar Wilde wrote, "Everything in the world is about sex except sex. Sex is about power."

Research confirms this thesis. Sex is about power. And addicts can never get enough. Many of us can identify with the line in *Top Gun*. We have an incredible "need for speed."

This speed comes in many forms – with sex at the top of the list. Like those who struggle with substances, impulse control disorders, or behavioral addictions, sexual addicts find themselves with ever-growing passions and ever-diminishing satisfaction.

This is what makes recovery so hard for so many. We want sobriety, but we also want power. We want to be in control. But we can't have both. Recovery is absolutely rooted in surrender.

How do we find victory? James offers clear insight. "Submit yourselves therefore to God. Resist the devil, and he will flee from you" (James 4:7).

Oswald Chambers was right: "If you have only come as far as asking God for things, you have never come to understand the meaning of surrender."

Recovery Step: Sex is power. But recovery comes by surrender to a greater power. It is done one day at a time. If you are tired of being in control and falling short, surrender to God. Today.

Purpose
January 25

"Why am I here?"

That is the yearning of every heart – to find God's purpose. Rick Warren correctly asserted, in *The Purpose Driven Life,* "Living on purpose is the only way to really live. Everything else is just existing."

But there is no universal agreement on what that purpose is.

That great theologian John Lennon wrote an iconic song, *Imagine*, in which he offered his view on the purpose of life. "You may say I'm a dreamer, but I'm not the only one. I hope someday you'll join us and the world will be as one."

Solomon had a different take. "The end of the matter is this: Fear God and keep his commandments, for this is the whole duty of man. For God will bring every deed into judgment, with every secret thing, whether good or evil" (Ecclesiastes 12:13-14).

Did you catch what Solomon said? God will bring every secret thing to light. That is why we need to "fear God and keep his commandments."

You can exist, or you can really live. To choose life is to choose God. And by choosing God, you choose recovery.

Recovery Step: God's purpose is this – that you fear him and keep his commandments. The fear of God is where the road to recovery begins.

Off the Cliff
January 26

John Bevere has produced the best YouTube video on addiction recovery I have seen. Look it up. It's called *The Cliff Killing Kryptonite*. In the video, a blind man is slowly walking toward a cliff and an inevitable death. His only hope is two men who see him. They debate whether they should risk offending the man by telling him how to walk or to "love" him with only words of affirmation. At the end, they decide to "love" him – as he disappears off the edge.

James admonishes his readers, "My brothers and sisters, if one of you should wander from the truth and someone should bring that person back, remember this: whoever turns a sinner from the error of their way will save them from death and cover over a multitude of sins" (James 5:19-20).

We all know people who are headed over the edge. And God has strategically placed us in their way. Their hope is us. Let me say that again – *their hope is us*.

Who do you know who is struggling with addiction? More importantly, what are you doing about it?

When you help others, you help yourself. So ask God to lead you to the person you can lead to him.

Recovery Step: Help someone who is struggling today. In the process, you will help yourself.

The Wrong Source
January 27

Years ago, a bearded man dressed in a robe showed up outside a church service in Chapel Hill, North Carolina. He claimed to have the power to heal people suffering from any disease. For hours, he tried to convince the church that he possessed these healing powers. Then someone challenged him: "The hospital is just down the street. Let's go there so we can watch you heal all the patients."

The man led the procession to the hospital, and they rode elevators to the cancer floor. With dramatic effect, the man pronounced healing over all the patients. But none of them was healed.

We read in Scripture, "Behold, I will bring to them health and healing, and I will heal them and reveal to them abundance of prosperity and security" (Jeremiah 33:6).

Step 2 of the 12 Steps says, "We came to believe that a Power greater than ourselves could restore us to sanity."

We all need healing because we are all sick. But we must go to the Primary Care Physician who has never lost a case.

Recovery Step: If you struggle with compulsive behaviors, you need help. And you can find that help – in God as your Higher Power.

The Real Thing
January 28

One day, Charlie Brown lamented, "Someday, we will all die." Snoopy replied, "True, but on all the other days, we will not."

If you are among the readers who are alive today, you need to define what it means to really live. Let me help you with that one. To live is to love others – *really love others*.

The Bible says it like this: "Don't just pretend to love others. Really love them" (Romans 12:9).

The problem is that rather than loving people, we use people. And usually, we don't even see it – especially in our addiction.

St. Augustine described the love we are to express for one another. "What does love look like? It has the hands to help others. It has the feet to hasten to the poor and needy. It has eyes to see misery and want. It has the ears to hear the sighs and sorrows of men. That is what love looks like."

Indeed, love "has the eyes to see misery and want." So look around. What will you find? Someone who is hurting, addicted, and alone. Your job is not to judge them nor condemn them. Your assignment is to love them . . . period.

Recovery Step: Augustine was right. Love has the hands to help others. So get after it. As God brings someone in need into your life, love them. *Really love them*.

The Great Disconnect
January 29

Founder of Authentic Intimacy, Dr. Juli Slattery wrote, "Sex outside of marriage is doing with our bodies what we aren't doing with our lives."

Paul warned, "Flee from sexual immorality. Every other sin a person commits is outside the body, but the sexually immoral person sins against his own body" (1 Corinthians 6:18).

Such counsel is not popular in modern American culture. According to Waiting Till Marriage, Inc., only three percent of Americans wait until marriage to have sex. Among the highly religious that number climbs as high as 20 percent.

So why is sexual activity so prevalent outside of marriage? Why are we so willing to do with our bodies (intimacy) what we aren't doing with our lives?

It's simple. We want instant gratification.

Divya Srivastava wrote an article, "The Psychology of Bad Decision Making." Srivastava asserts, "According to research, impulsive people dislike waiting, so they choose instantaneous rewards. People able to delay gratification do so because they imagine a future with better rewards."

If you are not married, you can follow your impulses. Or you can "imagine a future with better rewards."

Recovery Step: Flee sexual immorality. Look to the rewards that come with waiting for God's perfect plan.

Brave Heart
January 30

In the closing scene of *Braveheart*, William Wallace was being tortured and executed for leading a rebellion against the evil English king. Even at the moment of his greatest pain, he still longed for his countrymen to experience something he was giving his life for – freedom.

With freedom comes tension. The apostle wrote, "For you have been called to live in freedom, my brothers and sisters. But don't use your freedom to satisfy your sinful nature. Instead, use your freedom to serve one another" (Galatians 5:13).

Let's talk about it. Thucydides said, "The secret to happiness is freedom, and the secret to freedom is courage."

Indeed, it takes courage to use freedom wisely.

You are free to make bad decisions. You are free to satisfy your sinful nature whenever and however you want. But anyone can do that. You are better than that. Do what you know is right. Have the courage to do what *is* right instead of what *feels* right.

Recovery Step: God has set you free through faith in Christ. You can now go in one of two directions. You can use your freedom to satisfy your sinful nature, or you can use your freedom to serve others. One road is easy. The other is paved with courage. The next move is yours.

Build It Up or Tear It Down
January 31

Pastor and humorist Charles Lowry is a trained psychologist. Speaking on the subject of sex addiction, he writes, "We either build up the fantasy and tear down reality or we build up reality and tear down the fantasy."

The real definition of sexual sobriety is progressive victory over lust. And lust begins in the mind.

The Bible has a lot to say about the mind. It warns us against impure thoughts. "Finally, brothers, whatever is true, whatever is honorable, whatever is just, whatever is pure, whatever is lovely, whatever is commendable, if there is any excellence, if there is anything worthy of praise, think about these things" (Philippians 4:8).

Fantasy is a huge problem. But there is an answer. The way to rid our minds of impure thoughts is to fill them with pure thoughts. That's how we tear down the fantasy and build up reality.

Buddha was right: "We are shaped by our thoughts; we become what we think." I'm guessing you want to win the battle for purity. It begins in the mind. It begins with your next thought – and then the one after that.

Recovery Step: A pure life follows a pure mind. So starting today, fill your mind with those thoughts that are holy and pure.

How Does God See Me?
February 1

Russian author Maxim Gorky said, "A good man can be stupid and still be good."

As addicts, we often struggle to find a strong sense of personal worth. In our acting out, it's easy to just say, "I do bad things because I'm a bad person."

But how does God see us?

When he created man – the most selfish, conniving, and, to use Gorky's word, stupid – of all his creation, he paused, and then knowing every sin we would ever commit and every addiction we would ever embrace . . . he said, "This is very good" (Genesis 1:31). Not just good, but *"very good."*

All of us have wandered from God's intended pastures and perfect plan. But he still sees us, whether in the middle of life's fairway where we live life best, or in the rough, or even out of bounds. And wherever he finds us, his opinion of his finest work has not changed. "Very good." Sometimes stupid, too often reckless and self-centered, but still *"very good."*

Even in the midst of our addiction, we must never forget that there is nothing we can ever do that will make God love us more, and there is nothing we can ever do that will make him love us less.

Recovery Step: Repeat these words: "There is nothing I can ever do that will make God love me more, and there is nothing I can ever do that will make him love me less."

Breaking Free
February 2

A mailman with a new route came to a house with a mean-looking dog on the porch. When he approached the mailbox, the dog jumped 20 feet in the air, and then sat down. The owner walked out to check on the commotion.

The mailman asked in amazement, "Why did your dog do that?"

The owner replied, "We removed his chain yesterday, but he doesn't realize it."

Like many of us, the dog was living in the past. He assumed that yesterday's chains still had him bound today. The mailman triggered his reaction. He jumped and barked, but acted like he was still chained to his past.

Freedom from your addiction is a daily choice. Yesterday's chains do not bind you today; only today's choices can do that. Like the dog, you will be triggered sometime today. That is not a choice. But how you respond is a choice.

The Bible tells the story of a man bound by chains. When he was set free, for the first time in his life he was found "in his right mind" (Mark 5:15).

Sobriety does that. It puts us in our right minds. But we can only be set free by our Higher Power, Jesus Christ. Trust him to set you free. Then live in freedom, and reject the chains of the past.

Recovery Step: Pray for power to overcome your triggers today. Then claim the freedom God promises those who truly seek Him.

Desperation
February 3

Hippocrates said, "Desperate times call for desperate measures." The man seemed to understand addiction. Desperation is the birthplace of recovery. You will never find lasting, sustainable recovery without it. You have to want recovery more than anything else.

I can't think of a more desperate situation in the Bible than that of Lazarus. The man was dying, so his sisters came to Jesus and pled for him to heal their brother. Jesus responded, "This sickness will not end in death" (John 11:4). And then, two days later, Lazarus died.

So what gives?

Notice what Jesus *did not say*. He didn't say Lazarus wouldn't die. He said the sickness would not *end in death*.

Think about it. If Jesus had healed Lazarus before he died, he would have just been another nameless guy in the Bible. What made Lazarus famous was not his healing, but his resurrection.

God is the master of the resurrection. Think about your own recovery. Your addiction may have killed your marriage, your job, your finances, and your self-esteem. But God's promise is that it won't end there. God always gets the final word.

Addiction brings death. But in death, we find resurrection and recovery. When we rely fully on him, we discover that, as with Lazarus, "this sickness will not end in death."

Recovery Step: Become desperate for recovery as you've never been desperate for anything else in your life.

Deciding is Not Enough
February 4

Five frogs sat on a log. Three decided to jump off. How many remained on the log? Answer: five. Here's the thing. *Deciding* to do something and *actually doing it* aren't the same thing.

A million times, I decided to stop acting out in my addiction. But I didn't really stop. Why? Because decision and action are two different things.

James warned his readers, "Be doers of the Word, and not hearers only, deceiving yourselves" (James 1:22).

Addiction is all about deception. We deceive ourselves into thinking we can stop anytime, that we are really in control, that we don't need God's help. And when we decide to stop our destructive routines, we think that this decision will be enough.

Decisions are not enough. They must be followed by action.

Zig Ziglar said, "It was character that got us out of bed, commitment that moved us into action, and discipline that enabled us to follow through."

Every addict needs that discipline. Decide to be sober and in recovery. Then do something about it. Follow through: go to meetings, pray, get a sponsor, seek God daily.

Are you ready for real recovery? Then get off the log. It's time to jump!

Recovery Step: Do today what you said you would do yesterday.

Getting Honest
February 5

Americans lie – a lot. *USA Today* recently cited statistics from a book, *The Day America Told the Truth*. They reported that 91 percent of Americans lie routinely. Specifically, 36 percent tell "big lies," 86 percent lie to their parents, 75 percent to their friends, 73 percent to their siblings, and 69 percent to their spouse.

What are we lying about? Eighty-one percent lie about their feelings, 43 percent about their income, and 40 percent lie about sex.

Solomon said, "The Lord hates a lying tongue" (Proverbs 6:17).

Guess who else hates "a lying tongue"? Your wife or husband. Recovery taught me something that decades of marriage never did. My wife values honesty more than anything. That's why it was so important for me to give full disclosure of my past, accompanied with a polygraph – not just once, but several times.

William Shakespeare wrote, "Honesty is the best policy. If I lose my honor, I lose myself." One of the first things you must do to get sober is to get honest – with yourself, your spouse, and your God. Until you get completely honest, you will lose your sobriety. Worse yet, you will lose yourself.

Recovery Step: Decide right now – no more lies. Get completely honest, with yourself, your family, and your God. Start with today. Commit to 24 hours of sobriety – and honesty.

Grieving the Loss
February 6

I have a sign hanging on my wall that reads, "Your mountain is waiting, so get on your way." That is the message every addict and spouse need to hear. Yesterday's crisis opens the door to tomorrow's blessing. But we have to walk through that door.

At the age of 137, Abraham lost his beloved wife, "and Abraham went to mourn and to weep over her" (Genesis 23:2). Death brought grief. But it didn't end there. The response of Abraham is a parable for the addict and his spouse. Your addiction has killed your self-esteem, integrity, and perhaps marriage. But the story doesn't have to end there. The process of recovery can now begin.

First, there is death. When Sarah died, part of Abraham died with her. When you were discovered, it was like death. For many of us, our addiction was our closest companion.

Second, there is mourning. Abraham wept and mourned. The addict must mourn his addiction. The transition toward sobriety is one of turmoil and uncertainty . . . and a lot of pain.

Third, there must be a burial. Burying his wife was so important to Abraham that he paid 400 pieces of silver for a burial plot. The burial represents the addict's sobriety date. To get well, he must mark the final time and place he acted out.

Fourth, we must move on. Abraham lived another 38 years after Sarah's death. He even remarried. For the addict to get well, he must move on from his past. Indeed, your mountain is waiting, so get on your way.

Recovery Step: Accept the death of your past, take time to mourn, set a date for a new beginning – then move forward.

A Dog's Life
February 7

Heaven will be full of Westies. I know this because heaven is a perfect place and my Westie is the perfect dog. But Heidi has this slightly annoying habit. On our daily walks, she sometimes throws up. And then, on our way back home, she'll sniff her own vomit and lick it up – unless I intercede on her behalf. I must do for her what she cannot do for herself.

The Bible describes addicts that way. When we return to our habit, we are like the dog who returns to its vomit (2 Peter 2:22).

I have no good explanation for why a dog returns to its vomit. Nor does my dog understand why I returned to my addiction – over and over – for 30 years.

My Westie and I share a lot in common. If left to our own natural desires, we do dumb, destructive things. Our only hope is for our Higher Power to do for us what we cannot do for ourselves.

Pastor Chuck Smith says simply, "Where God guides, God provides." When you are tempted to *act out*, there is always a *way out*. Make a call. Say a prayer. Turn to God – over and over. He never tires of hearing your cries for help.

Recovery Step: Walk close enough to your Master today that you can feel his gentle tug when he needs to pull you away from returning to the insanity of your addiction.

The 4-Letter Word of Recovery
February 8

There is a four-letter word for recovery. *Rest*. It is not an option. It's in the Ten Commandments. "You have six days in your week to work, but the seventh day is a day of rest" (Exodus 20:9).

Why is rest important to our recovery? Because it offers a break from stress, and stress triggers addiction. There's an old acronym in recovery we call "H.A.L.T." We tend to act out when we are *hungry, angry, lonely,* or *tired.*

The National Sleep Foundation says we need seven to nine hours of sleep every day. The National Institute for Occupational Safety and Health has found 12 benefits to a day of rest. The first is that it reduces stress. And nothing triggers addiction like stress.

I suggest you go a step further. Some of the best advice my sponsor ever gave me was to have a Recovery Day every month or so. A Recovery Day is a day of rest. It includes solitude, reading recovery material, meditation, and prayer.

William Wadsworth wrote, "Rest and be thankful." Embrace rest. It's God's four-letter word for recovery. Every seven days you need a day of rest. Your recovery depends on it.

Recovery Step: Plan a day of rest this week. And plan a Recovery Day this month. Mark both dates on your calendar and make them a priority.

Winning the Gold
February 9

On this day in 2018, the Winter Olympics began, hosted by South Korea. For the next 17 days, the city of PyeongChang and surrounding areas played host to the world's greatest athletes, representing 90 countries and competing in 102 different events.

The United States sent 240 athletes to compete. Among them was Shani Davis, the 35-year-old speed skater from Chicago, who is the first black skater to win gold. Winner of 13 medals from the past three Winter Games, Davis reveals the key to his enduring success with one word – "discipline."

Recovery is not a single event. And past success is no guarantee of future sobriety. We must keep competing – every day. Davis was successful at the Winter Games, in full sight of millions of viewers, because he has been hard at work when no one is watching.

It's what you do when no one is watching that will keep you sober for today. Using the athletic metaphor, Paul told young Timothy, "Athletes cannot win the prize unless they follow the rules" (2 Timothy 2:5). There is no shortcut to success. There are exercises to be done and rules to be followed. In recovery, we must follow certain rules and maintain a regimen of disciplined activities. Recovery does not come easily, nor does it come quickly. But it does come if we work at it.

Recovery Step: Make a commitment today to the daily disciplines that will keep you sober.

Your Hidden Weapon
February 10

When we are discovered, we are overwhelmed with shame. Shame (not God) defines us by our addiction. It renders us emotionally impotent. It tells us we are not worthy of God's favor or blessings.

One day, Jonathan, the son of King Saul, unknowingly violated an edict of his father. Thinking deprivation would secure God's favor, Saul had ordered his army to abstain from food for a day.

This left them in a weakened state. "But Jonathan had not heard his father's command" (1 Samuel 14:27). Then he ate some honeycomb and was "refreshed." Others noticed the difference it made in his life.

One of the keys in recovery is to understand our addiction has not diminished God's desire to bless us. John Calvin said, "God has put before us a table at which to feast, not an altar on which to die." Yes, work on recovery. But be good to yourself along the way.

I have found several ways to be good to myself: a scoop of ice cream, a walk on the beach, a scoop of ice cream, time on the water in my kayak, or a scoop of ice cream. The fact that you are in recovery says a lot about your integrity and values. It is easy for you to be hard on yourself. But it is better to be good to yourself.

Recovery Step: Do something good for yourself today.

Knocking on a Brothel's Door
February 11

G.K. Chesterton said, "Every man who knocks on the door of a brothel is looking for God."

The biochemical model of addiction tells us why competent, intelligent people can easily be sidetracked by their pursuit of sex. Dr. Michael Herkov writes, "Studies indicate that food, abused drugs, and sexual interests share a common pathway within our brains' survival and reward systems. This pathway leads into the area of the brain responsible for our rational thoughts and judgment."

Dr. Robert Weiss, the founder of The Sexual Recovery Institute, says, "What sex addiction is really about is an intimacy disorder."

In other words, there is something deeper than sex that drives the addict to his bottom line behaviors. That is why the addiction is referred to as "cunning and baffling" in sex addiction literature.

So what is the answer? For the addict, his addiction is not just a bad problem. It's a bad solution. He is knocking on the wrong door, searching for a God he may not even know exists. And the whole time, God is seeking him. That's where surrender comes into play. The addict's intimacy vacuum can only be filled by God.

Hear God's voice. "Here I am! I stand at the door and knock. If anyone hears my voice and opens the door, I will come in and eat with that person, and he with me" (Revelation 3:20).

Recovery Step: Quit knocking on doors and answer the door to your heart. God is waiting for a relationship with you. Let Him in.

The Untold Price We Pay
February 12

The Bible tells the story of a man named Amnon who fell in love with Tamar, his half-sister (2 Samuel 13). Here we find the progressive nature of addiction. What Amnon took in with his eyes became lust. Lust led to fantasy, which resulted in acting out.

Then we discover the final chapter in every episode of acting out. Amnon's brief moment of ecstasy was followed by an overwhelming sense of shame. What happened in Amnon's life is the story of every addict. He wanted what he shouldn't have and didn't want it once he had it.

Immediately after he committed his sin, "Suddenly Amnon's love turned to hate, and he hated her even more than he had loved her" (13:15). Amnon became a permanent wreck. Amnon discovered a hard truth: the one thing more painful than not feeding our lust is feeding our lust.

The next time you fantasize about crossing the boundaries God has put in place, pause just long enough to play out the end of the story in your head. It never ends well.

When you do cross those lines, even if just in your head, keep the words of Watchman Nee close by. "Now is the hour we should humbly prostrate ourselves before God, willing to be convinced afresh of our sins by the Holy Spirit."

Recovery Step: When you are drawn toward lust in your heart, remind yourself how the story always ends.

It Only Takes an Hour
February 13

I recently heard about a pastor who, in five minutes, lost his entire reputation. It doesn't take long. Saul, the first king of Israel, is a perfect example. Though a mighty warrior and strong leader, he lost it all – in one hour.

Israel was at war with the Philistines. Things looked bleak. "Saul stayed at Gilgal, and his men were trembling with fear" (1 Samuel 13:7). Samuel had instructed the king to wait until he arrived, and then he would make a burnt offering to the Lord. But after seven days, Saul grew impatient. His anxiety overtook his better judgment, so he made the offering himself, in violation of the law and Samuel's commands. When he arrived, Samuel told Saul that his sin would have consequences. "Your kingdom must end" (13:13).

If Saul had waited another hour, he would have kept his kingdom. But like many of us, he lost it all – in order to control things himself – for just one hour.

When the urge to act out hits, know that this will pass. It always does. When the urge hits, only focus on the next hour. Pray. Make a call. Read Scripture. Take a walk. If you can make it for an hour, you can make it!

You make your decisions, then your decisions make you. Be alert. Be on guard. All the recovery you have built up over the past several months or years can come crashing down – in less than an hour.

Recovery Step: Be alert, and have a game plan already in place for the next time a wave of temptation comes against you.

Love
February 14

Today is Valentine's Day – the day of love. Love is a key to recovery. We must embrace God's love for us, while we express that same perfect love toward others, such as our spouse, children, and friends. But we must also learn to love ourselves.

Jesus was asked to name the greatest command. He said, "You must love the Lord your God" (Matthew 22:37). Then he added, "A second is equally important: 'Love your neighbor as yourself'" (22:39).

With these two commands, Jesus narrowed the 600-plus Jewish laws emanating from the Law of Moses. A better two-point summary of the Twelve Steps cannot be found: Love God, love others.

But notice something else. Jesus said to love others "as you love yourself." In recovery, we must connect with God and with others, but also with ourselves. The best way you can love yourself is to stay sober.

Rob Lowe said, "Sobriety was the greatest gift I ever gave myself." Love yourself enough today to give yourself the gift of sobriety. To maintain sobriety, we must work as though it all depends on us, then pray as though it all depends on God. Partner with him to maintain sobriety. Today, love God. Love others. But don't forget to love yourself.

Recovery Step: Love yourself enough today to do the things that maintain sobriety for the next 24 hours.

Realignment
February 15

Charlie Brown commented on what it meant to have a good day. "I know it's going to be a good day when all the wheels on my shopping cart turn the same way."

If ever there was a time when our lives needed to be in alignment, it is in our personal recovery. That means having all our wheels headed in the same direction – therapy, meetings, prayer, working the steps, calling our sponsor, surrender, honesty. If we try to maintain sobriety with even one of the wheels out of alignment, we will live a life of constant frustration.

The good news is the road to recovery is well-lit. "The Lord says, 'I will guide you along the best pathway for your life'" (Psalm 32:8). God is committed to your personal recovery.

Martin Luther King, Jr., said, "Faith is taking the first step, even when you don't see the whole staircase."

When I got into recovery, I didn't see the whole staircase. But I always saw the next step. And that is enough.

Recovery Step: Be proactive. Do the things that keep your cart headed in the right direction. Follow God's plan for your life – one day at a time.

Father Damien
February 16

Tourists visit the Hawaiian Island of Molokai to enjoy the beaches and charm. But Father Damien came for a different reason. He came to help people die. You see, lepers came here first, starting in about 1840. They lived in isolation, on a tract of land set aside just for them.

When Father Damien heard of their plight, he begged with his supervisors to let him move to Molokai, to live with the lepers. The year was 1873. Damien said, "I want to sacrifice myself for the lepers."

Damien entered the world of the lepers. He dressed their sores, hugged their children, and buried their dead. Eventually, he would contract their disease. On April 15, 1889, Father Damien died of leprosy.

Father Damien did for the Molokai lepers what Jesus did for each of us. Not content to simply "treat" man, Jesus became a man. He joined the human race. The Bible says, "It was necessary for him to be made in every respect like us so that he could be our merciful and faithful High Priest before God" (Hebrews 2:17).

You can overcome every temptation because of what Jesus has done. Not content to look down on us from above, he has joined us. You are not alone. Because he became man, Christ knows exactly what you are going through, and he will walk with you every step of the way.

Recovery Step: Recognize that you are not alone. Embrace the one who understands every temptation you will ever face – because he's been there. In fact, he still is.

Celebrate Success!
February 17

Early in recovery, it is natural for an addict to look around the room in a 12-step meeting and conclude, "There are guys here with years of sobriety! I have so far to go!"

We need to celebrate early success in our recovery. In the Old Testament, we read about the determination that led the Israelites to rebuild the Temple, their sacred place of worship. "When the builders completed the foundation of the Lord's Temple, they clashed their cymbals to praise the Lord, just as King David had prescribed" (Ezra 3:10).

Did you catch that? The builders didn't hold off the celebration until the Temple was *finished*. They celebrated when the Temple was *started*.

Recovery is never finished. If you wait until you have reached perfection, until you have "arrived" to celebrate, you can leave the cymbals in the box.

The fact that you are reading this right now is something. Even the smallest of steps in early recovery are to be celebrated. If you attend a 12-step meeting, you will hear about the 24-hour desire chip. When someone claims that chip, they are committing to sobriety for the next 24 hours – not 24 days, weeks, or years.

The builders celebrated the laying of the foundation of the temple. You have begun to lay a foundation on which to build a life of recovery. That's huge! Take time to celebrate!

Recovery Step: Take a moment now and celebrate one small step you have successfully taken on the road to recovery.

Close the Window
February 18

It happened on April 17, 1790. Ben Franklin died from sitting in front of his window. Here's what happened. Franklin was a big believer in fresh air. So every night, he slept with the window open. He wrote, "I rise every morning and sit near the window in my chamber without any clothes, regardless of the season."

April of 1790 started like any other time in the 84-year-old's life. But this time, Franklin developed an abscess in his lungs, which his doctors attributed to his many hours sitting naked in front of an open window. The abscess burst on April 17, and he died a few hours later.

Many of us suffer from open windows. We open the window to temptation – just a little – and we are okay. Until we're not.

Peter warned, "Keep away from worldly desires that wage war against your very souls" (1 Peter 2:11).

Maintaining sobriety is a war. It will probably be the most difficult battle you ever face. One of the keys to victory is to keep the window of temptation nailed shut. Don't even crack the window just a bit. This may mean you need to avoid certain places, television shows, or toxic relationships. If you allow the window of temptation to remain open, you will soon find yourself like Ben Franklin – naked and helpless.

It's time to shut the window.

Recovery Step: Identify the open windows of your life. Then do whatever is necessary to nail those windows shut. Your recovery depends on it.

Do What Doesn't Make Sense
February 19

Sometimes, in order to find lasting recovery we have to do things that don't make sense at first. For example, it is recommended that you attend ninety 12-step meetings in your first ninety days of recovery. The addict rarely sees the benefit of this until he looks back ninety days later.

There was a man in the Bible who had to do what didn't make sense, in order to get well. His name was Naaman. "Though Naaman was a mighty warrior, he suffered from leprosy" (2 Kings 5:1). He called for the prophet Elisha to come and heal him. "But Elisha sent a messenger out to him with this message: 'Go and wash yourself seven times in the Jordan River. Then your skin will be restored, and you will be healed of your leprosy'" (5:10).

At first, Naaman balked. Why? Because he wasn't desperate enough. Having nowhere else to turn, he eventually hit bottom. Then he did what made no sense. "Naaman went down to the Jordan River and dipped himself seven times, as the man of God had instructed him. And his skin became as healthy as the skin of a young child, and he was healed!" (5:14).

Recovery requires doing things we don't always understand. For example, I don't know why going to meetings works, but it does. I go to two meetings a week, for one reason. It works.

You need a sponsor. More importantly, you need to do the things your sponsor says. Lean on his experience. Your own best thinking got you in this mess in the first place. It's time for a little humility. Do what may not make sense in order to find what you've never had.

Recovery Step: Do something for recovery that doesn't make sense, just because someone with more experience said to.

Lesson from the Frog
February 20

There is an old fable about a scorpion and a frog. The scorpion asked the frog to carry him on his back across a creek. When they were halfway across, the scorpion stung the frog.

"Why did you do that?" asked the frog. "Now I will die, and you will drown, too!"

The scorpion replied, "I know, but it's just my nature to sting."

The scorpion represents the attack of outside forces that seek to undermine your recovery. J.I. Packer wrote, "Satan has no constructive purpose of his own; his tactics are simply to destroy."

You are in a spiritual battle. Even the most secular among us must admit that seven of the twelve steps of recovery have a spiritual component to them.

We cannot negotiate with our "scorpions." Each temptation brings what Paul called the "sting of death" (1 Corinthians 15:56). When we try to live a normal life while still carrying our addiction on our backs, we, like the frog, will drown.

When we get in recovery, the enemy's work has just begun. David McGee writes, "Every source of blessing is a point of attack." The enemy exists to bring you down. He says that he, just like the scorpion, just wants to go along for the ride.

Don't believe it.

Recovery Step: Remove every temptation and trigger that you can.

Fresh Start
February 21

I am grateful that we serve a God of second chances. King David serves as the ultimate example of a man who made a mess of things. But God never gave up on him. Following his sin of adultery and true repentance, David wrote, "What joy for those whose record the Lord has cleared of guilt" (Psalm 32:2).

No matter what you've done in the past, hear this – *The rest of your life can be the best of your life!* We serve a God of second chances.

Inspirational author Carl Bard said it like this: "Though no one can go back and make a brand new start, anyone can start from now and make a brand new ending."

We serve a God of second chances.

What you did yesterday is history. What you do today is a choice. God has given you a whole new set of choices to make today. And after you make your choices, your choices will make you. So proceed with caution. Start small. Do the little things right. Take advantage of a fresh start.

We serve a God of second chances.

Recovery Step: Every fresh start begins with a single step. Take that step today. And never forget that we serve a God of second chances.

Safety Net
February 22

Andy Stanley says the greatest question ever is: *What is the wise thing to do?* But the answer is not always clear. This leads to what Andy calls the second greatest question ever: *What do you think is the wise thing to do?*

Solomon said it like this: "Plans go wrong for lack of advice; many advisers bring success" (Proverbs 15:22). He also wrote, "There is safety in having many advisers" (Proverbs 11:14).

It's what I call the safety net. In recovery, none of us is as strong as all of us. Michael Leahy, the founder of BraveHearts, says that only one man in 10,000 gets well on his own. We need each other.

To find successful recovery, you will need several people in your corner: a therapist, a pastor or priest, a sponsor, sponsees, 12-step friends, and others.

When I am struggling, I call my pastor. Sometimes I call a mentor in the field of sex addiction. Other times, I call my sponsor.

The important thing is not *who* you call, but *that* you call. Can you surround yourself with helpful advisers and still slip or relapse? Absolutely! But if you go it alone, I can almost guarantee you will have a relapse. You need many advisers. That is about the best safety net you will ever find.

Recovery Step: Make a list of five people you can lean on for wise counsel and support.

This Is Who God Blesses
February 23

A man saw a sign that offered a reward for anyone who found a lost dog and returned it to its master. The man looked for the dog but was unsuccessful. He showed up at the dog owner's house anyway, to claim the reward. "I looked for your dog," he said, holding out his hand.

"But you didn't find my dog, did you?" asked the dog's owner.

"No, but I want a reward just for the effort."

Of course, the man went away empty handed. No one rewards someone simply for the search. Well, there is one who does that – God.

"God rewards those who sincerely seek Him" (Hebrews 11:6).

When we are empty, lonely, or depressed, there is still Good News. We don't have to figure it all out and live the perfect life to find God's favor. Recovery is about progress, not perfection. You don't have to "arrive" to get the blessing. Recovery is more about direction than destination.

Start seeking God today. It is the search that God rewards. He likes to bless those who are in the fight, on the path and seeking him.

Recovery Step: Focus less on your destination and more on your direction. Seek God in your recovery, and the blessings will begin to flow.

The Blessing of Mistakes
February 24

Coach John Wooden used to tell his players, "Experience does you no good. It is learning from your experience that makes the difference."

The Apostle Paul learned from his mistakes. After his friend John Mark had abandoned him during the first missionary journey, Paul wrote him off. He never gave him a second chance or traveled with him again. But late in his life, Paul recognized his folly. In his dying letter written from the cell of a prison, Paul wrote, "Bring Mark to me. He is helpful to me in my ministry" (2 Timothy 4:11).

How could a man who had abandoned Paul be described as "helpful"?

The answer isn't that John Mark changed (though he did). The difference was that Paul had changed. He learned from his mistakes.

Rick Warren says, "We are products of our past, but we don't have to be prisoners of it." Johann Wolfgang von Goethe said it like this: "By seeking and blundering we learn."

The fact is, we all have a past. We all have made huge mistakes in our lives. And it's okay to visit the past from time to time. But it's not okay to live there. Allow yesterday's mistakes to prepare you for tomorrow's blessings.

Recovery Step: Take a second to reflect on a huge mistake in your past. Then ask God to show you a lesson from this mistake. Then take your next step . . . forward.

Learn from the Snail
February 25

Nineteenth-century preacher Charles Spurgeon taught what he called "the lesson of the snail." He said, "By perseverance the snail reached the ark."

Nothing will bring you victory over lust like perseverance. Never give up. Failure is the path of least persistence.

Consider the honey bee. To produce one pound of honey, he must visit 56,000 clover heads. Since each head has 60 flower tubes, he must make 3.36 million visits to produce one pound of honey.

Lust. A second look. Fantasy. We all battle these temptations – and more. And none of us has been victorious every time. But that's okay. The key to victory is perseverance. Stay in the battle. Keep swinging.

Your job is simple. Do the next right thing. Then do that again tomorrow. Take small steps – one day at a time. Paul said it like this: "Never tire from doing the right thing" (2 Thessalonians 3:13).

Think of yourself as the snail and the ark as recovery. You can get there. It won't be easy, and it won't come fast. But it can happen – if you have perseverance.

Recovery Step: Do one thing that takes you in the right direction today.

Never Satisfied
February 26

Lust is progressive. It never satisfies. There's an old story about God's people returning from exile to Jerusalem. They started to rebuild the Temple, but when they faced opposition, they quit. In frustration, they turned inward, building lavish homes for themselves instead of furnishing God's House. For them, life was about taking the easy path and indulging in the pleasure of the moment.

In stepped a prophet named Haggai. He wrote, "Look what's happening to you! You have planted much but harvested little. You eat but are not satisfied. You drink but are still thirsty" (Haggai 1:5-6).

That is the picture of every addict. We eat but are still hungry. We drink, but are still thirsty. There's a reason for this.

We are chasing temporary solutions to permanent problems.

I have acid reflux. That causes a burning in my esophagus. Sometimes, I do the right thing and drink a disgusting tasting liquid before bed. And I sleep all night. But other times, I eat a bowl of ice cream. Why? Because it tastes better in the moment. And it actually coats my throat, so it feels better for a few minutes. The problem is that in four or five hours, the pain returns, and I end up having to drink the medicine anyway.

Every day, we are tempted to drink in the lust. And it feels good in the moment. But it only coats the real pain. What's the solution? Drink of the Living Water that never runs dry.

Recovery Step: Turn to Jesus today. Bring him your hurts, habits, and hang-ups. Then leave them there.

Universal Principle
February 27

There is a universal principle that applies to addiction. It's called sowing and reaping. The ancient prophet Hosea said, "Plant the good seeds of righteousness, and you will harvest a crop of love" (Hosea 10:12).

The mistake most of us make is that we want good results without doing the things that produce those results. We want the blessing of the crop without the pain of the work.

Muhammad Ali said, "The crown is never won in the ring. It's just recognized there. The crown is won on the streets, where I run miles when no one is watching, and in the gym, where I put my body through hell so I will be ready to go 15 rounds."

Recovery is never won in the first round. You have to go the distance. But tomorrow's victory is decided by today's work. If you want to be well tomorrow, you need to pray today. If you want to be strong tomorrow, go to a meeting tonight. If you want to see a good harvest, start planting seeds now.

Pete Rose, baseball's all-time hit king, said, "My father taught me that the only way you can make good at anything is to practice, and then practice some more." Jackson Brown said, "You can't hire someone to practice for you."

Everything significant that happens to you tomorrow will have already been determined by the things you did today. What you sow today you will reap tomorrow. That is a universal principle of life.

Recovery Step: Do one thing today that will fuel your recovery tomorrow.

Dark Clouds
February 28

C.S. Lewis called pain "God's great unwanted gift." Nothing brings more pain than losing our sobriety. The disappointment, shame, and guilt can feel overwhelming. In those moments we feel all alone. Even God has left us.

Or has he?

There is an interesting verse tucked away in one of the least read books of the Bible. At a time when King Solomon and the Israelites were facing a bleak future – largely due to their own poor decisions, the Bible says, "God spoke from a dark cloud" (2 Chronicles 6:1).

It's easy to see God in a sunrise or sunset. It's easy to feel his presence on a mountain, by a stream, or on the beach. When the choir hits the high note, when the preacher hits a home run, and when we experience showers of blessing, we see, hear, and touch God.

But what about in the hard times? Hear it again: "God spoke from a *dark* cloud."

Here's the good news. If the storm clouds have gathered, if the pain is massive, and if sobriety seems elusive, God is still there. When recovery seems to be no more than a mirage in the desert, God is still speaking.

So don't wait for the sunshine to return, for times to get better, or for sobriety to come easy. Listen for God's voice *now*; seek his face *now*; lean into Him *now*. Claim one of the Bible's great promises. *"God spoke from a dark cloud."*

Recovery Step: Take five minutes to listen for God's voice. Don't talk. Just listen.

Mousetraps
March 1

Every person who has fallen into sin has the same story. It is the story of Lot, nephew of Abraham. When the day came for them to separate, we read that "Lot cast his tent near Sodom" (Genesis 13:12). It took exactly one chapter for Lot to complete his relocation. In just a few days, Lot moved from *near* Sodom to *in* Sodom (Genesis 14:12), and it nearly cost him everything.

There's an old proverb that says, "Free cheese is always available in mouse traps." Lot got in trouble because he chose to hang around a big mousetrap where he could sniff the cheese.

The key to staying sexually *pure* is to avoid that which is sexually *impure*. Block the channel. Delete the phone number. Change the route. End the relationship.

Avoid the mousetrap.

Yes, each of us who has fallen has the same story. I have yet to meet the man who said, "I viewed porn in order to wreck my marriage." The enemy doesn't tempt us that way. Had someone walked up to Lot and said, "Hey, why don't you move to Sodom, the most wicked place on earth?" he would have surely turned away.

The temptation is to camp on the hill near Sodom, to smile at the new lady at work, or to quickly browse the internet site. And then we fall. Like Lot, we only meant to sniff the cheese.

There is only one answer. Avoid the mousetrap.

Recovery Step: The key to staying pure is not to avoid the cheese, but to avoid the mousetrap. Identify one trap in your life that you need to avoid at all costs – then run the other way!

When Hope Seems Gone
March 2

When "Susan" got the call, she couldn't believe it could possibly be true. She had been married to "Todd" for 20 years. There were no signs, not the slightest hint of infidelity. But her friend saw Todd coming out of the restaurant across town with another woman. So the next night, while Todd was asleep, Susan went through his phone – just to be sure her friend was wrong.

What Susan saw told the story of a man she didn't know. There were phone numbers, pictures, dating sites – the works. Life as she knew it was now over.

"How could I have been so naïve? Who is this man? How did I not see any of this coming? What do I do now?" These are just some of the thoughts that raced through Susan's mind.

Perhaps you've been there. The most blessed man of the Old Testament was also its most depressed man. Solomon wrote, "I will never forget this awful time, as I grieve over my loss. Yet I still dare to hope when I remember this: the faithful love of the Lord never ends! His mercies never cease" (Lamentations 3:20-21).

It's okay to feel pain and abandonment. If you are "Susan," no one can tell you how to feel. But while I can't tell you how to feel, I can tell you where to look.

On the other side of the darkest valley is a mountain you cannot yet see. But it's still there. The only way to find it is to keep walking. You only lose if you stop. So keep walking. There will be plenty of time to answer your questions about "Todd." Today is not about you and Todd, but you and God.

I promise you, your pain will yield to peace, and your grief will be baptized in grace. But only if you keep walking.

Recovery Step: Look to God for hope. Then keep walking, one day and one step at a time.

Did Jesus Really Say That?
March 3

Jesus came upon a man who had been sick for 38 years. We can assume the man had tried everything: doctors, religion, and home remedies. Still, he was sick. He had played his last card. He was out of options. So he looked to Jesus.

And Jesus asked him the strangest question: "Do you want to be well?" (John 5:6). Was that a serious question? Sure, he wanted to be well! Who wouldn't?

But Jesus' question really wasn't one of desire, but desperation. "Do you *really* want to be well?" He told the man – who could not walk – to pick up his mat and walk. That required a willingness to look the part of a fool. What if the healing didn't really take place?

But when he did the improbable, Jesus did the impossible. And the man was healed.

The first key to freedom is desperation. Most of us are more comfortable with old problems than new solutions. So we never find freedom.

Real freedom comes when we are more desperate for God than his blessings.

St. Augustine said, "To fall in love with God is the greatest romance; to seek him the greatest adventure; to find him, the greatest human achievement."

Perhaps you have been mired in years of pain and struggle. The answer is found in the question. Do you want to get well? *Really?*

Recovery Step: Seek God with a desperate heart.

The Spiritual Connection
March 4

Compartmentalization. It gets us all in trouble. We separate the physical, spiritual, emotional, and mental. But the fact is, they are all intertwined.

John addressed a friend, "Dear friend, I pray that you may enjoy good health and that all may go well with you, even as your soul is getting along well" (3 John 2). There is a connection between the physical and the mental.

A study by Purdue University found that people who practice their religion regularly develop only half as many medical problems as nonbelievers. "We have recently completed a systematic review of over 1,200 studies on the effects of religion on health," the study concluded. "The vast majority of these studies show a relationship between greater religious involvement and better mental and physical health, and lower use of health services."

A spiritual connection is not a guarantee for sobriety, but it is foundational.

The AA "Big Book" says, "It is easy to let up on the spiritual program of action and rest on our laurels. We are headed for trouble if we do" (page 85).

Philosopher Teilhard de Chardin said it like this: "We are not human beings having a spiritual experience. We are spiritual beings having a human experience."

You can read all the literature, go to meetings every day, get a sponsor, and do all the right things. But if you are not connected to the ultimate source your power will run out before you do.

Recovery Step: Spend 15 minutes with God every day. Find the spiritual connection.

Jesus Is for You!
March 5

Jesus is all about recovery. He stated his mission clearly. "The Spirit of the Lord is on me because he has anointed me to proclaim good news to the poor. He has sent me to proclaim freedom for the prisoners and recovery of sight for the blind, to set the oppressed free" (Luke 4:18-19).

By fulfilling the promise of Isaiah 61, Jesus was claiming to be the Messiah in unmistakable terms. But he was also offering hope to four groups: the poor, captive, blind, and oppressed.

That's us!

Sometimes we mistake the Bible for a book of doctrine. We leave it to scholars to interpret. The complexities of understanding 66 separate books can be intimidating. But it was never intended to be that way. The purpose of God in Jesus Christ is simple – he came for us.

Jesus didn't come for the rich, famous, powerful, or elite. He came for the poor, captive, blind, and oppressed.

For the hurting there is hope, for the lonely there is love, and for the grieving there is grace.

Recovery Step: Jesus came to set us free from our bondage and addictions. In him, you can find a life of true recovery. Seek him, trust him, and find him today.

When Times Are Still Hard
March 6

One of the things many fail to understand early in their recovery is that coming clean and seeking sobriety doesn't magically make all our problems go away. We say we are all in, and we mean it. But the temptations of our addiction and the suspicions of our friends remain.

There's a great example of this in the Old Testament. The prophet Habakkuk sought God on behalf of his people. He came with a heart of repentance and sincerity. He prayed for God's blessings out of total surrender. And he meant it.

But God's blessings did not all come at once. Still, Habakkuk remained true to his commitments and to his God.

"Even though the fig trees have no blossoms, and there are no grapes on the vines; even though the olive crop fails, and the fields are empty and barren; even though the flocks die in the fields, and the cattle barns are empty, yet I will rejoice in the Lord! I will be joyful in the God of my salvation" (Habakkuk 3:17-18).

It's easy to live in sobriety when we are heavily rewarded. But it's what we do when our wife doesn't come home, when we still lose our job, when our friends still turn away, that counts.

Are you seeking recovery as a bargain with God? He doesn't make bargains. Unless you are seeking recovery simply for the prize of being in recovery, it won't work. The fact is, recovery is its own best reward.

Recovery Step: Are times still hard? That's okay. Stay at it. Do the right things. Recovery is its own best reward.

Self-Control
March 7

A man was standing in line at a grocery store check-out when he witnessed another man struggling to control his son, about two years of age. The boy was trying to grab everything in sight and toss it into the shopping cart. The dad kept repeating, "Just be calm, Albert. Don't act up, Albert. Don't make a scene, Albert. Control yourself, Albert. Don't act like a child, Albert."

The bystander approached the man with praise. "Sir, I couldn't help but overhear you. I just want to say how impressed I am with the way you just handled little Albert."

The man responded, "Sir, the boy's name is Jimmy. My name is Albert."

Albert is like most of us. We have a much easier time controlling others than ourselves. We are like Lucy, who told Charlie Brown, "I plan to change the world – starting with you."

In recovery, there is no silver bullet. While there are principles to be embraced, Scriptures to be read, meetings to be attended, and steps to be followed, there is this one thing we all must have.

Self-control.

The good news is self-control is prayed down, not worked up. It is the result of a spiritual connection. Paul wrote, "The Holy Spirit produces this kind of fruit in our lives: love, joy, peace, patience, kindness, goodness, faithfulness, gentleness, and *self-control*" (Galatians 5:22-23).

You can't make it without good old-fashioned self-control. And you find that in God.

Recovery Step: Seek God and ask him for the gift of self-control.

The First Step
March 8

"I want you to paint it," Pope Julius II told Michelangelo Buonarroti.

The artist was stunned. "This job is beyond me. Get Raphael to do it."

"Nonsense," said the Pope. "The assignment is yours."

So with one stroke of his brush, Michelangelo began the overwhelming task of painting the ceiling of the Sistine Chapel. Month after month, each day was the same. The artist worked alone, lying on a scaffold and painting the ceiling above his head. As paint dripped into his eyes, his entire body ached from the arduous work. But Michelangelo stayed at the task. Four years later, one final stroke completed the immense project.

While the final stroke was one of ecstasy, imagine the first. That first stroke seemed without purpose to the casual observer. Only in the eye of the great artist did it mean anything.

Every journey begins with a first step. The same is true in recovery. The first step is the most important, for every step that follows is dependent on the first one.

Mark Twain said, "The secret of getting ahead is getting started."

Moses' successor was a man named Joshua. The task of leading Israel into the Promised Land fell to him. The time for planning had ended; it was time to take the first step. "So the people crossed over opposite Jericho" (Joshua 3:16).

Recovery is about taking the first step. What are you waiting for?

Recovery Step: Face the direction you know is right – and take the first step.

Still a Leper
March 9

Once an addict, always an addict? That is a question that has been debated for years. My intention is not to answer that question, other than to say that God is the master at using our pasts – if we don't run from them.

There was a man in the Bible who hosted Jesus and a group of his friends in his house one day. His name was Simon, better known as "Simon the Leper." Scripture tells us, "Jesus was in Bethany in the home of Simon the Leper" (Matthew 26:6).

We can assume that Simon was actually no longer a leper, or he would not be allowed in the presence of the crowds. Leprosy was thought to be highly contagious and deadly. Clearly, Simon was a *former* leper. Yet he still identified with his past.

God doesn't want us to run from our past. In fact, God doesn't use us *despite* our past, but *because* of it. Your past becomes God's purpose, and your problem becomes your platform.

As a former pastor, it took me a while to get comfortable with the idea of leading with my past. Being known can be scary. We make the mistake that our past invalidates God's ability to really use us.

Lisa Bevere wrote, "If you think you've blown God's plan for your life, rest in this: You, my friend, are not that powerful."

You have a past. We all do. Here's the good news. Your past is not a deterrent to God using you in the future; rather, it opens up new opportunities you never knew existed.

Recovery Step: Let your past become God's purpose and your problem become your platform.

Two-for-One Deal
March 10

Augustine said, "God loves each of us as if there were only one of us." There is nothing you can ever do to invalidate that love.

But life often feels like a battlefield.

Five hundred years before the birth of Jesus, God's people were discouraged. They had lost much because of their faithfulness. But God gave them this promise: "Return to your fortress, you prisoners of hope; even now I announce that I will restore twice as much to you" (Zechariah 9:12).

God gives two blessings for every trouble.

Your job is to be faithful; God's job is to take care of you. And his promise is that no matter how steep the hill or tough the battle, the blessings on the other side are worth it.

Recovery is a daily battle. But it is a battle with its own reward. Every time you are tested – and found faithful – you will know peace that passes all understanding.

Better yet, God's two-for-one blessing comes with a purpose. Warren Wiersbe said, "God doesn't bless us to make us happy; he blesses us to make us a blessing."

Recovery Step: In the midst of the battle, remain faithful. That's all God asks. And know that the blessing from him will be twice the magnitude of the trials you face to get there.

The Power of Confession
March 11

Sin can only destroy us if we let it. John said, "If we confess our sins, he is faithful and just and will forgive us our sins and purify us from all unrighteousness" (1 John 1:9).

I love the story that unfolded in a Houston courtroom in April, 1994. Arthur Hollingsworth was on trial for the armed robbery of a Sun Mart convenience store.

Harris County prosecutor Jay Hileman asked Hollingsworth, "You're guilty, aren't you?"

Hollingsworth responded, "No."

Hileman repeated, "Mr. Hollingsworth, you're guilty, aren't you?"

Hollingsworth said it again: "No."

Hileman stayed at it. "Mr. Hollingsworth, you're guilty, aren't you?"

Hollingsworth eventually caved. "Yeah, I guess I am."

Lee Strobel writes, "Few things accelerate the peace process as much as humbly admitting our own wrongdoing and asking forgiveness."

F.B. Meyer said simply, "Confess sin immediately."

There is power in confession. Until you come clean and admit to God your wrongdoing, you will never know God's peace. Perpetual sin will destroy you – but only if you hang onto it instead of confessing it to God.

Recovery Step: Confess your sin to God in order to receive his forgiveness and peace.

Good Grief
March 12

"Big boys don't cry." Every child of my era heard that – repeatedly. Crying was seen as a sign of weakness. I was once told, "John Wayne doesn't cry." I remember thinking, "What does John Wayne have to do with my skinned knee?"

But there are certain things that *should* bring us to tears. They include personal struggles and failings. Case in point – King David.

David was a man's man. He was a bare-handed killer of bears and lions and a slayer of giants. He was a brilliant military strategist and decisive national political leader. But David cried – a lot. He cried out loud. When confronted with his sin, David baptized his couch in tears.

David said, "I am worn out from my groaning. All night long I flood my bed with weeping and drench my couch with tears" (Psalm 6:6).

Jack Hyles used to say, "Laughter means nothing unless there have been tears."

It's good to laugh. But it's also good to cry. You probably won't find recovery any other way. It is in the heart that cries bitter tears of remorse that God is about to do something special. It is in our grief that we find God's grace, in our pain that we find his peace, and in our loss that we find his love.

Recovery Step: Bare your heart to God. Confess your failings openly and freely. Approach him with your heart, not just your head.

Truth & Consequences
March 13

On his last day in office, Governor Bill Richardson of New Mexico did what every other governor had done for the past 130 years. He refused to issue an official pardon for notorious outlaw Billy the Kid.

Also known as Henry McCarty, "The Kid" was responsible for at least 20 deaths. But in 1879, New Mexico Governor Lew Wallace promised him a pardon in exchange for his testimony against three men accused of killing a one-armed lawyer during the Lincoln County Wars. But Wallace reneged on his promise, and Billy the Kid escaped from prison, killing four guards. He was eventually tracked down and killed on July 14, 1881.

To this day, there are those who still call for Billy's pardon. But that pardon has not come, and probably never will.

Here's the deal – choices have consequences.

The old prophet said, "The soul that sins will surely die" (Ezekiel 18:4). Addiction will take you further than you want to go, keep you longer than you want to stay, and cost you more than you want to pay.

You don't need to apologize for an addiction. But what you do about it is on you.

Recovery Step: Come clean. Admit your struggle to God and others. Then pay the price of lasting recovery.

Anger Management
March 14

Anger is one of the strongest triggers of inappropriate behavior. In 12-step meetings, we often hear of the "big four" known as H.A.L.T. We are at our greatest risk when we are *hungry, angry, lonely,* or *tired*.

Untreated anger makes true recovery impossible. Anger gives birth to bitterness, and bitterness blocks healthy progress.

Paul understood the danger of anger when he wrote to the church, "In your anger do not sin" (Ephesians 4:26).

Ridding ourselves of anger is not always easy. Mark Twain's strategy was simple: "When angry, count to four. When very angry, swear."

Colin Powell said, "Get mad, then get over it."

But anger is not something we just "get over." It is like our other character defects. Anger must be surrendered to God. You can do that today. Tell God about your anger, and ask him to remove it, just like every other defect that stands in the way of sobriety and recovery.

Recovery Step: Pray the 7th Step Prayer – "My Creator, I am now willing that you should have all of me, good and bad. I pray that you now remove from me every single defect of character – including anger – that stands in the way of my usefulness to you and to others. Grant me strength, as I go out from here, to do your work."

Trading Up
March 15

We only give in to our urges and passions in the moment for one reason. We make the decision to trade what we want *most* for what we want *now*.

There was a man in the Bible named Samson. He was given to wild impulses. One day, he decided that rather than seek a wife within his faith, he would explore more exciting options. So "Samson said to his father and mother, 'I have seen a Philistine woman in Timnah; now get her for me as my wife.' His father and mother replied, 'Isn't there an acceptable woman among your relatives or among all our people? Must you go to the uncircumcised Philistines to get a wife?'" (Judges 14:2-3).

Samson chose a woman based on one thing – how she looked. He sought to marry her based on what he saw when he had not even met her. She came from a different faith background, and Samson had almost nothing in common with the woman. But she looked good at the moment. For Samson, that was enough.

Samson traded what he wanted most – his integrity – for what he wanted now.

Barbra Streisand said, "I need instant gratification." Meryl Streep said, "Instant gratification is not soon enough."

When you are tempted to give in to your sexual urges, remember you do so at a cost. You will be trading what you want most for what you want now. And when you look back, that will be a trade you will regret – every time.

Recovery Step: Make a list of the things you want most from life. Then determine that you will never trade what you want most for what you want now.

It's Why We Are Here
March 16

W.H. Auden said, "We are all here on earth to help others. Why they are here, I have no idea."

Auden is actually on to something. We are here for others, not ourselves. Les Brown said it like this: "Help others achieve their dreams, and you will achieve yours." That is especially true in recovery.

Charles Plumb was an American pilot in the Vietnam War. When his plane was shot down, he ejected and parachuted into the jungle, where the Viet Cong captured him and held him captive for six years. Years later, Plumb was dining at a restaurant with his wife when a stranger approached him. He said, "You are Charles Plumb, aren't you? You were shot down over Vietnam."

Plumb asked the stranger who he was. "I'm the man who packed your parachute that day. I guess it worked!"

Plumb gives speeches across America. He tells that story, then asks his audiences, "Who packed your parachute?"

Recovery is a team sport. We find recovery by helping others find recovery. One of the best things you can do to secure your own recovery is to help someone else secure theirs.

The Bible says, "There will never cease to be poor in the land. Therefore, I command you, 'You shall open wide your hand to your brother, to the needy and to the poor, in your land'" (Deuteronomy 15:11).

Recovery Step: Reach out to someone today who is on the road to recovery, and help them "pack their parachute."

Delayed Gratification
March 17

For many of us, the real problem is that we are addicted to chaos. We may be so used to living in crisis that we don't know how to enjoy the calm. Life in recovery even seems boring in comparison to our old lifestyles. Many in recovery miss the excitement. They don't enter recovery because the rewards seem too slow in coming.

We live for instant gratification. Carrie Fisher went even further when she said, "Instant gratification takes too long."

The Good News is that God wants us to have rewarding and fulfilled lives. But victory requires surrender.

Jesus said it like this: "Whoever wants to be my disciple must deny himself and take up his cross and follow me" (Matthew 16:24).

Recovery is a trade-off. It's called delayed gratification. We trade the pleasures that don't last for the peace that does. In taking the deal, we must remember that by denying ourselves immediate pleasure, we will reap a harvest of rich rewards in this life and in the life to come.

Recovery Step: You must make a fundamental choice. Will it be gratification in the moment that only leads to shame and guilt? Or will you choose the lasting peace that only comes by walking with God in total surrender?

12th Step
March 18

Recovery is not complete until we work the 12th Step: "Having had a spiritual awakening as the result of these steps, we tried to carry the message to others." Recovery is not just about what God is doing *in* us; it's about what God is doing *through* us.

Poet Ella Wheelcox said it like this: "There are only two kinds of people on earth today, two kinds of people, no more, I say; not the good and the bad, for 'tis well understood, that the good are half bad and the bad are half good. No, the two kinds of people on earth I mean are the people who lift and the people who lean."

It's never too soon to practice the 12th step. From day one, you need to start giving back. When you go to your next 12-step meeting, find the newcomer and give him your number. Help set up the room. Look for the person who doesn't seem to fit in and become his friend. Find the man with no sobriety and praise him for just showing up.

One day, Jesus bragged on a woman who gave very little, but who gave it all. Comparing her to bigger givers, he said, "They all gave out of their wealth; but she, out of her poverty, put in everything – all she had to live on" (Mark 12:44).

Martin Luther King, Jr., wrote, "Somewhere along the way, we must learn that there is nothing greater than to do something for others."

Recovery Step: Learn to give back. Find someone who needs a word of encouragement, and give it to them. And by being the healer, you will be healed.

God's Strength
March 19

The year was 1911. The South Pole was not the vacation paradise it is today. But a Norwegian explorer named Roald Amundsen changed all that when he set out to become the first man to reach the South Pole. While assembling his team, Amundsen chose expert skiers and dog handlers. His strategy was simple. The dogs would do most of the work as they pulled the group 15 to 20 miles a day. Rather than rely on their own strength, they would rely on the strength of the dogs. It worked, as Amundsen became the first man to reach the South Pole.

The road to recovery is one of exploration. None of us got it right the first time. And as long as we sought sobriety in our own strength, we found no recovery at all.

The key to lasting recovery is surrender to our Higher Power. As Roald Amundsen relied on the strength of his dogs, we must rely on the strength of our God.

King David wrote, "The Lord is the strength of my life; of whom shall I be afraid?" (Psalm 27:1).

The troubles of this life multiply and can become overwhelming – downright scary. And if we don't learn to rely on God's strength, we become gripped by fear.

Alexander MacLaren nailed it when he said, "Only he who can say, 'The Lord is the strength of my life' can also say, 'Of whom shall I be afraid?'"

Recovery Step: You aren't strong enough to find recovery on your own. Turn your life and will over to the care of God. Rely only on him, or you'll never reach your Promised Land.

Waiting
March 20

I have a friend who just celebrated 16 years of sobriety. "How did you do it?" he was asked. His answer was simple: "One day at a time."

My friend said that recovery never becomes easy. We will struggle with temptation and triggers while facing our pain and our past. But there is a coming day when the struggles will all end.

Paul wrote to the church, "We who are still alive will be caught up together to meet the Lord in the air. And so we will be with the Lord forever" (1 Thessalonians 4:17).

In his old age, former president John Quincy Adams was walking down a street in Boston. An old friend asked how he was. Adams replied, "John Quincy Adams is quite well. But the house in which he lives is becoming quite dilapidated. I believe Mr. Adams will be moving out soon."

Philip Yancey wrote, "I know a woman whose grandmother lies buried under 150-year-old live oak trees in the cemetery of an Episcopal church in rural Louisiana. In accordance with the grandmother's instructions, only one word is carved on her tombstone – 'Waiting.'"

Life is about waiting. We wait on the fruits of our recovery work. We wait on the pain to slowly ebb away. And mostly, we wait on the One who will come again, and take us home where each of us will be free at last.

Recovery Step: Keep working your recovery. But never take your eyes off Jesus. Look fully to him as you wait for that glorious day.

Pride
March 21

The most dangerous state in America is the state of overconfidence. That is especially true in recovery. Overconfidence is code for pride, and pride comes before fall – every time.

God says simply, "I hate pride" (Proverbs 8:13).

C.S. Lewis had much to say about pride. In *Mere Christianity*, he wrote, "As long as you are proud, you cannot know God."

The real problem with addiction is that it is progressive. What satisfied yesterday has lost its thrill for tomorrow. Pride says, "I deserve it. I've earned it. And I want more."

Another C.S. Lewis quote: "Pride gets no pleasure out of simply having something, but out of having more of it than the next man. It is the comparison that makes you proud: the pleasure of being above the rest. Once the element of competition has gone, pride is gone."

I hear it all the time. "My wife isn't meeting my needs. I work hard. I deserve to be happy. This isn't hurting anyone, anyway."

Pride has only one purpose – to convince you that you deserve whatever you want. Pride is the 1,000-pound weight tied around your ankle. Until you cut it loose, you will never be free.

Recovery Step: Take a hard look at yourself. Do you have unhealthy pride? Confess it to God and let it go.

Today
March 22

The Latin phrase *carpe diem* means, "Seize the day."

Recovery cannot wait until tomorrow. If you wait until you are ready, you will never get well. If you wait until the feeling is right, your mood is right, and the timing is right, you will never find sobriety.

The devil's strategy is not to tell you to not enter recovery. He will tell you, "Get in recovery. Your life depends on it." Then he says, "But wait until tomorrow."

The problem is, tomorrow is the one day you won't find on the calendar.

Carpe diem!

Jesus said, "But about that day or hour no one knows, not even the angels in heaven, nor the Son, but only the Father. As it was in the days of Noah, so it will be at the coming of the Son of Man" (Matthew 24:36-37). He was saying life is unpredictable. Live for today.

Carpe diem!

Francis Schaeffer said, "Life is like a clock with no hands. It's ticking, but you never know when it's going to strike midnight." So live for today. Albert Einstein said, "Learn from yesterday, but live for today."

Carpe diem!

Recovery Step: Get started in recovery today. Don't wait another second. *Carpe diem!*

Ready for War
March 23

When you get in recovery, you are entering a major war zone. You are in the fight of your life – especially if your issue is sex or porn addiction. I've had recovering cocaine addicts tell me that beating cocaine is much easier than beating sex addiction. So get ready for war.

Peter wrote, "Your adversary the devil, is a roaring lion, seeking whom he may devour" (1 Peter 5:8).

The battle gets the most intense when you get the most serious about your recovery. David McGee said, "Every source of blessing is a point of attack."

So get ready.

But make no mistake. While you are in a spiritual battle for your very mind, you can win.

In a popular 1970s sitcom, Flip Wilson famously and repeatedly said, every time he was caught doing something wrong, "The devil made me do it."

If you are serious about your recovery, you have a target on your chest. The enemy is coming after you with everything he's got. But make no mistake. The devil can't make you do anything. You can win the battle of addiction – but only if you are willing to join the fight.

Recovery Step: Submit to God and get ready for battle. Your fight for sobriety will be the longest and most difficult of your life. But you can win – if you want it badly enough.

Winning Tomorrow's Sobriety Today
March 24

I owe today's sobriety to the actions of yesterday. Tomorrow's sobriety remains unfinished business. The prophet Hosea wrote, "Sow righteousness for yourselves, reap the fruit of unfailing love, and break up your unplowed ground; for it is time to seek the Lord, until he comes and showers his righteousness on you" (Hosea 10:12).

The fruit we reap tomorrow will mostly be determined by the time we go to bed tonight. What we sow today, we will reap tomorrow. Matthew Henry wrote, "Every action is seed sown." And it cuts both ways.

The key, Hosea said, is to "break up your unplowed ground." That means to spend serious time with God, asking him to soften our hearts, to unearth that which we have buried deep beneath the rocky soil. And then we plant new seeds, knowing that no seed is too small.

C.S. Lewis wrote, in *Mere Christianity*, "The smallest good act today is the capture of a strategic point from which, a few months later, you may be able to go on to victories you never dreamed of. And an apparently trivial indulgence in lust may launch an attack otherwise impossible."

Today, you have two choices. You can ask God to soften your heart and then do a "good act." Or you can surrender to "an apparently trivial indulgence of lust." And either way, you will probably be okay for today.

But tomorrow's another story. Today you make your choices. Tomorrow your choices will make you. Every action is seed sown.

Recovery Step: Do one small, right thing today, to prepare tomorrow for a day of victory.

Satisfaction
March 25

There is really only one reason we ever get in trouble. We buy into the false narrative that we need something more in order to be truly satisfied.

A man explained why he bought a new car. "I was faced with the choice of buying a $50 battery for my old car or a new car for $50,000. And they wanted cash for the battery."

Jay Leno was once asked why he had 300 classic cars. He said, "Because 200 wasn't enough." That's the American dream, isn't it? I'm not satisfied with what I have, so I must need more of it.

The Bible offers a different way. "Be satisfied with what you have" (Hebrews 13:5).

G.K. Chesterton said it like this: "There are two ways to get enough. One is to accumulate more. The other is to desire less."

Addiction is a progressive disease. At first, you don't even know you have it. The patient never notices when his temperature hits 98.7. The addict takes in a glance here, a second look there. He watches an "R" movie, becomes casual on the Internet, and pretty soon, he has crossed over to a world he never knew. And what satisfied yesterday no longer does it for him today.

Satisfaction is not a destination, but a choice. If you are tired of crossing all the wrong boundaries, choose satisfaction. If you are tired of grabbing what you were never intended to have, only to find it's never enough, choose satisfaction.

"Be satisfied with what you have" (Hebrews 13:5). It really is enough.

Recovery Step: Make a list of your three greatest blessings. Then thank God that what he has given you really is enough.

Letting Go
March 26

Most of us aren't very good at letting go. We hang onto old stuff, bad memories, and unmet expectations. Americans are hoarders. That's why there are 32.8 million storage units in the U.S., covering over 2.3 billion square feet of space.

But recovery is all about letting go. We must let go of toxic relationships, lingering triggers, and unfulfilled desires. We must quit chasing the rainbow that doesn't really exist, the one "fix" that will finally be enough.

The children of Israel had the Promised Land staring them in the face. But first, they heard this: "Do not take any of the things set apart for destruction, or you yourselves will be completely destroyed" (Joshua 6:18).

Alexander Graham Bell said it well. "When one door closes, another opens; but we often look so long and so regretfully upon the closed door that we do not see the one which has opened to us."

Recovery is only achieved by moving forward – through the open doors we miss if we keep looking back. No matter how hard the struggle or deep the valley, know this:

Your current situation is not your future destination.

God has a future for you beyond your imagination. But in order to grasp your future, you must release your past. That which threatens to destroy you can do so only on one condition – if you choose to not let go.

Recovery Step: Ask God to show you the one thing you need to let go of, then start looking for open doors to a better tomorrow.

No Place Like Home
March 27

Joyce Meyer says, "God not only sees where you are; he sees where you can be."

The sweet spot of God's will is like being home. It is a place of security and peace. And that is what every addict is looking for.

Dignitaries lined the street when the funeral procession passed. Thousands waited just to catch a glimpse of the coffin. In fact, the people of the United States and all parts of the world loved and revered the deceased man so much that his remains were de-interred in Tripoli and brought to the United States for a magnificent funeral. His name was John Howard Payne.

You probably haven't heard of him. But this well-loved poet was best known for composing one simple verse: *"Mid pleasures and palaces, though oft I may roam; be it ever so humble, there's no place like home."*

If you have strayed from God and his plans for your life, he is calling you home. If you have hit bottom and are ready for the climb back up, he is calling you home. And by finding your way home, you find peace and serenity you can't imagine.

God spoke through the prophet Jeremiah: "For I know the plans I have for you; plans to prosper you and not to harm you, plans to give you hope and a future" (Jeremiah 29:11).

Recovery Step: Take one step toward home, and God will pick up your feet for the rest of the journey.

Hard Work
March 28

G.K. Chesterton said, "The Christian ideal has not been tried and found wanting; it has been found difficult and left untried."

That statement applies to recovery. The reason we don't find lasting sobriety is not that we have engaged the principles common to recovery and found them lacking, but that we took a hard look at the demands of recovery, then turned and walked the other way.

My problem was never a lack of knowledge, but a lack of action. The words of Jesus ring true. "Now that you know these things, you will be blessed *if you do them*" (John 13:17).

Therapy. Meetings. Three-day intensive. Disclosure. A sponsor. Step work. More meetings. These are just some of the things you will need to take seriously if you want recovery to be your lifestyle and not just the rainbow you only imagine.

Blaise Pascal said, "The strength of a man's virtue should not be measured by his special exertions, but by his habitual acts."

Successful recovery is the result of habitual acts, done over and over. Will you find true recovery? That's up to you.

Recovery Step: Recovery is about establishing habits that don't come easy. There is no better time to start than right now.

The Greatest Gift
March 29

Solomon became king at the age of 20. His kingdom was so formidable that Pharaoh, the powerful Egyptian monarch, formed an alliance with him by giving Solomon his daughter in marriage. Because he understood that his youth and inexperience could topple the kingdom, Solomon cried out for God's help, seeking his approval and guidance.

The young king offered 1,000 burnt offerings in an effort to secure God's blessings. Then God appeared to him in a dream, offering Solomon anything he wanted. Imagine such an offer from God. What would you ask for?

Solomon did not hesitate in his response. "Give your servant a discerning heart to govern your people and to distinguish between right and wrong" (1 Kings 3:9).

Solomon prayed for wisdom.

No man or woman has ever found recovery apart from wisdom. It comes from several directions. We find wisdom from experience. Leonardo DaVinci stated, "Wisdom is the daughter of experience."

We also find wisdom from Scripture. Samuel Chadwick wrote, "No man is uneducated who knows the Bible, and no one is wise who is ignorant of its teachings."

Seek God. Seek wisdom. Find recovery.

Recovery Step: Seek wisdom. In wisdom, you will find recovery.

Humble Pie
March 30

Tax collectors were among the most despised citizens in Jewish society, whereas Pharisees were the most respected. Jesus was cognizant of this reality when he made a hero out of a tax collector in the following story.

"Two men went to the Temple to pray. One was a Pharisee, and the other was a despised tax collector. The Pharisee stood by himself and prayed this prayer: 'I thank you, God, that I am not like other people – cheaters, sinners, adulterers. I'm certainly not like that tax collector!' But the tax collector beat his chest in sorrow, saying, 'O God, be merciful to me, for I am a sinner.' I tell you, this sinner, not the Pharisee, returned home justified before God. For those who exalt themselves will be humbled, and those who humble themselves will be exalted" (Luke 18:10-14).

It is the humble heart that opens the door to God's blessing. It is when we think we have arrived that we are behind. Let me say it like this. Your past victories are no guarantee of future success.

Ernest Hemingway wrote, "There is nothing noble in being superior to your fellow man; true nobility is being superior to your former self."

Don't compare yourself to the tax collector. And don't compare yourself to the guy with less sobriety – or more. Just commit, one day at a time, to be superior to your former self.

Recovery Step: Escape the comparison trap. Don't worry about tomorrow. Just decide on sobriety for today. And thank God for that gift, because it is unattainable without him.

Holy Habits
March 31

Baseball Hall-of-Famer Al Kaline said, "You've got to develop good habits before the season begins. That way when the big play comes – and you never know when that will be – you will be ready."

Your sobriety tomorrow will be determined by what you do today. It's all about developing the right habits.

Camel cigarettes knew this 50 years ago. They came out with an ad, in which they invited people to take the "30-day test." They asked people to try Camel for 30 days, knowing that by that time, they would be both loyal and addicted.

There was a man in the Bible who was the master of holy habits. His name was Daniel. When he was thrown to the lion's den, the king said, "May your God, whom you serve continually, rescue you!" (Daniel 6:16). King Darius had observed Daniel "distinguish himself by his exceptional qualities" (6:3) for 30 days – and longer. And it was the character developed by those habits – such as praying three times a day at the same place and time – that saw Daniel through.

Gandhi said, "Your actions become your habits, your habits become your values, and your values become your destiny."

Do you want sobriety tomorrow? Then develop holy habits today – prayer, Scripture reading, worship, meetings, recovery work. The more you do the right thing today, the harder it will be to do the wrong thing tomorrow.

Recovery Step: Start developing one holy habit today in order to find real recovery tomorrow.

Shadows
April 1

Addiction thrives in the darkness.

Psychiatrist Carl Jung refers to our problem as a "shadow." The shadow is a metaphor for everything about us that we hide. We take our junk and hide it, repress it, deny it, and stuff it. We don't want anyone to see what's really going on inside of us. But there's just one problem.

Addiction thrives in the darkness.

In his marvelous book, *No More Secrets*, Dennis Swanberg writes, "If we cannot get rid of our secret, we try to get rid of ourselves by doing something that numbs us, amuses us, or makes us forget who we are." This only makes the problem worse.

Addiction thrives in the darkness.

There are 196 references and warnings in Scripture – about darkness. The psalmist wrote, "They do not know nor do they understand; they walk about in darkness. All the foundations of the earth are shaken" (Psalm 82:5). Our only hope of redemption is to step into the light, to be known, to embrace our better future. We must come out from the shadows. Why?

Addiction thrives in the darkness.

Recovery Step: You must be known, not by everybody, but by somebody. Decide today to take that leap and share your story with someone you can trust. You must do this because addiction thrives in the darkness.

Don't Stand Alone
April 2

He was the world's most famous recluse, the hermit's hermit, and the richest man alive. His name was Howard Hughes. An aviator, industrialist, and film producer, Hughes began showing signs of mental illness while in his 30s. On Thanksgiving Day of 1966, he moved into a suite at Las Vegas' Desert Inn. He refused to leave his room. When they insisted, he bought the hotel. Howard Hughes never found the peace that comes from healthy relationships. Fittingly, ten years later, he died alone.

We were never intended to do life alone. Few find recovery on their own. Gandhi said, "The best way to find yourself is to lose yourself in service to others." The man who stands alone will surely fall.

An elderly lady stood in line at the post office once a week, to buy stamps. The line often took about 30 minutes. An employee noted this pattern and approached the lady one day. "You do know you can buy your stamps from the stamp machine, don't you? Why do you stand in line for 30 minutes when you could get them so much quicker?"

The lady replied, "It's simple. When I get to the counter, the young man working there speaks to me. But that stupid stamp machine never says a word."

We need others in order to win the race of life. That's why Solomon wrote, "Though one may be overpowered, two can defend themselves. A cord of three strands is not quickly broken" (Ecclesiastes 4:12).

Recovery Step: You can't do this alone. You need others in your life if you are to maintain sobriety. Join a 12-step group. Get a sponsor. Sponsor others. You can't do this alone.

Tough Love
April 3

Soren Kierkegaard said, "God creates out of nothing. Wonderful, you say. Yes, to be sure, but he does what is still more wonderful: he makes saints out of sinners."

Jude said it like this: "Save others by snatching them from the fire; to others show mercy, mixed with fear – hating even the clothing stained by corrupted flesh" (Jude 23).

God is in the business of turning sinners into saints and addicts into agents of recovery for others. He finds us in our dark denials and deep despair. But he does not leave us there. While we come as we are, he does not leave us that way.

For the addict, finding recovery is not enough. We are called to help others, to "snatch them from the fire, to show mercy."

You are sober today because someone showed you mercy. Who do you know who needs a healthy dose of mercy today? Give it to them – in abundance. Then step back and watch the work of the Master Creator.

Indeed, God "does what is more wonderful: he makes saints out of sinners." He did it for you, and he can do it for others. Join him in the work. It will be the best participation award you ever receive.

Recovery Step: God is in the business of turning sinners to saints. And what he has done *in* you he can do *through* you. Join him in reaching out to others starting today.

How to Help Others
April 4

British musician Ken Hensley says, "It is hard to understand addiction unless you have experienced it."

I couldn't agree more. One of the reasons we don't help those who are suffering is that we don't understand their pain. Another reason is a misunderstanding of what it takes to get well.

Hippocrates said, "Healing is a matter of time, but mostly opportunity."

No one suffered more than a man named Job, from the Old Testament. In a short time, he lost his farm, sheep, farmers, servants, and children. Then his friends came "to comfort him" (Job 1:11). And for the most part, Job's three buddies did an awful job of offering comfort. They became critical and judgmental.

But they started well. When they first heard of their friend's troubles, "they sat on the ground with him for seven days and seven nights. No one said a word to him, because they saw how great his suffering was" (Job 2:13).

What people want more than your words is your presence. Did you catch what Job's friends did? They just sat with him in utter silence *for seven days!* We can't go seven seconds without talking. They went seven days. That's how you help others. Do you know someone who is suffering from an addiction? Your job is not to judge them or correct them – but to join them.

Recovery Step: Ask God to bring to mind one person who is suffering, then reach out to that person. Set up some time just to be there. Don't preach, teach, or advise. Just show up!

Run!
April 5

The Bible says, "Flee youthful lusts" (2 Timothy 2:22). That doesn't mean to back away from lust or take a quick glance and look away. It means *run!* And don't look back.

I love antique car shows. Every car has a sign that says, "Look, but don't touch." That's good advice for cars, but horrible advice for lust. When it comes to someone attractive from the opposite sex, we need to learn to neither look nor touch.

That's not how we are wired. We want to get as close to the cliff as we can without going over. We enjoy the intrigue, the tease. And we are playing with fire.

Dennis Swanberg illustrates this brilliantly, in *No More Secrets*, "If you wanted to hire a driver to drive you up a narrow one-lane highway in the Andes Mountains with a sheer drop-off of 2,000 feet, would you ask for a driver who could drive as close to the edge as possible? Would you ask him to keep half of the wheel over the edge in thin air? Probably not. You would want a driver who hugged the side of the mountain and stayed as far from the edge as possible. Go then and do likewise."

Lust writes checks it cannot cash. It leaves us bankrupt and alone. Presbyterian theologian Frederick Buechner said it like this: "Lust is the craving for salt of a man who is dying of thirst."

Recovery Step: You don't need to go looking for lust; it will find you. And when it does, look the other way – and then run!

Self-Control
April 6

Actor Matthew Perry, who has been public about his bouts with addiction, says, "A lot of people think that addiction is a choice. A lot of people think it's a matter of will. That has not been my experience. I don't find it to have anything to do with strength."

Perry is right, and he is wrong. Overcoming lust does require strength, but it is not a manufactured strength. It is a strength that flows from our growth in our relation to our Higher Power.

Here's the process: "Supplement your faith with a generous provision of moral excellence, and moral excellence with knowledge, and knowledge with self-control" (2 Peter 1:5-6, NLB).

From faith comes moral excellence; from moral excellence comes knowledge, and from knowledge comes self-control. The first three lay the foundation for self-control, but they don't guarantee it.

Webster defines self-control as "the ability to control oneself, in particular, one's emotions and desires." I like the way entrepreneur Robert Tew says it. "You are always responsible for how you act, no matter how you feel."

Addiction is not a choice, but acting out is. That's where self-control comes into play. But self-control only works when it is plugged into the right source.

Recovery Step: To overcome lust you need self-control. But that only comes from God. So plug into the Source and draw near to him.

Secrets
April 7

Secrets kill.

There is a story about a man named Achan. He cost Israel 36 lives and a huge upset loss to the army of tiny Ai. Israel had just defeated mighty Jericho. But they soon learned that yesterday's success is no guarantee of tomorrow's victory. They became overconfident, and they lost. Worse yet, Achan broke God's command by keeping a few valuables from the previous battle. He confessed, "I coveted the silver and gold and buried them under my tent" (Joshua 7:21). And what he buried became his undoing. It would cost him his life.

Secrets kill.

The danger of our secrets is that they are our secrets. They define us, whether we know it or not. French novelist Andre Malraux wrote, "Man is not what he thinks he is; he is what he hides."

Secrets kill.

Patrick Kennedy says, "No one is immune from addiction; it afflicts people of all ages, races, classes, and professions." If anyone should have been immune to addiction, it should have been Patrick Kennedy. But what he saw alcohol do to so many in his family, it did to him. And he did not find sobriety until he exposed his struggle to those around him. It took Kennedy years to learn this, but when he did, it saved his life. Patrick Kennedy learned this . . .

Secrets kill.

Recovery Step: What are you hiding today? The only way you can kill the enemy is to expose it. Get it out into the open. Tell somebody. Today. Because secrets kill.

Never Alone
April 8

In the United States, there are 400,000 children living in foster care. One-fourth of those are ready to be adopted, but there aren't enough parents to take in all these precious children.

Our sin has left us as orphans, separated from God. But fortunately, he is in the adoption business. As my pastor likes to say, "Jesus was, is, and always will be a come as you are Savior. But he never was and never will be a leave you as you are Lord."

The goal is transformation. The means is connection. When we connect with God and walk with him, we find the strength to overcome.

Jesus promised his followers, "I will not leave you as orphans; I will come to you" (John 14:18).

When the great John Wesley was asked to reflect on the benefits of God, he said, "The best thing of all is God is with us."

We all have something wrong with us. And regardless of the problem, the solution is the same.

God's love is unconditional and always waiting for us. Turning our life and will over to God involves opening the door of our heart to his love. Filling up on God's love helps us to avoid relapses. It meets us at our deepest need and overcomes our most powerful insecurities.

Claim the foundational promise to recovery – you are not alone.

Recovery Step: Embrace God in prayer today. Take a moment to reflect on his love, forgiveness, and most of all – his presence. Rejoice, for you are not alone.

Possibilities
April 9

That great theologian Billy Joel said, "I'd rather laugh with the sinners than cry with the saints."

There is something to be said for laughing – even from the valley of addiction. Keeping things bottled up always makes things worse. But to whom do we turn? Who do we tell? I know this. You better find that person, because keeping your struggle to yourself only leads to implosion from within.

Following his sin with Bathsheba, King David went through a period of a cover-up. He hid his sin, and to make matters worse, had Bathsheba's husband put to death in order to have her for himself. It was all a part of a master plan to cover up what he had done.

And that worked – until it didn't. David would soon acknowledge, "When I kept silent my bones roared" (Psalm 32:3). He was saying, "Until I confessed what I had done to God and one other person, the pain shot down to my bones."

Secrets make us sick.

Dr. Alex Lickerman wrote, in *Psychology Today*, "Confession opens up possibilities we would otherwise miss."

What possibilities are you missing because of your secrets? A closer walk with God? A real connection with another human being? It's time to get it out. Tell someone. Then get ready to see possibilities you would otherwise surely miss.

Recovery Step: Tell your secrets to someone, so the healing may begin.

Time to Fly
April 10

Larry Walker wanted to fly. It was his greatest passion and dream. Not born with wings, he had to become rather creative. So he hitched up 45 helium-filled balloons to his lawn chair. He strapped himself in, with a snack, soft drink, and pellet gun. His plan was to rise 30 feet into the air, then shoot the balloons to bring about a slow, gentle landing.

He overshot his target. Larry's lawn chair rocketed to heights of 16,000 feet! He then shot his balloons until he landed in some power lines. When arrested, he told the police, "A man can't just sit there."

Recovery is nothing more than redirected passion. It calls us to a universe where the impossible becomes possible, the unimaginable reality.

We really can be free! We can fly – above circumstances, temptations, and our past. But it starts with a passion for going where we have not been and for doing what we have not tried.

Yogi Berra said it like this: "If all you do is what you've done, all you'll get is what you've got."

God said it like this, speaking to Moses: "The Lord had said to Moses, 'Leave your country, your people and your father's household and go to the land I will show you'" (Genesis 12:1).

God has big plans. You've been grounded by your addiction long enough. It's time to fly.

Recovery Step: Pray for the impossible. Pray for a life free from the bondage of addiction and for the freedom to fly above it all. Then seek God with everything you've got.

Kryptonite
April 11

When I was a kid, I liked to dress up like Superman. I jumped off furniture as if I could fly. I dreamed of powers I didn't really have. Superman was every boy's hero. But even Superman could be brought down – by something called kryptonite. Kryptonite is a fictitious substance from a radioactive element from Superman's home planet of Krypton. When we watched the show on Saturday mornings, we couldn't really see the kryptonite, but we knew it was there.

That's how it is with recovery. It's what no one can see that matters. We can do all the right things, attend meetings, say prayers, and have a sponsor. By all outward appearances, we are sober and well.

But we have kryptonite that nobody else can see. It's called our heart. We are holding onto something – a fantasy, a person, an intrigue. It's deep inside of us. But if left untreated, it is the disease that will bring us down.

Jesus said, "What goes into someone's mouth does not defile them, but what comes out of their mouth, that is what defiles them" (Matthew 15:11).

It's what is going on inside of us that matters most. Ralph Waldo Emerson is credited with these memorable words: "Sow a thought, and you reap an action; sow an action and you reap a habit; sow a habit, and you reap a character; sow a character, and you reap a destiny."

You can learn to fly like Superman – victorious over temptation. But beware of your thought life. That's the kryptonite that can bring you down.

Recovery Step: Set your mind on the things of God. Focus on your thought life, and right actions will naturally follow.

Unstuck
April 12

The Tartar tribes of central Asia spoke a certain curse against an enemy. They didn't call for their enemy's swords to rust or for the people to die of disease. Instead, they said, "May you stay in one place forever."

In recovery, it is critical that we keep moving forward. When we quit working the steps, going to meetings, and making the calls, we get stuck. And before long, we lose the ground we have worked so hard to gain.

The Bible says, "But as for you, be strong and do not give up. Your work will be rewarded" (1 Chronicles 15:7).

For most of us, recovery is not a linear journey. There are a lot of ups and downs. It is not uncommon to experience setbacks, especially early in the process. When temptation comes – as it will – the worst thing we can do is not to give *in*, but to give *up*.

A St. Louis doctor met a young man in high school who had lost his hand at the wrist. When the doctor asked him about his handicap, the boy said, "I don't have a handicap, sir. I just don't have a right hand."

That is the spirit of recovery. We are only handicapped by our past, failures, and addictions if we give up if we get stuck. So keep moving, one day and one step at a time.

Recovery Step: Are you stuck in your recovery? Then it's time to get unstuck. Take one short step today that leads down a pathway to freedom and blessing.

The Person God Uses
April 13

In recovery, it is important to get outside ourselves and help others on their journey to freedom. But I hear it all the time: "How can God use me, given my messed up past?"

I have good news. God uses messed up people to do his work. In fact, God *only* uses messed up people. Consider a few examples from Scripture.

Noah got drunk and exposed himself to his sons. Abraham lied about his wife and slept with her maid. Jacob deceived his blind father. Moses killed an Egyptian he had never met. Gideon had 70 sons with his wives and another son with his concubine. Abimelech killed all 70 of his half-brothers. David slept with another man's wife, then had the man killed so he could take her as his wife. Peter denied Jesus three times. Paul dragged Christians through the city streets.

Let's go back to King David. No one did more for the kingdom's work than David. We know he was a fornicator, adulterer, and premeditated killer. But we know something else. God said, "I have found David son of Jesse, a man after my own heart; he will do everything I want him to do" (Acts 13:22).

Yes, God uses messed up people.

Peter Drucker, the father of modern management, said, "The great mystery isn't that people do things badly, but that they occasionally do a few things well."

God can mop up your biggest mess. You are exactly the kind of person he uses.

Recovery Step: Bring your messed-up life to your clean-up God. Submit to him, then get ready for him to use you as never before.

Unprocessed Shame
April 14

Debbie Ford has written a helpful book, *Why Good People Do Bad Things*. She writes of the battle of good vs. evil that is common to each of us. "Within each of us a war rages between the good self and the bad, the light and the dark, the id and the ego, the Jekyll and the Hyde."

Then, Ford offers great insight into the real problem that holds so many of us back. She says that the real obstacle to recovery is not the bad that we have done, but what she calls "unprocessed shame."

With addiction comes shame. We define ourselves by what we have done, rather than by who we are. Don't misunderstand. A little shame is alright; it's what we do with it that matters. It is *unprocessed shame* that will kill us.

One night, Peter promised Jesus he would never deny him. And then he denied him – three times. A short time later, Jesus asked Peter, "Do you love me?" (John 21:17). When Peter admitted he loved Jesus, but not with the highest form of love – *agape* love – Jesus didn't blink. He said, essentially, "That's okay. I'll use you anyway."

You have made mistakes – serious mistakes. And you've paid the price. So now it's time to move on. It's time to process your shame.

Recovery Step: Think about the thing you've done that has brought you the most shame. Then turn it over to God – and move on.

Sincerity Isn't Good Enough
April 15

Sincerity is not enough.

Charles Whitman was sincere when he shot and killed 16 people from the tower at the University of Texas. The young Arab terrorist was sincere when he drove his carload of explosives into the Marine barracks in Beirut, killing 241 American peacekeepers. Sirhan Sirhan was sincere when he killed Robert Kennedy. Adolf Hitler was sincere when he wrote *Mein-Kampf*. Benedict Arnold was sincere when he betrayed his country on the banks of the Hudson. And Judas was sincere when he sold his soul for 30 silver coins.

Sincerity is not enough.

You can be sincerely wrong. That's no good. Or you can be sincerely right. But that's not good, either, unless you do something with your sincerity.

Sincerity is not enough. But coupled with discipline, it can move mountains.

Solomon said, "For the commands are a lamp, this teaching is a light, and the corrections of discipline are the way to life" (Proverbs 6:23).

Peter Drucker said it this way: "Plans are only good intentions unless they immediately degenerate into hard work."

Recovery begins with sincerity, but it cannot end there. Sincerity + discipline = freedom. There's no other way.

Recovery Step: What is it that you sincerely wish to do to achieve sobriety? Take one step in that direction today. Then, tomorrow, take another.

It's How God Loves
April 16

C.S. Lewis wrote, "Though our feelings come and go, God's love for us does not." God wants you to do the right thing today. But if you don't, he will still love you as if you had. He loves us – even in the depths of our addiction – with unconditional love.

Paul said, "God demonstrates his love toward us in this: While we were still sinners, Christ died for us" (Romans 5:8).

Let me illustrate. When you play on a league softball team, your team will seek a corporate sponsor. This is a person or business who pays a little money, then puts his name on the back of your jersey. Let's say it's Mike's Auto Repair. You are now part of Mike's team – before your first at-bat. Whether you hit four homers or strike out every at-bat, his name stays on your jersey. It is unconditional – not dependent on your personal performance. Your bond to Mike's Auto Repair was established pre-performance.

That's how it is with God. When you come to him by faith, he accepts you. You now have the jersey. There will be days in the Christian life when you will knock it out of the park. Other times, you will strike out. But you're still on his team. You may stray, but God never does.

St. Augustine said it so well: "God loves each of us as if there was only one of us."

In recovery, you should expect ups and downs. But you can also expect this: The God of the universe will be there with you, his love undeterred by even your worst at-bat.

Recovery Step: Walk in confidence today – confidence that you are accepted by the King of the universe, not because of what you have done for him, but because of what he has done for you.

///

Three Keys to Sobriety
April 17

There is no story in literature full of more lessons than that of the Good Samaritan. After the priest and Levite passed the fallen man, a Samaritan approached. Then he did what neither religious leader dared to do. He got his hands dirty.

"He went to him and bandaged his wounds, pouring on oil and wine. Then he put the man on his own donkey, brought him to an inn and took care of him" (Luke 10:34).

Martin Luther King, Jr., wrote, in *Strength to Love*, "I imagine that the first question the priest and Levite asked was, 'If I stop to help this man, what will happen to me?' But the Good Samaritan reversed it. He thought, 'If I don't stop and help this man, what will happen to him?'"

Jesus is the Good Samaritan who came to save us. And in this passage we discover three keys to recovery.

First, the sufferer must be helpless – and know he is helpless. The fallen man knew he had no chance of recovery apart from the intervention of someone else.

Second, there must be surrender. The man had to place complete trust in the Samaritan – to take care of his needs, bandage his wounds, and take him places he could otherwise never go.

Third, there must be community. The Samaritan needed the aid of the innkeeper and others. Recovery involves a team: 12-step groups, sponsors, therapists, and more.

Recovery Step: If you have fallen, you need three things: helplessness, surrender, and community. Miss any of these and you will miss God.

Bottoms Up
April 18

Every person I've seen get well had one thing in common. They all hit bottom.

The Old Testament tells the story of such a woman. When a new widow was out of food and had become desperate, she cried out to Elisha for help. Without her husband to provide for her, the widow feared she would lose her sons to slavery. She needed to provide for them immediately, but she had precious few resources, and her family was hungry. Elisha asked her what she had in the house.

The widow had only a little oil. "She went and told the man of God, and he said, 'Go, sell the oil and pay your debts. You and your sons can live on what is left'" (2 Kings 4:7). In obedience, she started to fill the jars with oil, and God miraculously multiplied the oil.

The woman shifted her focus from what she had *lost* to what she had *left*. And then the blessings began to flow.

F.B. Meyer said, "We must get to the end of ourselves before God can begin in us." Teddy Roosevelt said it like this: "When you reach the end of your rope, tie a knot and hang on."

Perhaps you've come to the end of your rope. That's a good place to be. That means you have hit bottom. You have nowhere else to turn but to the God you should have turned to all along.

Recovery Step: If you are to the end of your rope, if you are truly desperate, you are in a good place. Why? Because it is only when you let go that God takes over.

Your Value to God
April 19

God knows everything about you. Jesus said, "The very hairs of your head are numbered. Don't be afraid; you are worth more than many sparrows" (Luke 12:7).

There are some things you probably didn't know about hair. Blondes were given 150,000 hairs to start with. Brunettes have 100,000 and redheads just 60,000. The average eyebrow has 550 hairs. Ten percent of men shave only with an electric razor, while 30% of women do. The typical beard has 15,500 hairs. Half of Caucasian men go bald, compared to 18% of African Americans. Fifty percent of men have gray hair by age 50. You are hair today and gone tomorrow.

And God has your hairs numbered. Granted, that is not a big deal for the follically challenged, but it's still pretty impressive. God knows us intimately.

God sees every thought, fantasy, and desire. Still, he loves you. And that gives you great value.

The value of something is measured by what someone is willing to pay. Jesus was willing to pay everything he had to ransom you from your sin – and from your addiction.

Albert Einstein said, "Try not to become a man of success, but a man of value."

The good news is that we are already men and women of value. The God who numbers the hairs on our heads loves us so much that he gave everything he had for us – on a bloody Roman cross.

Recovery Step: Take a moment and reflect on this: The God of the universe loves you so much that he counts every hair and forgives every sin. It doesn't get any better than that!

Don't Quit Now!
April 20

One of the keys to successful recovery is the determination to never give up, even in the face of slips and relapse. We only lose when we quit fighting.

No one personified this spirit better than Abraham Lincoln. He knew failure first-hand. In 1816 his family was forced out of their home. Two years later, his mother died. In 1831 he failed in business. The next year, he ran for the Illinois state legislature and lost. He lost his job as well. In 1833 he borrowed money to live on and needed 17 years to pay it back. In 1835 his fiancé died. This led to a nervous breakdown that had Lincoln in bed for six months. He would lose races for Congress, the Senate, and Vice President before being elected President of the United States.

Reflecting on his losses, Lincoln said, "The path was worn and slippery. My foot slipped from under me, but I said, 'It's only a slip, not a fall.'"

We must see our failures as slips and not falls. The key is to keep at it. Recovery is a marathon, not a sprint.

I love the Book of Nehemiah. When called back to his homeland to lead the rebuilding of the wall around Jerusalem, Nehemiah faced a prodigious task. But with the help of God and those closest to him, he prevailed.

What worked for Nehemiah will work for you. "So we rebuilt the wall till all of it reached half its height, for the people worked with all their heart" (Nehemiah 4:6).

Recovery Step: When progress comes slowly, keep at it. Recovery will come, if, like the people on Nehemiah's team, you "work with all your heart."

Happy Endings
April 21

I love the story of the little boy whose mother took him to the animal shelter to pick out a dog. He chose the homeliest looking puppy, but one whose tail was wagging briskly. His mom asked the boy why he picked that particular dog. The boy said, "I wanted the dog with a happy ending."

We all like happy endings.

Here's the good news. We win. For those whose faith is in their Higher Power, there is coming a day when "He will wipe every tear from their eyes. There will be no more death, no more tears, no more sorrow, and no more pain" (Revelation 21:4).

You may be in a battle today – for custody of your eyes, purity of thought, and sobriety. And while you may not win every battle, you will win the war. Your story has a happy ending.

Robin Sharma, Canadian writer and speaker, says, "Starting strong is good. Finishing strong is epic."

Billy Sunday offered a baseball analogy. "Stopping at third adds no more to the score than striking out. It doesn't matter how well you start if you fail to finish."

Keep your eye on the prize. There is coming a day when you will be victorious. The road ahead will be marred by potholes, occasional detours, and moments of discouragement. But I've read the end of the Book. There is a happy ending.

Recovery Step: Take a moment today to reflect on the fact that by faith in God, your journey will end well. There will be a happy ending. For that, you can be thankful.

Acceptance
April 22

The hardest step for most addicts is acceptance. Before I got into recovery, I said it a thousand times. "I can do this on my own; I can stop these destructive behaviors when I'm ready."

After all, I have four degrees, planted a church, pastored three churches, was a university board chairman, picked the best wife in the world, and we raised the best son in the world. And while I'm no natural mechanic, I taught myself to change my oil, my radiator, and my valve cover gaskets. I could change everything – except myself.

I just couldn't accept the fact that I am powerless. But that's where God comes in.

The Bible offers great encouragement for those of us who accept our powerlessness. "As a father has compassion on his children, so the Lord has compassion on those who fear him; for he knows how we are formed, he remembers that we are dust" (Psalm 103:13-14).

Psychotherapist Nathaniel Branden said, "The first step toward change is awareness."

That is why we need to echo the prayer attributed to Reinhold Niebuhr every day. "God grant me the serenity to accept the things I cannot change . . ."

You can't address a problem you have not yet accepted. Your only hope is to accept today what you can get to work on tomorrow.

Recovery Step: Accept that you struggle, you are an addict, and you can't fix yourself.

The War Within
April 23

We often get this idea that the Apostle Paul had it all together, that he had risen above the common sins and temptations that derail the rest of us. Nothing could be further from the truth. Hear him in his own words:

"I know that good itself does not dwell in me, that is to say in my sinful nature. For I have the desire to do what is good, but I cannot carry it out" (Romans 7:18).

That is the war that rages within each of us. We want to do the right thing, but find ourselves coming up short. But I suggest that this struggle, of itself, is not a bad thing.

Frederick Douglass wrote, "Without a struggle, there can be no progress."

So which side will win the battle? I suggest it is the side you feed the most. If you feed your addiction, expect a rough road ahead. But if you feed your recovery, expect success. And along the way, know that you will not likely win every battle.

Pope Paul VI said, "All life demands struggle."

Recovery may be the biggest struggle of all. But you only lose if you quit fighting. So stay in the fray, whether it feels like you are winning or not.

Recovery Step: Engage the enemy today. Whatever the temptation, keep fighting. Feed your recovery with the things you know will work. Then keep at it. Eventually, freedom will be yours.

Sex and Ice Cream
April 24

I still remember my first "fix." I was in my late 20s. I'm not sure how I discovered my new "drug," but when I did, I was hooked. From the first time I indulged, the image has been firmly lodged in my mind – for 30 years. Sometimes, I have gone several months without my "drug," while other times, I only abstain for a few days at a time. But the image is always there.

I'm talking, of course, about a strawberry soda from LaKing's Ice Cream Parlor in Galveston, Texas. They do it the old-fashioned way. To step into LaKing's is to step in 1920s America. They make their own taffy, candy, and strawberry sodas. I've been known to down three of them in one sitting. And then I'm satisfied – for a day or two. And no matter how many strawberry sodas I've had, I always want one more.

I identify with Oscar Wilde, who said, "I can resist anything except temptation."

Whether it is ice cream, tobacco, alcohol, or sex, we become slaves to our appetites. And then they own us. But it doesn't have to be that way.

Paul determined, "I will not be mastered by anything" (1 Corinthians 6:12).

The temptations do not go away. The key is to see that as an opportunity, and not a trap. As Ralph Waldo Emerson wrote, "We gain strength through the temptations we resist." Sometimes, it's as simple as that. We must learn to resist, to not give in. Each day we do that, we get just a little bit stronger.

Recovery Step: Identify your "drug." What is it that captivates your thoughts and imagination? Determine today to "not be mastered by anything," including that drug.

Happy, Healthy, or Holy?
April 25

One day, Jesus approached a crowd of people. Most of them were well. But Jesus noticed the lame man. He always notices the lame man. Jesus walked up to the man who had not walked in 38 years, and he healed him.

But then the story took a strange turn. A brief time later, Jesus encountered the man in town, walking free of his limp. And then Jesus said to him, "Stop sinning, or something worse may happen to you" (John 5:14).

"Something worse?" the man must have thought. "What could be worse than being crippled for 38 years?"

Let me ask you a question. If you could pick one, which would you choose: happy, healthy, or holy?

This man was now *healthy*. And this restored his standing in the community. He had to be *happy* about that. But for Jesus, the bigger issue was *holy*. The only thing worse than being physically handicapped for 38 years is to be spiritually handicapped for 38 seconds.

A.W. Tozer said, "No man should desire to be happy who is not first holy. He should spend his efforts in seeking to know and do the will of God, leaving to Christ the matter of how happy he should be."

God cares more about your character than your comfort. He may want you to be healthy and happy. It's hard to say; the day he healed the lame man, he did not heal the others. But I do know this. He wants you to be holy. And that will only happen if you stop sinning. You must remove yourself from your destructive behaviors.

Recovery Step: Stop sinning and acting out, or something "worse" will happen. That's not my threat. It's God's promise.

Change
April 26

About 2500 years ago, Chinese philosopher Lao Tzu said, "If you do not change direction, you may end up where you are headed."

Another, more modern philosopher named Yogi Berra said it like this: "If all you do is what you've done, then all you'll get is what you've got."

They are both right. Progress requires change.

The prince of prophets said, "See, I am doing a new thing! Now it springs up; do you not perceive it? I am making a way" (Isaiah 43:19).

The easy way out is to change your circumstances. But that rarely works. That leaves us with the real solution to recovery. In the words of Victor Frankl, "When we are no longer able to change a situation, we must change ourselves."

I suggest you pray the Serenity Prayer every day. Don't miss the second part of the prayer: "God grant me the serenity to accept the things I cannot change, *the courage to change the things I can*, and the wisdom to know the difference."

Gandhi said, "You must be the change you wish to see." That can start today. Submit to the one who promised, "I am doing a new thing!"

Recovery Step: Pray for the courage to change – starting with your heart, and then your behavior.

Perfectionism
April 27

Golfer Bernhard Langer had one putt that would decide the Ryder Cup winner, between Europe and the United States. He missed the putt. But he told a reporter afterward, "If I had made that putt, it wouldn't have made God love me more. And by missing it, it didn't make God love me less."

Langer learned what most of us never do – perfectionism is the impediment to progress.

No one does recover perfectly. It's all about progress – and understanding that God's approval is not determined by the accuracy of our next shot.

Brene Brown has authored four New York Times best-sellers. She is an expert on the subject of perfectionism. After years of study, Brown has concluded, "Perfectionism isn't about self-improvement; it's about approval and acceptance."

If you are to find healthy recovery, you need to understand that flawless sobriety doesn't move the needle of God's love one bit. He loves you right now, this very moment. So quit living *for* God's approval and live *from* God's approval.

The Bible says, "The Lord knows all human plans; he knows that they are futile" (Psalm 94:11).

Even if you could reach the apex of perfectionism, it wouldn't matter. The best we bring to God is "futile" apart from his blessing. Just present yourself to God today, the only way you can – just as you are.

Recovery Step: Say goodbye to perfectionism and hello to progress. This will free you up to live a life of *real* recovery.

Lessons from Golf
April 28

I am to golf what rap is to music. Technically, I am a golfer, as I have hacked at the ball an average of once a year over the past ten years. One day I was playing out of the rough. There was a tree directly between me and the green. God knew my ball would be right there, but he stuck a tree in my path anyway. I never hit my target, so I aimed right for the tree. Then it hit me – the ball, that is. It didn't hit the trunk of the tree, just a small branch. But that was enough. It turned a promising double bogey into something much worse.

Bobby Jones was right when he said, "Golf is the closest game to the game we call life."

I'm not sure Jones would have said that had he seen me play. But there is a lesson, for sure. Be careful what you are aiming at because you just might hit it.

I know guys who mess around on their phones, browsing dating sites and soft-porn sites. They never intend to actually line up a meeting with a woman, nor do they plan to click on the porn sites. But inevitably, they do. Why? Because what we aim at, we hit. And then it hits us.

Paul warned the church, "Whoever sows to please their flesh, from the flesh will reap destruction; whoever sows to please the Spirit, from the Spirit will reap eternal life" (Galatians 6:8).

Whatever captures your eye today will own your heart tomorrow. So be careful where you look – in golf and in life.

Recovery Step: Make a covenant with your eyes, to only look at those things that feed your spirit and starve your addiction.

Sharpening Your Ax
April 29

Deliverance is the product of preparation.

Moses was the greatest leader Israel ever had. The nation was depending on him to lead them to the Promised Land. But God had other plans. He intended for Moses' #2 man, Joshua, to complete the task. But it wouldn't be easy.

God told his children, "Moses my servant is dead. Now then, you and all these people, get ready to cross the Jordan River into the land I am about to give them" (Joshua 1:2).

Don't miss two words. They were the keys to victory: "Get ready."

A call to success – in anything – is a call to prepare. Abraham Lincoln understood this as well as anyone. In the midst of repeated disappointments, he said, "I will prepare, and someday my chance will come." Lincoln also said, "Give me six hours to chop down a tree, and I will spend the first four sharpening the ax."

For five years, I was blessed to serve as a chaplain for the Houston Rockets. James Harden may be the greatest basketball player I've ever seen up close. (And he never missed chapel.) But what makes him great is what happens before the cameras start rolling. Harden takes hundreds of practice shots before chapel every night – from the 3-point line. It's called preparation.

That's how it works with recovery. Success doesn't just happen. You will be able to avoid the second glance, the fantasy in your head, and the occasional slip or relapse – by what you do to prepare for the inevitable temptation. It's the private prayers, quiet readings, and daily re-commitments to sobriety that will get you through. The battle is coming, so "Get ready."

Recovery Step: Do the work of preparation today, before you face the battle tomorrow.

The Tool Box
April 30

I loved to help my dad work on the family car. We each had distinct roles. I handed him the tools, and he used them. One time, he asked for a socket wrench. I gave him a screwdriver. He said, "Why did you hand me the screwdriver?" I said, "Because when I opened the toolkit, it was on top. In order to get to the socket wrench, I would have had to get my hands dirty."

Any significant achievement in life requires hard work. You have to get your hands dirty. But the good news is that in recovery, God has given you all the tools you need.

Paul said, "God is able to make all grace abound to you, so that having all sufficiency in all things at all times, you may abound in every good work" (2 Corinthians 9:8).

John Piper describes life's daily struggle with his typical brilliance. "Darkness comes. In the middle of it, the future looks bleak. The temptation to quit is huge. Don't. You are in good company. You will argue with yourself that there is no way forward. But with God, nothing is impossible. He has more ropes and ladders and tunnels out of pits than you can conceive. Wait. Pray without ceasing. Hope."

God will give you every tool you need to achieve recovery. The reason we don't find success is not that we don't have the right tools, but that we only use the ones we like, and leave the rest in the box.

Recovery Step: You have all the tools you need in your toolbox – prayer, readings, meetings, counseling, a sponsor, Scripture, and most of all – God. Open the box, and put to good use the tools that work, even if it is hard, and even if you get your hands dirty.

Weak Is Okay
May 1

The average man can bench press 135 pounds. That means that for every guy who can lift 270 pounds there is another man who can barely lift a finger. But that's okay. *Weak is okay*.

It is in our weakness that we look to God's strength. David understood this when he penned, "God knows how we are formed; he remembers that we are dust" (Psalm 103:14).

Robin Williams, who fought addiction throughout his life, said wryly, "Reality is just a crutch for people who can't cope with drugs."

Williams had a point. Where a lot of us get into trouble is not that we are weak. It's that we aren't okay with being weak. To find recovery, we must embrace weakness as a true gift from God himself. He has allowed us to be weak in order to recognize our need for him.

Step 1 says it right off the bat. It is the foundation for recovery: "We admitted we were powerless and that our lives had become unmanageable."

D.L. Moody said it like this: "The definition of faith is placing your weakness into God's strength." The fact is, you are weak. Otherwise, you probably wouldn't be reading this right now. But that's okay. Embrace your weakness. Take it to God. In him, you can be made strong.

Recovery Step: Take your weakness to God today. Admit your powerlessness over your struggles and lean into his strength.

Empty Desire
May 2

In his book of satirical stories, *Fuzzy Memories*, Jack Handey writes, "There used to be this bully who would demand my lunch money every day. Since I was smaller, I would give it to him. But then I decided to fight back. I started taking karate lessons. But then the karate lesson guy said I had to start paying him five dollars a lesson. So I just went back to paying the bully."

It is easier to pay the bully than figure out how to defeat him.

The Apostle Paul understood this well. He had a constant inner struggle between what he knew was the right thing to do and the temptation to do the exact opposite. In a moment of inspired candor, Paul confessed, "I have the desire to do what is right, but I can't carry it out" (Romans 7:18).

That is every man's battle. It has no more difficult arena than that of sexual purity. We don't lack information. We know what we are supposed to do and what we are supposed to not do. It's actually doing what we desire to do that is so very, very hard.

Working against us is the sin nature into which we are all born. Tony Campolo sums this up with these words: "Each of us comes into the world with a disposition to live in such a way as to inflict pain on those who love us most, and to offend the God who cares for us infinitely."

And so the battle continues. My advice for us today is simple. Don't give up. Stay in the fight. You only lose when you quit fighting.

Recovery Step: Admit the wickedness of your natural desires to God and pray for the strength to do the right thing – one day at a time.

Slaves
May 3

Addiction has become an accepted way of life in American culture. The Substance Abuse and Mental Health Services Administration (SAMHSA) receives 1,594 calls of desperation per day. No area of compulsive behavior is growing like that of porn and sex addiction. It is estimated that there are 15-20 million sex addicts in the United States. A recent national survey found that one in five men have solicited a prostitute. Sex Addicts Anonymous (SAA) now has over 1,000 meetings around the country every week. But clearly, most who need help are not seeking help, as 856 condoms are sold every minute.

Millions of adolescents and adults have become slaves to their sexual appetites.

Paul warned against such trappings. "Even though I am allowed to do anything, I must not become a slave to anything" (1 Corinthians 6:12).

So what is the answer? I have found a three-step process of freedom that works when we work it. First, there must be *desire*. We have to want the benefits of freedom more than the pleasures of sin. Second, there must be *death*. Another word is surrender. We only get over what is supposed to be under us after we get under what is supposed to be over us. Third, there must be *disclosure*. We heal only once we are known.

Recovery Step: Are you ready to break free? Take these steps: desire, death, and disclosure. Only then can the chains begin to drop away.

Better than Happiness
May 4

"Stop sinning or something worse will happen to you" (John 5:14).

Those were the words of Christ – directed at a man who had been crippled for the last 38 years. The man was a beggar, with few friends, and with no means of personal sustenance. He was likely both homeless and hopeless. It's hard to imagine being in a worse state. Then Jesus healed him. A short time later, Jesus found him at a place of worship. It was then that he told the man:

"Stop sinning or something worse will happen to you."

What could be worse than being homeless? Lame? Poor? One thing – enduring the consequences of a lifestyle of habitual sin.

Getting "clean" is a most difficult, laborious, and painful journey. But the cost of not getting "clean" is greater than being a homeless beggar, unable to walk.

J.C. Ryle acknowledged the battle we are in. "There is no holiness without warfare." So fight for personal holiness. Fight for purity. Fight for integrity. Let happiness come on its own terms.

A.W. Tozer was right when he said, "No man should ask to be happy who is not first holy." So enter the battle for holiness. That is your job. Wait on happiness. That is God's job. You think you've got problems now?

"Stop sinning, or something worse will happen to you."

Recovery Step: Take the necessary steps to get "clean." Engage the enemy. Fight the battle. It won't be easy. But it will be worth it.

It's Not Your Battle
May 5

Writing about the Battle of Gettysburg, William Faulkner observed that for every Southern soldier, "There is the instant when the brigades are in position behind the rail fence, the guns are laid and ready in the woods and the furled flags are already loosened to break out . . . and it's all in the balance, it hasn't happened yet, it hasn't even begun yet. For these soldiers, the tension was palpable. Their hearts pounded in their chests as they anticipated the battle ahead."

We all have a battle raging within us. It is a battle for purity, freedom, and sobriety. But it is not a battle we can fight alone – if we want to win.

There once lived a giant named Goliath, who taunted the people of Israel. Day after day he stood there, daring them to bring out their best warrior to face him. And day after day, I can hear the prayers of the Israelites: "Please, God, remove Goliath. Take him out. Rescue us from the battle."

But God had other plans – plans to rescue them *in the battle*.

Young David volunteered to face the giant. And mere moments before confronting him, David declared, "The battle is the Lord's" (1 Samuel 17:47). Two verses later, Goliath was dead.

God could remove your battle. He could take out your giant. But he probably won't – until you enter the battle. Dale Carnegie said, "If you want to conquer fear, don't sit home and think about it. Get busy."

In our fight for sobriety, it is past time to sit at home and think about it. It's time to get busy. But keep in mind, when you step to the front lines, the battle is the Lord's.

Recovery Step: You are in the fight of your life if you have committed to personal purity. You must do two things: encounter the enemy, and remember the battle is the Lord's.

A Watchman
May 6

Stephen Covey writes, "Accountability breeds response-ability."

The only thing harder than maintaining personal purity with the support of others is to do it on your own.

The ancient prophet Ezekiel was given a critical assignment. God appointed him "watchman" over his people, in the face of enemy attack. God told Ezekiel, "I have made you a watchman for the people of Israel; so hear the word I speak and give them warning from me" (Ezekiel 33:7).

Matthew Henry describes the role of the watchman. He is "to discover the approaches and advances of the enemy, and to give notice of them immediately by sound of trumpet."

To enjoy lasting sobriety, you need to *have* a watchman, and you need to *be* a watchman.

First, you need to *have* a watchman. This is a sponsor or someone else with successful long-term recovery. They will see the threats to your sobriety that you don't yet recognize.

Second, you need to *be* a watchman. Even in your earliest days of recovery, you can help others. Look for the newcomer who needs a friend. Share what is working for you. Help him to recognize the hidden pitfalls to early sobriety.

A watchman – it's who you need, and it's who you are if you want to achieve recovery.

Recovery Step: Identify someone with successful recovery and become accountable to him or her. And become a watchman to someone new to recovery, as well.

Treasures
May 7

Jesus said, "Where your treasure is, there will your heart be also" (Matthew 6:21).

What do you treasure in this world? Is it your family? Your career? Your reputation? Maybe security? Those are all worthy of your pursuit. But none of them rises to the level of your personal sobriety and recovery. God cares more about your character than your comfort. To pursue him with all your heart, body, mind, and soul is life's highest calling.

The reason so many of us keep falling back into our temptations is that while we want sobriety, we don't treasure it. Sobriety has yet to capture our hearts. Because we treasure pleasure, comfort, and success more than we treasure personal purity, sobriety remains an elusive target.

Henry Ward Beecher said it like this: "Heaven will be inherited by every man who has heaven in his soul." Doing right has to become more than something we'd like to have. It has to consume us.

No one knows more about accumulating wealth than Warren Buffet. I love his plan, different from most whose fortunes don't begin to match his own. Buffet says, "Diversification is for people who don't know what they're doing."

Here's the point. You don't achieve purity by diversifying the portfolio of your heart. You must pursue God, purity, and sobriety above all else. You must go all in. Why? Because where your treasure is, there will your heart be also.

Recovery Step: Make personal recovery your great, unyielding task. Go all in. Treasure your recovery and personal walk with God more than anything else in this world.

Taking Out the Garbage
May 8

John Piper tells the story about the time he had a fight with his wife early in their marriage. He needed a break from the argument, so he left the house to take the garbage down the street to the pick-up spot. He says, "As I walked down the driveway toward the street where we set the garbage, the sun broke through the morning clouds. To this day, the profoundness of that moment grips me. Here I was huffing and puffing with my hurt feelings and desires for vindication, and God, who had every right to strike me dead, opened the window of heaven and covered me with pleasure. I recall stopping and letting it soak in. It felt like paradise – garbage in hand."

The Bible says, "The heavens declare the glory of God; the skies proclaim the work of his hands . . . In the heavens God has pitched a tent for the sun" (Psalm 19:1, 4).

What was true for John Piper is also true for you and me. We all have garbage we need to take out. We need to take it to the cross, God's pick-up spot. That's where we lay our garbage down.

There is an interesting promise for those of us willing to release our garbage. We experience God's glory and his redeeming grace in the process. God does not wait until we are garbage-free to reveal his glory. He has "pitched a tent" of blessing for each of us who are in the process of taking out the garbage.

What garbage have you been hanging onto? It's time to let it go. Then prepare for the blessing in the journey, not just the destination.

Recovery Step: We all have garbage to take out. Start bagging it up today, then take it to the cross. And prepare to meet God along the way.

Falling Forward
May 9

Chuck Swindoll wrote a book, decades ago, called *Falling Forward*. His premise was that we all fail. And we all fall. What matters most, he wrote, was not *whether* we fall, but *how* we fall. The fall is only a permanent failure if we don't learn from it. By letting God use the mistakes of our past, we learn to fall forward.

John wrote, "Everyone born of God has overcome the world. This is the victory that has overcome the world, even our faith" (1 John 5:4).

Soichiro Honda understood a little bit about failure. He built bicycles for a living, with a focus on small motors he would attach to the bikes. Have you ever heard of the Honda Bike Company? Probably not. But you may have heard of the Honda Motor Company. When the bike thing didn't work out, Mr. Honda put all of his efforts into making cars. What he began in a simple shop in 1948 has evolved into one of the premier companies in the world. The key? Mr. Honda fell forward. Looking back at the keys to his success, he wrote, "Success is 99 percent failure."

There was an angry farmer who took out his frustration on his hard-working horse by throwing it in the trash dump to die. He had his crew pour trash on him every hour to bury the horse alive. But each time, the horse shook off the trash and stomped on it. Each time he did this, he rose a little higher. By the third day, he walked free.

It's time you learned to walk free. Own your past. Admit your mistakes. Confess your failures. When others have tossed you in the trash heap of failures, keep climbing. It's okay to fail once in a while. Just remember – when you fall, fall forward.

Recovery Step: In what ways have you failed? Bring your past before God. Then turn the page to a whole new beginning.

Rock the Boat
May 10

I love the words of Joni Eareckson Tada. "God allows what he hates in order to accomplish what he loves."

The fact is, God can use the dark moments of your past. In some cases, he actually created them. Why? Because he allows what he hates in order to accomplish what he loves.

In God's own words, "I form the light and I create the darkness. I make peace and I create evil" (Isaiah 45:7).

One day, a little boy was playing with his toy boat on the pond. Then his boat drifted away from him, and he tried everything he could to get it back, but he couldn't reach it. All of a sudden, as he was watching the boat and trying to figure out what to do, he saw a man throwing rocks toward the boat. "What are you doing?" he asked the man. "I'm trying to help you," he said. "I'm throwing the rocks just past your boat, creating waves that are bringing your boat back to safety."

God is the ultimate rock-thrower. He will do whatever is necessary – even if it causes a few unexpected waves – to bring you back to him.

We all prefer to sail in calm waters. But sometimes it is in the storms of life that we best hear the voice of God. So when you see rocks falling around you, don't blame God. He may be the one who created them.

Recovery Step: Is your life bumpy right now? If so, quit blaming God and start thanking him, even when times are hard. Never forget, God allows what he hates in order to accomplish what he loves.

Fun for a Season
May 11

Why do many of us keep returning to our destructive habits? It's not complicated. We feed our addictions because they bring us pleasure, if only in the moment.

W.C. Fields famously said, "I spent half my money on gambling, alcohol, and wild women. The other half, I wasted."

Sin is fun – for a season. That is why we need to adopt the attitude of Moses. The Bible says, "He chose to be mistreated along with the people of God rather than enjoy the pleasures of sin for a season" (Hebrews 11:25).

A crazy thing happened one day on the streets of Wilkes-Barre, Pennsylvania. A man was walking down the street when he found a wallet. When he opened it up, he discovered hundreds of dollars in cash, as well as a driver's license. The wallet belonged to a man who was performing in town that week – Steve Martin. Now he had a choice – keep the cash or return the wallet. He returned the wallet, refusing a generous reward. He could have enjoyed the cash – for a time.

Acting out our addictions brings instant gratification. But I've never met a man or woman who looked back at those periods in their lives and said, "Feeding the pleasure of my addiction was a good idea." God has a better plan. Trade the pleasures of the moment for blessings that will never end.

Recovery Step: Identify one bad habit or addiction in your life. Recognize the pleasure it may bring in the moment. Then confess it to God and trade up for his blessings that have no end.

Beyond the Pain
May 12

As you walk the trails of recovery, you will lose some of your defective ways of coping. You will discover that your addiction is not a bad problem as much as it is a bad solution. Your real problem is an intimacy disorder. Or an unresolved conflict. Or isolation. These all brought pain into your life. Your addiction is the way you have dealt with that pain.

The Old Testament tells the story of a man named Jacob, who was devoted to his wife. But then Rachel died. Notice how Jacob dealt with the pain.

"So Rachel died and was buried on the way to Ephrath. Jacob set up a stone monument over Rachel's grave, and it can be seen to this day. Then Jacob moved on" (Genesis 35:19-21).

Did you catch that last sentence? *"Then Jacob moved on."*

You have suffered enormous pain in your past – probably due to no fault of your own. But you turned to unhealthy and destructive habits in order to cope. It's time to take those habits and put them away. Grieve the loss, then bury them.

Helen Keller said, "Only through suffering can the soul be strengthened." You have suffered long enough. It's time to bury the unhealthy ways you have coped in the past. It's time to grieve the loss. And it's time to move on.

Recovery Step: How have you coped with your pain? Take each of those unhealthy habits and bury them. Grieve the loss. Then move on.

Never Alone
May 13

You need to find recovery. But you can't do it alone. You need other people in your life; we all do.

Dr. Susan Whitbourne wrote an article that was published in *Psychology Today* on March 26, 2013, titled *15 Reasons You Need Friends*. At the end of the article, Whitbourne concludes, "You are a product of your friends, even if they are no longer your friends."

One of the things many addicts resist is joining a 12-step group. I hear it all the time: "I don't have anything in common with the group." "The group is secular, and not Christ-centered." "I may be seen walking into the building by someone who knows me."

All of those statements may be true. But they are excuses – not reasons – to not join a group. I attend two meetings a week. I need the fellowship and accountability these groups offer.

Some of my most enjoyable moments have been spent in the stadium or arena, celebrating an Astros World Series win or a Rockets playoff win with thousands of people with whom I had virtually nothing in common. And some of my best recovery moments have come in the rooms where fellow addicts gather – for support and encouragement.

There is actually a direct link from meaningful relationships to personal recovery. The Bible says, "Above all, love each other deeply, because love covers a multitude of sins" (1 Peter 4:8).

You have a problem for which there is hope. That hope is that you can find recovery. But you can't do it alone.

Recovery Step: Ask God to bring one person into your life with whom you can walk the road of recovery.

The Struggle Continues
May 14

Marilyn Monroe said, "I am good, but I'm no angel. I am just a small girl in a big world trying to find someone to love."

With those words, Marilyn Monroe spoke for all of us. If you struggle with compulsive behaviors, you are still a good person, locked in a struggle for sobriety and sanity.

The man closest to Jesus admitted, "If we claim to be without sin, we deceive ourselves, and the truth is not in us" (1 John 1:8).

You may feel awkward about bringing your recurring sins before the Lord. You may be embarrassed by the number of times you have had to deal with the same issues – issues that stubbornly refuse to go away. You may imagine that God is collecting a long list of repeated offenses to be used against you. But the truth is this – if you recognize your mistakes and confess them to God, he will forgive you.

The goal is 100 percent sobriety – no more slips and no more relapses – ever. Never accept anything less as your goal. But if you do fall short from time to time, don't kick yourself. We all continue to struggle. And God is in the business of forgiveness and restoration.

The struggle will be with you for the rest of your life – every single day. You can find victory. That's God's promise. But if you fall short, you can also find forgiveness. That's God's nature.

Recovery Step: Admit you are in the battle of your life. Don't run from the battle; engage it. And commit to personal recovery today. But if you find yourself coming up short, return to the battle. More importantly, return to God.

Why Men View Porn
May 15

Dr. Jay Springer's groundbreaking study of 3,800 men who struggle with porn has produced an interesting conclusion. The one consistent characteristic of men who view porn is not that they are bad, were abused as children, or lacked personal discipline. The dominant reason men view porn, Springer says, is that they lack a real purpose in life.

Specifically, men who admit to having no clear purpose for their lives are seven times more likely to be chronic viewers of pornography than the general population.

Porn is a not a bad problem; it's a bad solution. The problem is a purposeless heart.

Winston Churchill said, "It's not enough to have lived. We should be determined to live for something." This has been the heartbeat of every generation – the desire to know one's purpose.

This explains why Rick Warren's book, *The Purpose Driven Life*, has sold more than 34 million copies. Warren writes, "The basic question everyone faces in life is 'Why am I here?'"

Peter answered that question for each of us. He said we are "called out of darkness into God's wonderful light" (1 Peter 2:9).

Claim that promise today. Find your purpose in a daily walk with the creator of the universe, who has made you to walk in his wonderful light.

Recovery Step: Face the light and take one step forward. Tomorrow, take another step. In so doing, you will discover God's wonderful light – and your purpose for being here.

Isolation
May 16

Pitcairn Island is one of the most remote places on earth. Set in the Pacific Ocean, it is home to just 50 residents, and for good reason – you can't get there. You must fly to Tahiti and then sail for 1,200 miles. Then you transfer to a ruby dinghy, take your climbing gear and eventually scale the 900-foot rock cliffs to the tiny village.

Pitcairn Island is a metaphor for loneliness and isolation. Pitcairn Island is a metaphor for addiction.

Solomon wrote, "Whoever isolates himself seeks his own desire; he rejects sound judgment" (Proverbs 18:1).

Addicts come in all shapes and sizes. Addiction knows no color or creed, race or religion. But if you look hard enough and long enough into every addict's past, you will find the same thing.

Isolation.

Hear the words of John Lennon's hit song from 1970: *"People say we've got it made. Don't they know we're so afraid? We're afraid to be alone. Everybody got to have a home."*

The facts are these: Nobody has it made, we're all afraid, we don't want to be alone, and we've all got to have a home.

Here's the thing. Isolation is not a condition as much as it is a choice. So join the family of God, get in a support group, and get outside yourself. Why? Because if you don't defeat the demon of isolation, the demon of isolation will defeat you.

Recovery Step: Join a group. Get in a church. Make some new friends. That is the key to sanity, hope, and freedom.

It Only Takes a Smile
May 17

San Francisco's Golden Gate Bridge is one of the most beautiful places in America. But behind her majestic glory lies a series of tragedies – men and women who have scaled the apex of the great edifice, only to jump, taking their own lives.

Several years ago, a young man added his name to the list of suicides at the great bridge. Mired in loneliness and depression, he left a note on the dresser at his apartment. It read, "I'm going to walk to the bridge. If one person smiles at me on the way, I won't jump." Sadly, no one smiled, so he jumped.

In her article, *The Power of a Smile*, Kaitlin Roig-DeBellis writes, "There is an immense power found within a smile. It conveys feelings of happiness and hope."

The world needs more happiness. It really needs more hope. The key to successful recovery is not capturing that hope for yourself, but giving it away. And that's where a smile comes into play.

One of the steps on the road to recovery is helping others. And anyone can do it. Sure, you may not have the right words to say, but you do have the right smile to give. So go ahead. Give someone hope today – and be blessed in the process. It only takes a smile.

Solomon said, "A glad heart makes a cheerful face" (Proverbs 15:13). Do you have a glad heart? Then tell your face!

Recovery Step: Find one person who seems down today. Smile at them. It only takes a second, but it can make their whole day. And you will be blessed in the process.

It's All God Asks
May 18

In *Chase the Kangaroo*, Charles Cos wrote, "God calls me to be faithful. The end result is in his hands, not mine."

That flies in the face of our results-driven world. We live in an age whose god is the scoreboard, bank balance, and bathroom scale. The ends don't merely justify the means; the means no longer matter.

But in God's playbook, *the game is the scoreboard*. How you play the game matters. Then, when the game is over, the scoreboard goes black, and the players are carried off the field on the backs of angels.

In recovery, pay close attention to the journey. The destination will take care of itself.

Samuel said, "Only fear the Lord and serve him faithfully with all your heart. Consider what great things he has done for you" (1 Samuel 12:24).

Today, don't choose to be great, successful, or happy. Choose to be faithful. Live with a single focus. "Fear the Lord and serve him faithfully with all your heart."

Recovery Step: Walk faithfully before the Lord today. Then leave the rest in his enormous hands.

The Tell-Tale Heart
May 19

Edgar Allan Poe's short story, *The Tell-Tale Heart*, tells the gruesome story of a murderer who hides his victim's body under the floorboards of his house. He is so confident that he cannot be discovered that he invites police investigators into his house, where he cheerfully answers all of their questions while standing just above the corpse.

Then the murderer hears the sound of a beating heart from below his feet. He wonders why the police don't seem to hear it, as the beating gets louder. Though the officers know nothing, the man finally loses it and confesses his crime.

Geoffrey Chaucer said, "The guilty think all talk is of themselves." In other words, the guilty become consumed in the destitution of their souls.

The Bible says, "Whoever conceals his sins does not prosper, but the one who confesses and renounces them finds mercy" (Proverbs 28:13).

John Adams said, "Great is the guilt of an unnecessary war."

One of the most unnecessary wars is the one that rages in the heart of a man who has something to hide. A man is crippled by his guilt and buried by his secrets. The key to recovery is not living a sin-free life. It is outing our mistakes before they destroy us.

Recovery Step: Confess your sins. Share your struggles. Reveal your past. And in the process, embrace a God who loves, forgives, and is the creator of the second chance.

Defining God's Will
May 20

In 30 years as a senior pastor, I heard this question all the time: "What is God's will for my life?" Paul answers that for each of us. "It is God's will that you should be sanctified: that you should avoid sexual immorality" (1 Thessalonians 4:3).

How does that work, exactly? Andrew Dhuse said it well: "God's will is not an itinerary, but an attitude."

We often diminish God's will to a linear map we can track from point to point. We see God's will as a destination when it is a journey.

God's will is not about our next step, but God's next step, often hidden from the naked eye. Paul calls this *sanctification*. That's a big word that simply means "to become like him." It's a process.

And when we engage that process, the rest of God's will unfolds: we avoid sexual immorality. Don't confuse the order. We don't become like God by avoiding sexual immorality; we avoid sexual immorality by becoming like God.

It's all about attitude. Quit focusing on purity and focus on Jesus, because here's the deal. If you seek God's will, you will be frustrated. But if you seek God, it will find you.

Recovery Step: Draw near to God, through prayer, meditation, and Scripture readings. Focus your mind on him with an attitude of total submission.

Foxholes
May 21

Researchers who analyzed church attendance in the wake of the 9/11 attacks noted a spike in attendance directly following the tragedy. One megachurch in Dallas saw their attendance jump from 13,000 on September 9 to 21,000 on September 16. It was a time of unprecedented openness to God's leading, of individuals searching for stability and answers. Unfortunately, the mood soon passed.

This is what is known as the "foxhole faith" syndrome. When the heat is on, and the shells are whizzing overhead, we suddenly seek God.

We take on the attitude of David, who wrote, "Whoever dwells in the shelter of the Most High will rest in the shadow of the Almighty. I will say to the Lord, 'He is my refuge and my fortress, my God, in whom I trust'" (Psalm 91:1-2).

Most addicts turn to God because of a crisis. Then, when the crisis passes, so does their desire for God. But it doesn't have to be that way.

While serving in the Obama Administration, Rahm Emanuel famously said, "Never let a serious crisis go to waste. It's an opportunity to do things you didn't think you could do before."

Plug in the word "sobriety" in place of "things." You may be in a crisis time, seeking God in a foxhole you didn't know existed a few days ago. It's okay to be in a crisis. What's not okay is to let it go to waste.

Recovery Step: If you are in a crisis right now, find a foxhole. Seek cover in God, but when the crisis ends, let your reliance on him go deeper and deeper.

57 Rules
May 22

A sign hanging on a wall in a small business read, "The 57 Rules of Success: Rule #1 – Deliver the goods. Rule #2 – The other 56 rules don't matter."

When I was a young boy, we had a milkman who "delivered the goods" right to our front door. The grocery store did the same thing. Mom never accepted excuses. They either delivered the goods or they were in real trouble.

Jesus "delivered the goods" like no man before or after. But he kept things pretty simple. While the religious crowd was all about rules, Jesus had just one for his earliest followers. When he saw these would-be disciples, Jesus said, "Come, follow me" (Matthew 4:19).

Sure, other rules would follow – rules about how to love God and others, rules about how to care for the hurting and minister to the poor. But it was Rule #1 that served as a foundation for all the others. "Come, follow me."

St. Augustine said it like this: "Love God, then do what you want."

The Christian life is not about rules; it's about relationship. And that's good news for those of us with hurts, habits, and hang-ups. Jesus didn't tell Peter, James, and John to figure it all out and *then* follow him. Why? Because we can't figure it all out *until* we follow him.

Recovery Step: Follow Jesus today. Save the rest of the rules for later.

When the Party Ends
May 23

For millions of Americans, life is one big party. Janis Joplin confirmed, "Life is a party. But the party always ends. Then what?"

Parties come in many shapes and sizes. For some, the party is a rock climb. Others chase the thrill of water skiing. Some remodel old houses, cars, or themselves. Some seek the high of a financial deal or chase after that one elusive relationship that will surely satisfy.

And some turn to porn.

Whether your party involves relationships, material goods, alcohol, drugs, or porn, Janis Joplin is right. The party always ends.

The man who had the most understood this the best. Solomon wrote, "I have seen all the things that are done under the sun; all of them are meaningless, a chasing after the wind" (Ecclesiastes 1:14).

What are you chasing after to fill the void? As Billy Graham often said, there is in the heart of every person an emptiness that only God can fill. You can try to fill that void with many other things. But remember, they don't last. The party ends. Then what?

Recovery Step: The pleasures of this world are both elusive and fleeting. Put your faith in Christ, because when this party ends – and you know it will – his party will just be starting.

TV Dinners and Pot Pies
May 24

We ate them once a week – TV dinners and pot pies. Six nights a week, mom and dad insisted that we sit around the table for family dinner at 6:00 pm sharp. But once a week – usually when *Batman* was on – we were allowed to eat in front of the television set.

The TV dinner was different from the pot pie, as each segment of the "meal" – meat, veggies, and dessert was in its own compartment. But the pot pie had it all thrown in together. The chicken or turkey was mixed with the carrots, peas, and mystery sauce.

There are two ways we can do life – like the TV dinner or the pot pie. But only one is healthy.

Addicts live the life of a TV dinner. Everything is compartmentalized. Each part of life – family, financial, faith, and fantasy – is separated from the rest. This leads to chronic fatigue and constant frustration.

God intended us to live life like a pot pie. We must not separate our sexual lives from everything else. It's all interconnected.

God wants your sexual life – but not *just* your sexual life. He wants it all. Proverbs 21:26 says, "The righteous gives and does not take back." In other words, we must give it all to God. Every day.

Recovery Step: Quit compartmentalizing. Either God is Lord of all, or he is not Lord at all. Make him Lord of all today.

Jephthah
May 25

Tucked away in the Book of Judges is the story of a man named Jephthah. The Bible says, "Then the Spirit of the Lord came on Jephthah. He crossed Gilead and Manasseh, passed through Mizpah of Gilead, and from there he advanced against the Ammonites. And Jephthah made a vow to the Lord: If you give me the Ammonites into my hands, whatever comes out of the door of my house to meet me when I return in triumph from the Ammonites will be the Lord's, and I will sacrifice it as a burnt offering" (Judges 11:29-32).

This commander of God's army made this vow, and he stuck with it. God's victory would be followed by man's sacrifice.

Ecclesiastes 5:4 says, "When you make a vow to God, do not delay to fulfill it."

What vows have you made to God? Have you said something like this? "God, if you bless me with (fill in the blank), I will never view inappropriate websites again." That is a vow worth keeping.

Robert Frost famously wrote, "The woods are lovely, dark and deep. But I have promises to keep and miles to go before I sleep."

Before you walk your next mile – or step – think about the promises you have made to God, your spouse, and others. Be like Jephthah. Keep your word as surely as God has kept his.

Recovery Step: Today is not a day to make new promises, but to keep the ones you've already made.

After the Temptation
May 26

Oscar Wilde said proudly, "I can resist anything except temptation."

Overcoming temptation is the focus of any person's sobriety. But what comes *after* the temptation must not be ignored.

The Bible tells us that "Jesus was led by the Spirit into the wilderness to be tempted by the devil. After fasting forty days and forty nights, he was hungry" (Matthew 4:1-2).

I see two lessons here.

First, we can be at risk *after* the temptation, not just *before* it. Jesus became hungry. Hunger puts us at a point of vulnerability.

Second, while the temptation can be exhausting, victory gives us strength and confidence for the next battle. John Bunyan said it like this. "Temptations, when we meet them at first, are as the lion that roared upon Samson, but if we overcome them, the next time we see them we shall find a nest of honey within them."

Temptation is a battle we all must face. But don't lose focus — because what comes next matters just as much.

Recovery Step: Are you facing temptation today? Then get ready for what comes next. In the victory, you may become overconfident and vulnerable. So get ready and stay strong.

The Proposal
May 27

The most unlikely couple in the Bible was Gomer and Hosea. Gomer (the woman) had a checkered past. But God told Hosea (the man) to pursue her anyway. And when Gomer persisted in her lifestyle as a prostitute, God gave Hosea amazing counsel.

"Go show your love to your wife again, though she is an adulteress" (Hosea 3:1). Then Hosea said to his wife, "You are to live with me many days; you must not be a prostitute or be intimate with any man, and I will behave the same way toward you" (Hosea 3:3).

God proposed that Hosea propose to his wife – a new beginning, launched from the pad of forgiveness.

We see two things here. First, adultery does not need to end a marriage. Second, sometimes, there must be a period of celibacy within the marriage so recovery can begin.

Perhaps you are a wounded spouse. You did not sign up for your mate's infidelity. And who can blame you if you file for divorce? I certainly wouldn't.

It takes a lot to stay with someone who turns out to be something less than advertised. But it's possible, and sometimes a blessing.

Marilyn Monroe said, "If you can't take me at my worst, you don't deserve me at my best."

Is the restoration of your marriage possible? Yes. Will it be easy? No. But as we say in our ministry every day, even in the face of adultery – *There's still hope.*

Recovery Step: If you've been wounded, just consider the possibility that the marriage doesn't have to end. Pray about it. Seek God's will. There are no easy answers, but – *There's still hope.*

Shoe
May 28

Jeff MacNelly used to write an old comic strip called *Shoe*. In one of the strips, Shoe was pitching in a baseball game. His catcher told him, "You've got to have faith in your curveball."

Shoe grumbled, "It's easy for him to say. When it comes to believing in myself, I'm an agnostic."

Charles Schwab said, "When a man has put a limit on what he *will* do, he has put a limit on what he *can* do."

If you are struggling to believe in yourself and your capacity for recovery, hear the words of Jack Canfield, who wrote *The Success Principle*. "Create a turnaround statement that affirms or gives you permission to be, act, or feel in this new way."

Scripture offers hope. It speaks of a Savior "who is able to do immeasurably more than all we ask or think, according to his power that is at work within us" (Ephesians 3:20).

Sobriety will not come easily, but it will come – if you believe in your Higher Power and yourself. Never put a limit on the overcoming power of two – you and God.

Recovery Step: Trust God and then trust yourself. Whatever obstacles you are facing can be overcome. How is this possible? Because we serve a God who can do more than we ask or think.

The Man God Wants
May 29

Mike Kollin, former linebacker for the Miami Dolphins, was talking to Coach Shug Jordan, who wanted his help with recruiting. "What kind of player do you want, Coach?" Kollin asked.

Jordan said, "See that player over there, who gets knocked down and stays down?"

Kollin said, "Sure, Coach, we don't want him, do we?"

Jordan said, "That's right. Now, see that other guy who gets knocked down, but he gets back up?"

"Sure, Coach. That's the kind of player we want, right?"

"Nope. We don't want him, either."

"Then which player do we want?"

Coach replied, "We want the guy who keeps knocking everyone else down!"

Jesus said, "The gates of hell will not prevail against the church" (Matthew 16:18). In other words, we are to play offense, not defense.

When you are tempted, don't crawl into a corner and recoil. Take the initiative. Don't wait for the enemy to attack you. Begin knocking down the strongholds that have captured your mind for too long. Sure, if you get knocked down, get back up. But better yet, do the things that will ensure that you don't get knocked down in the first place.

Recovery Step: Go on the offensive. Prepare for the day of battle so you can punch temptation in the face.

Sergeant York
May 30

Early in the classic movie *Sergeant York*, lightning struck the title character during a late-night thunderstorm in the backwoods. York, convinced that the bolt was a message from above, initiated a relationship with God. Later, York was called up for military duty in World War I and shipped off to Europe. Pinned down by enemy gunfire, York did not lose his faith – or his life.

The best thing about the movie is this: it really happened.

No one likes a crisis. They rarely fit our lifestyle, and they never fit our schedule.

Secretary of State Henry Kissinger once said, "There cannot be a crisis next week. My calendar is already full."

Fortunately, we serve a God whose calendar is always busy, but never full. David told his God, "Let all who take refuge in you rejoice" (Psalm 5:11).

Let your crisis be His opportunity. Like Sergeant York, find refuge in God. No matter how much the pain or how bad the timing, God is always good and he is always on time.

Recovery Step: Are you in a crisis moment today? Find refuge in God. And know this. In your loss there is love, in your pain, there is peace, and in your grief there is grace.

Detours
May 31

Those who live in the north know just two seasons – winter and road repair. The harsh winter conditions bring ice and snow, which often buckle roads and create potholes. The result is that drivers in March and April are often faced with detours from their normal routes.

Some detours are the fault of the driver. A missed turn, lack of concentration, or refusal to ask for directions. They all mean rerouting our course. We take detours.

Barbara Bush said, "When you come to a roadblock, take a detour."

Zig Ziglar added, "Failure is a detour, not a dead end street."

For many of us, our detour led us into a life of addiction. When we should have turned right, we went left. When we should have been in the Word, we were in the world.

But it's never too late to come back onto the main road. If you have driven off the intended path, there is an entrance ramp back to the thoroughfare of recovery. It's called "Jesus."

Jesus said, "I am the way" (John 14:6). Your habit has taken you off course. But it doesn't have to be a dead end. Follow Jesus back onto the road of sobriety and real recovery.

Recovery Step: If you have drifted off course, it's not too late to get back on the main road. Follow Jesus. He is the only one who can take you where you want to be.

Pray
June 1

"Pray continually" (1 Thessalonians 5:17).

You won't find a more straightforward verse than that one.

Unfortunately, too many of us pray too little. A report by *Newsweek* concluded that 91 percent of women pray, as well as 85 percent of men. That number rises to 100 percent among golfers once they reach the green. But most limit their prayers to quickies before a difficult putt or questionable meal.

For most of us, serious prayer is relegated to times of crisis. We are like the girl who prayed after taking a test in school: "God, either make Boston the capital of Vermont or lose my test paper by tomorrow morning."

Like that girl, we all face tests – especially those of us engaged in a fight for purity. We need to live like a mountain climber. When the wind comes against him, he gets on his knees.

Are the winds of temptation threatening to blow you off course? Then get on your knees today.

Robert Kennedy said, "All of us might wish at times that we lived in a more tranquil world, but we don't. And if our times are difficult and perplexing, so are they challenging and filled with opportunity."

The trials you face today are filled with opportunity – to grow, rely on God, and turn to him in prayer.

Recovery Step: When you are tempted, pray. Before you are tempted, pray. After you are tempted, pray. Get the point? Pray!

Knowing God
June 2

Any successful recovery is a spiritual recovery. It's not just about going to meetings, memorizing helpful principles, and working the steps. It's about making a spiritual connection. And for those who are blessed with years of genuine recovery, they have nothing to boast about, except for the Higher Power.

God told his children, "Let him who boasts boast in this, that he knows me" (Jeremiah 9:23).

Theologian J.I. Packer said it like this: "Once you become aware that the main business that you are here for is to know God, most of life's problems fall into place of their own accord. What makes life worthwhile is having a big enough objective, something which catches our imagination and lays hold of our allegiance; and this the Christian has in a way that no other person has. For what higher, more exalted, and more compelling goal can there be than to know God?"

We don't find God through recovery; we find recovery through God. If you seek recovery for the sake of recovery, you will be frustrated, like a man walking up a hill covered in butter. But if you seek God, recovery will find you.

Jim Elliot said it in typically concise terms. "Oh, the fullness, pleasure, sheer excitement of knowing God on earth!"

Make that your goal – to know God. Everything else comes later.

Recovery Step: Jesus said, "I am the way" (John 14:6). Through him, find God, and you will find hope and recovery. But always make knowing God your first priority.

Unknown Freedom
June 3

Juneteenth is an unusual holiday birthed in Texas. It is celebrated on June 19 across the country, commemorating the day in 1865 when Gordon Granger, a Union general, rode into Galveston, Texas, and announced that slavery had ended. Slaves were jubilant. However, the slaves had already been granted freedom when President Lincoln issued the Emancipation Proclamation on New Year's Day, 1863. The slaves in Texas were free for 2.5 years before they even knew it.

The slaves were free but didn't know it. Many of us live lives like that. God has provided a complete pardon through his son, Jesus Christ. Still, we remain behind the bars of our addiction and compulsive behaviors. The Sheriff has handed us the keys, but rather than unlock the doors, we remain captives in our own minds.

Paul wrote about such believers. "All of us also lived among them (non-believers) at one time, gratifying the cravings of our flesh and following its desires and thoughts" (Ephesians 2:3).

Martin Luther King, Jr.'s words ring as true as they did the day he first preached them, from the steps of the Lincoln Memorial on August 28, 1963. "Free at last. Free at last. Thank God almighty we are free at last."

You have been emancipated. You are no longer a slave to your addiction. So begin walking in the reality of that freedom.

Recovery Step: Claim the freedom God has already provided. Don't live to gain that freedom, but because it is already yours.

Make a Wish
June 4

Ever wonder how the Make-a-Wish thing all got started?

In 1980 doctors diagnosed Chris, age seven, with leukemia. He wanted to be a motorcycle police officer when he grew up. A friend of his family spoke to a member of the Arizona Highway Patrol, and within a few days, several officers came by to visit Chris.

After the meeting, the officers wanted to do more. They arranged for Chris to ride on a police helicopter and in a police car. They got him a police uniform and replaced his wheelchair with a battery-powered motorcycle. When he died, he was given full police honors.

This was the spark of the Make-a-Wish Foundation.

2 Thessalonians 1:11 says, "We pray that our God may make you worthy of his calling and that by his power he may bring to fruition your every desire."

Success begins when we make a wish. Why not make a wish today – for sobriety, sanity, and recovery? Then turn your wishes into reality. Walk out your wish, your desire.

Michael Jordan said, "Some people want it to happen, some wish it would happen, others make it happen."

Recovery starts with a wish. "I wish I was well." When put to action, Make-a-Wish becomes a foundation for a lifetime of recovery.

Recovery Step: State your wish for sobriety today. Then, do the things that help this wish come true.

Assume Nothing
June 5

One of our most vulnerable times is when things are going well. We let our guard down. Legendary tennis icon Rod Laver was right: "The time your game is the most vulnerable is when you're ahead; never let up."

If there was ever a man who could have taken his foot off the gas pedal, it was King David. But following his greatest triumph, he got a dire warning – and his response was perfect.

"A messenger soon arrived in Jerusalem to tell David, 'All Israel has joined Absalom in a conspiracy against you!' 'Then we must flee at once, or it will be too late!' David urged his men. 'Hurry! If we get out of the city before Absalom arrives, both we and the city of Jerusalem will be spared from disaster'" (2 Samuel 14:13-14).

Sometimes in recovery, we're on top of the world; we feel as though our problems are licked for good. At such times, it is tempting to relax and stop living one day at a time. But then life surprises us with an unexpected problem.

Colin Powell said, "A dream doesn't become reality through magic; it takes sweat, determination, and hard work."

Whether you have been sober for five minutes or five years, assume nothing. Take nothing for granted.

Recovery Step: Keep your guardrails in place. Prepare for battle. If you are sober today, that guarantees nothing for tomorrow. Take nothing for granted.

Keep It Simple
June 6

It's easy to make recovery – and life – more difficult than is necessary. I love the simplicity of the Christian life as expressed by 1960 World Series MVP Bobby Richardson.

During a Fellowship of Christian Athletes meeting, the group's leader asked Richardson to pray. In response, Richardson uttered eleven powerful and profound words: "Dear God, your will, nothing more, nothing less, nothing else. Amen."

Jesus told the story of a man who prayed a similarly simple but powerful prayer. A tax collector – someone the religious people of the day viewed with disdain and distrust – spoke a prayer of just seven words: "God, have mercy on me, a sinner" (Luke 18:13). Perhaps no one else has ever uttered a more sincere or powerful prayer.

Confucius said, "Life is really simple, but we insist on making it complicated."

Recovery is all about maintaining a centered life – around our Higher Power. Don't muddy the waters with unnecessary rules. Keep your eyes on Jesus – the Author and Finisher of your faith.

Recovery Step: Echo these words of Bobby Richardson. Whisper them to God right now: "Dear God, your will, nothing more, nothing less, nothing else. Amen."

When in Rome
June 7

Where did we get the mantra, "When in Rome, do as the Romans do"? Here's the story.

Before Augustine traveled to Rome from Milan, he shared a problem with Ambrose. As a young priest, Augustine wanted to know what he should do about celebrating the Sabbath. Rome celebrated the Lord's Day on Sunday, while Milan celebrated on Saturday. This discrepancy confused Augustine and caused him to take up the matter with Ambrose.

The elder priest advised Augustine, "When in Rome, do as the Romans do."

That is good advice for world travelers. But it is dangerous counsel for the person seeking to live a life of integrity – sold out completely to God.

Revelation 3:16 says, "So, because you are lukewarm – neither hot nor cold – I am about to spit you out of my mouth" (Revelation 3:16).

John Stott said, "Apathy is the acceptance of the unacceptable."

So go ahead. When in Rome, do as the Romans do. But if it is true recovery that you want, don't "do" as those around you. That's what got you in this mess in the first place.

Recovery Step: Stand out and take a stand. Don't cave to the norms of the crowd. Be willing to stand on principle, to live a life of honesty and integrity. Don't follow the crowd; lead the crowd. Don't cave to culture; create culture. Don't dream of integrity – model it for others.

When You Are Overwhelmed
June 8

King David prayed, "Though we are overwhelmed by our sins, you forgive them all" (Psalm 65:3).

Most of us need to desire something before we will wholeheartedly seek after it. Until we realize how much God loves us and cares about the details of our lives, we probably won't have the desire to pray to him. Until we sincerely believe that he has completely forgiven us, we will be ashamed to face him. If we hold to our misconceptions about God, this step will be a formidable chore rather than an indescribable pleasure.

The life of King David gives us hope. He had committed sins that would get any pastor fired, any president impeached, and any other person sued. But when he came to his senses, he came to his God. First overwhelmed by his sins, he became overwhelmed by God's grace.

Dorothy Hamill said, "At times I feel overwhelmed, and my depression leads me into darkness."

John Calvin wrote, "Seeing that a Pilot steers the ship in which we sail, who will never allow us to perish even in the midst of shipwrecks, there is no reason why our minds should be overwhelmed with fear and overcome with weariness."

Perhaps you have driven your "ship" into the darkest, most stormy waters. But it is in the desperation of your darkest moment that God shines his brightest light. Do you feel overwhelmed by sin, guilt, and shame? That's okay – God is about to do what he does best.

Recovery Step: If you are feeling overwhelmed by the mistakes of the past, confess that to the one who stands ready to overwhelm you with the forgiveness of all eternity.

Your Inheritance
June 9

Let's talk inheritance today. Statesman Patrick Henry stated his greatest inheritance. "What I possess is all the inheritance I can give to my dear family. The religion of Christ will give them one which will make them rich indeed."

Peter, one of Jesus' first followers, wrote, "We have an inheritance that can never perish" (1 Peter 1:4).

It's interesting that a man – Jesus – who had so little could give so much. He shunned the riches of this world to tap into the endless resources of heaven.

Soren Kierkegaard wrote, "In the understanding of the moment, never has anyone accomplished so little by the sacrifice of a consecrated life as did Jesus Christ. And yet in this same instant, eternally understood, he had accomplished all, and on that account said with eternity's wisdom, 'It is finished.'"

It was by "the sacrifice of a consecrated life" that Jesus changed the world. And that is what God requires of each of us. He doesn't ask you to be perfect – in life or recovery. But he does ask for the sacrifice of a consecrated life. Want the greatest inheritance ever? It can be yours, but remember this – a consecrated life is the price of admission.

Recovery Step: Make the sacrifice of a consecrated life today, and the blessing of heaven will be yours forever.

Love and Light
June 10

Which is more important – love or light? One defines how we live, and the other defines what we see. I suggest we need both.

J. Charleton Steen wrote, "God is light. That which professes to be light yet lacks love, is not of God, while that which calls itself love, but is not according to light is equally not of God."

I hear it all the time from men seeking to conquer their worst behaviors. "I don't just want to get right myself; I want to help others." This requires the best kind of love, which is guided by the brightest kind of light.

1 John 4:20 says, "Whoever does not love their brother or sister cannot love God."

St. Augustine said it like this: "What does love look like? It has the hands to help others, the feet to hasten to the poor and needy, the eyes to see misery and want, and the ears to hear the sighs and sorrows of men. That is what love looks like."

The light tells us where to go, while our love tells us what to do once we get there.

George Burns jokingly said, "Happiness is having a large, loving, caring, close-knit family in another city."

That may work for some families, but it doesn't work in addiction. You need relationships with fellow strugglers, where you are guided by divine light to share divine love in the power of a divine God.

Recovery Step: Pray for the light of God to guide you to a person with whom you can express the love of God today.

Let's Roll!
June 11

"Are you guys ready to roll?" Those were Todd Beamer's last recorded words.

The passengers who counterattacked the hijackers of United flight 03 on September 11, 2011, demonstrated that when a crisis strikes, ordinary people often rise to the occasion. The heroic actions of this group who took a stand against the hijackers probably prevented the destruction of another historic Washington D.C. building – either the U.S. Capitol or the White House.

In a taped phone conversation, Todd Beamer, one of the passengers, recited the Lord's Prayer and Psalm 23. Then he prayed, "Jesus, help me," before leading the attack on the hijackers. Undoubtedly, Beamer and his fellow passengers were scared. But faced with this challenge, his faith in Christ kicked in. He took action, uttering those now famous words, "Let's roll." Although Beamer's story ended tragically in a farmer's field in Shanksville, Pennsylvania, it stands as an inspiration to all who will never forget the shock of that infamous day.

Like Beamer's courageous call to action, Queen Esther's statement, "If I perish, I perish" (Esther 4:16), perfectly expresses the do-or-die quality of active faith. Esther's decision to speak on behalf of her threatened people, knowing that the king could execute her, demonstrates that God provides courage in crisis to people who are willing to step out in faith.

Mark Batterson wrote, "When you look back on your life, the greatest moments will be the moments when you went all in."

Do you want a successful recovery for the rest of your life? It can happen, but only if you go all in. If you really want it, you can have it.

Recovery Step: It's time to take a stand in the face of the enemy. All of heaven is on your side. "Let's roll!"

Production Without Passion
June 12

God did not create human doings, but human beings. He is far more concerned with what is happening *in* you than what is happening *around* you or *by* you. He is not looking for production, but passion.

Oswald Chambers wrote, "The greatest competitor of devotion to Jesus is service for him."

Speaking to a church that was doing all the right things, God said, "Yet I hold this against you. You have forsaken the love you had at first" (Revelation 2:4).

We live in busy times. We fill our schedules with things that are all good, but God gets left out. In the story of Mary and Martha, we see two sisters seeking to please God in their own way. One gave Jesus her best effort while the other gave Jesus her heart. And that was the sister most blessed.

God longs for you to spend time with him. Read a few verses of Scripture, talk to him as a friend, and just sit in his presence. Set down your phone and pick up your Bible. Get off your computer and get on your knees.

I love the way John Piper said it. "One of the greatest uses of Twitter and Facebook will be to prove at the Last Day that prayerlessness was not from lack of time."

Forget about production and focus on passion. If you get your passion right, the production will take care of itself.

Recovery Step: Take five minutes to read a verse of Scripture, get on your knees, and open your heart to God. Replace production with passion, and God will replace anxiety with peace.

Ferrari vs. Pinto
June 13

A leading voice on the porn effects on millennials is Alex Lerza, founder and CEO of The Recovery Tribe. Lerza summarizes the struggle of teens and young adults with the illustration of a car. He says of the emerging generation, "When it comes to sex and porn, they have a Ferrari engine, a Pinto set of brakes, and no owner's guide."

King David prayed, "Do not remember the sins of my youth and my rebellious ways" (Psalm 25:7).

As a young man, David struggled with the same temptations of today's generation. (And it's not just *young* men.) So what do we tell this new generation of young people – with a Ferrari engine, Pinto brakes, and no owners guide? I suggest two things.

First, we tell them sex is not bad. Too often, in our effort to keep our kids on the "straight and narrow," we rely on shame. "All sex before marriage is sin," we tell them. Since they have not yet been married, what they hear us saying is, "All sex is sin." We tie sex to shame. That's bad.

Second, we give them the owner's guide. The good news is that we have an excellent owner's guide. We teach them biblical principles. We tell them that sex is beautiful, that they are beautiful, and that the God of sex created it for them – in the right time.

Recovery Step: Cut out the secrets and lift the veil. The way to guide your kids down the right path is not to remove their engine or add anti-lock brakes, but to introduce them to the owner's guide.

Progress, not Perfection
June 14

Let me say up front, there is no license to acting out. It is never right, and it should never happen. Once you enter recovery, it is possible to never again view porn, masturbate, or act out. And God's intended will is that you never break your sobriety – ever.

And for many, this will be the case. But hear this – *recovery is about progress, not perfection*. Nobody works his recovery perfectly. And if you do have a slip, remember . . . it's about progress, not perfection.

Paul told the local church, "I don't mean to say that I have already achieved these things or that I have already reached perfection. But I press on to possess that perfection for which Christ Jesus has possessed me" (Philippians 3:12).

Perfection is out of reach. Progress is not.

Plato warned us, "Never discourage anyone who continually makes progress, no matter how slow."

We are too quick to criticize God's unfinished work. I have rarely heard a man criticize the looks of a house while it was only half-finished. Most of us are barely half-finished. So if you are a work in progress not yet completed, congratulations. And if you know someone who is not yet complete, congratulate him.

Recovery Step: Encourage someone who is struggling to stay in the battle for sobriety. If they aren't perfect, try to remember two things – God's not done with them yet, and you probably aren't perfect either.

Comfort
June 15

P.T. Barnum said, "Comfort is the enemy of progress."

Recovery is not about being comfortable. It's about progressing to the next step – and then the next. And sometimes this is hard, painful, and even discouraging.

Solomon wrote, "Those who work their land will have abundant food, but those who chase fantasies have no sense" (Proverbs 12:11).

In the arena of sexual gratification, it's interesting to read the stories of famous men who chased their fantasies and then bragged about their personal exploits. Wilt Chamberlain famously said, "I have been with over a thousand different women." Just doing the math on that one will make your head spin!

A thousand different women? Seriously? Why not stop at 900? The answer is simple. Seeking sexual satisfaction outside of God's boundaries is like quenching your thirst with salt water. It looks good and seems like it should work, but it only makes matters worse. You can never get enough.

Chasing your fantasies is easy. Anyone can do that. But as Solomon said, it makes no sense. God has a better plan. Work the land God has given you. It's not easy or popular to stay on your own farm. But that is the only way you will ever have abundant food.

Recovery Step: P.T. Barnum was right. Comfort is the enemy of progress. So do what's sometimes hard and even mundane. Instead of chasing fantasies, work your own land. Only then will you enjoy the blessing of abundant food.

One Slip
June 16

One slip can bring you down.

I have known many good men and women who achieved years of sobriety. Then, the reputation they worked so hard to achieve was lost in a moment.

One slip can bring you down.

James said, "For whoever keeps the whole law and yet stumbles at just one point is guilty of breaking all of it" (James 2:10).

The problem is, most of us "stumble" over something. A recent article in *Clinical Psychology Science* puts the relapse rate as high as 80 percent. So each of us – including you – must remain diligent and on guard. We can perform at a high level, but fail in the moment and lose it all.

One slip can bring you down.

If you have had a slip, don't despair. Mary Tyler Moore said, "You have to fail in order to practice being brave." So be brave today. Turn the page from yesterday's failures to tomorrow's miracles. Many stumble, but that doesn't have to include you. Learn from your past in order to change your destiny. It's critical, because . . .

One slip can bring you down.

Recovery Step: Because one slip can bring you down, it is critical that you remain diligent. Produce a 24-hour game plan to stay sober for today.

God's Greatest Wrath
June 17

That great philosopher Groucho Marx said, "The secret of life is honesty and fair dealing. If you can fake that, you've got it made!"

Groucho was right about one thing – the value of honesty. Unfortunately, it can't be faked. And God has high regard for honesty.

The old prophet made God's feelings on the matter pretty clear. "Everyone who swears falsely will be banished" (Zechariah 5:3).

Don't miss the form of judgment reserved for the sin of dishonesty. God said the person will be "banished." God's greatest wrath is not functional – what he does to us. It is relational – what it does to our walk with him.

Said another way, God's greatest judgment is not what he takes away from us, but what he takes us away from. When we are dishonest – and this is the struggle of every addict – we put in jeopardy the intimacy of our spiritual walks.

It's bad enough to lose custody of our eyes, to engage in fantasy, or worse, to slip or relapse. But to cover it up is an act of dishonesty. And this brings the gravest of judgment.

Recovery Step: Come clean. Get current and get honest – before God, yourself, and one other person. To live in dishonesty brings a price you cannot afford to pay.

Personal Responsibility
June 18

One day, Peter came upon a lame beggar. The man had no hope apart from the kindness of those who passed his way. He couldn't get a job because he could not walk.

Enter grace.

Acts 3:7 says, "And Peter took him by the right hand and lifted him up. Immediately his feet and ankle bones received strength."

But now the man had to take ownership of his future. Peter (God, really) could help him up, but it was up to the man to start walking.

It is easier to find sobriety and stand for the first time than it is to keep walking. To move forward in our recovery requires belief in God and ourselves, followed by taking personal responsibility for what happens *after* the healing begins.

In her wonderful book, *Mindset*, Dr. Carol Dweck writes that the single most important factor in recovery is the belief that a person can change and grow.

Ben Shapiro said, "There is nothing less seductive than a lecture on personal responsibility."

God can bring healing. If he can raise the dead, he can heal the lame. But it's up to you to believe in God and yourself – then to take responsibility for the next step forward.

Recovery Step: Trust God to raise you up, but only if you're committed to the journey forward. Take ownership of your personal recovery.

Worse than Failure
June 19

Sometimes, the only thing worse than a bad decision is a no-decision. Aaron Burr said, "Error is better than indecision."

King Rehoboam suffered from paralysis by analysis. He recoiled in the big moments. He had the authority and power to meet every challenge successfully. But, crippled by his unwillingness to make decisions, he found himself in constant turmoil.

One day, the Bible says, "Some worthless scoundrels gathered around him and opposed Rehoboam, son of Solomon, when he was young and indecisive and not strong enough to resist them" (2 Chronicles 13:7).

Like Rehoboam, you have the authority and power to overcome. You have what it takes, and you have Who it takes. Your recovery will be driven by making the decisions God clearly puts before you.

It is most likely that when you fail, it is not for lack of knowledge, but due to indecisiveness. John Ortberg was right: "Greatness is never achieved through indecision."

Because he wouldn't make decisions, Rehoboam was "not strong enough to resist" the battles that came his way. Recovery only comes through the strength to resist, and the strength to resist only comes by making the decisions that are right in front of you.

Recovery Step: Knowing what is right is the easy part. Deciding to act on what you know is where the magic takes place. So get off the couch, out of the box, and into the game. The only thing worse than taking the wrong step is taking no step at all.

Bankrupted by Success
June 20

Bud Post won $16.2 million in the Pennsylvania lottery. He figured he was set for life. But his ex-girlfriend successfully sued him for a share of his winnings. And Bud's brother hired a hit man to kill him, hoping to inherit some of the fortune. Sadly, Bud's troubles didn't end there. Due to his fulfilling repeated requests for debt relief from friends and family and making a large investment in a failed business venture, Bud found himself over $1 million in debt within a year of winning the lottery. By the time he reached retirement age, the former multimillionaire was surviving on $450 a month and food stamps.

Post is not alone. Within five years of winning the jackpot, one-third of all lottery winners declare bankruptcy. Too often, we put our trust in our own wisdom.

Wise old Solomon offered a better way. "Trust in the Lord with all your heart and lean not on your own understanding. In all your ways submit to him, and he will make your paths straight" (Proverbs 3:5-6).

I'll admit it. My spiritual gift is worry. I want to figure it out, measure it out, then carry it out. I like to be in control. But this comes with a heavy price. Worry brings stress while achieving nothing else.

Martin Luther said, "Pray, and let God worry."

That's good advice. Like Bud Post, you might win the lottery. But be warned: the more you have, the less you trust. And recovery is a spiritual process, one that requires complete abandonment to your Higher Power. Remember, it was trusting in your own ideas that got you into trouble in the first place.

Recovery Step: Ask God for wisdom, then live based on the insight he gives.

Never Forget
June 21

Jim Valvano's story has inspired a generation. I still remember that awful night in Albuquerque, New Mexico. The date was April 4, 1983. North Carolina State, coached by Valvano, beat my beloved Houston Cougars for the NCAA men's basketball championship. Valvano proceeded to run all over the court looking for someone to hug. It was one of the great upsets in sports history.

Ten years later, almost to the date, Valvano lost a courageous battle with cancer at the age of 47. But it was his battle with cancer, not his success on the court that touched millions.

Treasuring every day and knowing his fate, Coach Valvano said, "I will thank God for the day and moment I have."

What Jim Valvano did, we all must do. Never forget your blessings, and never take today's moments for granted.

Titus 3:4-5 reads, "When the kindness and love of God the Savior appeared, he saved us, not because of righteous things we had done, but because of his mercy. He saved us through the washing of rebirth and renewal by the Holy Spirit."

We all have been blessed beyond what we deserve. F.F. Bruce wrote, "God bestows his blessings without discrimination." One of the best ways to secure tomorrow's recovery is to simply thank God for the gift of today.

Recovery Step: Take a moment to thank God for the blessings of your past and commit this day to him – not next week or next year – just today.

Living in the Present
June 22

Moses was one scared dude. God told him to lead his children out of Egypt and eventually into the Promised Land. But standing up to the leader of Egypt would be no easy task. Moses came up with every excuse in the book. He begged God to use someone else. Eventually, Moses succumbed to God's demands. He rose to the challenge.

But Moses knew he could not escape the grip of Egypt in his own strength. He had no chance apart from his Higher Power. But how would he refer to his God? he wondered. The answer he received was not the one he expected.

"God said to Moses, 'I am that I am.' And he said, 'Thus shall you say unto the children of Israel, I AM sent me to you'" (Exodus 3:14).

Moses said, "Huh?"

By calling himself "I AM," God was claiming the present. His message was that victory is not found in the memories of the past or the promises of the future, but in the power of the present.

Helen Mallicoat wrote, "I was regretting the past and fearing the future. Suddenly my Lord was speaking. 'My name is I AM,' he said. Then he paused. I waited, and he continued. 'When you live in the past, with its mistakes and regrets, it is hard. I am not there. My name is not I WAS. When you live in the future, with its problems and fears, it is hard. I am not there. My name is not I WILL BE. When you live in this moment, it is not hard. I am here. My name is I AM.'"

Recovery Step: You can only win today's battles with today's strength. Fight in the name of the great I AM. He is with you in the present. Call on him, lean on him, and trust him for today.

The End Game
June 23

In any sport, there is an end game. It is the final score that counts. In war, it's all about who wins. In a political race, it's about getting the most votes.

But what about sobriety? What is the end game? How do you know if you are winning or losing? It's not that clear. Recovery is more about direction than destination.

But for each of us, there is an end game. The winner is the man or woman who is found faithful when we cross the finish line.

Jesus said, "You must be ready because the Son of Man will come at an hour when you do not expect him" (Matthew 24:44).

Until that day, choose a life of sobriety, pleasing to God. As Elton Trueblood said, "Our life is a gift *from* God. What we do with it is our gift *to* God."

That final day – the end game – is closer today than it has ever been. We don't know when it will come, either by our death or his return. Our job is not to know when that day will come, but to be ready.

May we celebrate the end game in advance. That will be a day of no more temptation, addiction, or pain. Richard Bach framed it perfectly: "What the caterpillar calls the end of this world the Master calls a butterfly."

Recovery Step: Prepare for the end game by living today in a way that is pleasing to God, feeds your recovery and brings sobriety to your life and others.

Fully Known and Truly Loved
June 24

One of the hardest things for any of us to believe is that we can be (a) fully known, and (b) truly loved – at the same time, by the same person. Tim Keller wrote, "To be loved but not known is comforting but superficial. To be known and not loved is our greatest fear. To be fully known and truly loved is the greatest gift of all."

There once lived a prophet named Micah. A contemporary of the more popular prophet Isaiah, Micah prophesied during the reigns of three kings from Judah: Jotham, Ahaz, and Hezekiah, about 700 years before Christ. Micah lived in difficult times. He preached to a divided people. The Northern Kingdom faced judgment because of their idolatry, and the Southern Kingdom wasn't much better. Micah warned of God's justice while celebrating his love.

Micah pled for his people in the midst of their sins. Hearing of God's pending doom, he said, "Because of this I will weep and wail; I will go about barefoot and naked. I will howl like a jackal and moan like an owl" (Micah 1:8).

Did you catch that phrase, "barefoot and naked"? Micah was saying, "I'm desperate for a miracle of healing, God. I stand bare before you." By exposing himself, Micah was willing to be fully known. What he didn't expect was that he would be truly loved at the same time.

Whether or not you ever experience the blessing of being fully known and truly loved by another human being, know this. God already knows you – fully. And he loves you – truly. And that is more than enough to feed our recovery.

Recovery Step: Are you fully known and truly loved? Yes, you are. Celebrate that fact by expressing to God your enormous gratitude and fidelity today.

Cleaning House
June 25

We used to have a Cocker Spaniel named Duffy. She was one happy mess. Her bladder was unable to control her joy. We were always cleaning up after her. She slobbered horribly. When she'd run or shake her head, slobber went everywhere. What she messed up, we cleaned up.

One day, due to a back problem that is common among Cockers, Duffy became paralyzed. She couldn't walk or get to her food dish. We spent a king's ransom on her back surgery, knowing it may not be successful. Then we had to just wait and see. We fed her by hand and carried her outside where she could at least enjoy the view.

It took a few weeks, but eventually, she began to move again, and she fully recovered. But she was still a mess. So why did we continue to clean up after her, no matter how bad it got? It's simple. We loved our dog more than we hated her mess.

You are a mess. But know this. God loves you more than he hates your mess.

We have this guarantee from God: "Their sins and lawless acts will I remember no more" (Hebrews 10:17). That's a pretty amazing promise.

God is in the housecleaning business. What we mess up, he cleans up. Then it's our turn to respond.

A.W. Tozer said, "You have been forgiven, so act like it!"

You have made a mess, but God has cleaned house. Now you are forgiven – so act like it!

Recovery Step: Live like a child of the King. And if you ever make a mess of things again, remember this – God loves you more than he hates your mess.

Generational Curse
June 26

Israel suffered from a generational curse. "For a long time Israel was without the true God, without a priest to teach and without the law" (2 Chronicles 15:3).

Here's the story.

When Asa assumed the throne as king of Judah, he also inherited a terrible family tradition. For three generations his family had led the nation in the practice of pagan worship, with its accompanying sexual immorality and moral and spiritual decay. Asa knew that changing these long-established practices would alienate him from his relatives. But he determined that pleasing God was more important than pleasing his family. So King Asa destroyed all evidence of idol worship in Israel and repaired the altar of the Lord. He even removed his grandmother from her powerful and influential position as queen. Imagine the flak Asa must have received after making that decision!

Most importantly, Asa led Judah back to worshiping the one true God. He changed the course of his own personal life and in the process the course of an entire nation, for as long as he remained in office.

Perhaps addiction runs in your family. Studies show that sex addict parents tend to have sex addict children. But it doesn't have to be that way.

Robert Strand wrote *Breaking the Generational Curse*. He said, "The sacrifice of Jesus Christ on the cross is strong enough to break any curse." By the power of God, you can break free. Generational curses are real, but so is God's amazing, healing grace.

Recovery Step: Perhaps you come from a family of strugglers. Recovery will come harder for you. But it will come, for greater is the power of your God than the grip of a generational curse.

Strength, Not Outcome
June 27

As a young man, C.S. Lewis established a strong friendship with a woman named Joy Greshem. It turned to love, and they married. Soon, Joy was diagnosed with cancer. After a hard battle, she died. But there were many ups and downs along the way.

During a period when Joy was responding well to treatment, a colleague of Lewis' approached him with words of encouragement. "I know how hard you've prayed. God is answering your prayers," Lewis' friend said.

Lewis replied, "I didn't pray for that. I prayed because I can't help myself. The power of prayer is not that it changes my circumstances, but that it changes my heart."

Most of us pray what I call "outcome prayers." We seek God only for a particular outcome. Well, Joy still died, but C.S. Lewis went on to change the world. But before he changed the world, God changed his heart.

Paul spoke to this need when he said, "In the same way, the Spirit helps us in our weakness. We do not know what we ought to pray for, but the Spirit himself intercedes for us with groans that words cannot express" (Romans 8:26).

Let's put our "outcome prayers" on the back burner. Don't pray for temptations equal to your strength, but for strength equal to your temptations.

Recovery Step: Are you facing temptations and trials today? Shelve your "outcome prayers" and ask God for the strength equal to the challenge.

Stay Positive
June 28

If you are fighting for sobriety, you are in the fight of your life. With your memories of past failures, illicit images sewn into the fabric of your mind, and a flood of daily temptations, staying on track can be a daunting challenge. The key is your attitude.

John Maxwell says, "Your attitude will determine your altitude."

You will never rise higher than your attitude. Until you see it, you cannot be it. It's like driving a car. Where you are looking now is where you will soon be.

Frank Sonnenberg is an award-winning author of six books and 300 articles. An expert on leadership and small business success, he speaks a lot on the subject of attitude. His studies concluded that "a positive mental attitude can improve your health, enhance your relationships, increase your chances for success, and add years to your life." He says that "true happiness depends on how you view the world and who you look to for inspiration. It pays to be positive."

No one had a better attitude than Jesus Christ. Scripture teaches us, "In your relationships with one another, have the same mindset of Christ Jesus" (Philippians 2:5).

In recovery, we need to embrace this attitude. Andrew Dhuse offers challenging words: "God's will is not an itinerary, but an attitude." In other words, God is less concerned about what is going on around you than what is going on in you.

You can win the battle for sobriety. It starts now. And it starts with your attitude.

Recovery Step: Stay positive. You have little control over your circumstances, but a lot of control over your attitude. Remember, your attitude determines your altitude.

Wait a Second!
June 29

We serve the God of the second chance. In fact, rarely does a person get it right the first time – in recovery or in life.

James Braddock was a washed-up depression era boxer. No one would pay him to fight, and he was living on welfare. Then, one night a boxer couldn't get to town for a match, so Braddock stepped in at the last minute. Two years later, he defeated Max Baer for the heavyweight championship of the world.

Life is all about second chances.

Presidents Adams, Jefferson, Monroe, Jackson, Harrison, Buchanan, Fillmore, Johnson, Grant, Cleveland, Nixon, Reagan, and Bush were all elected – on their second try.

Michael Jordan is the greatest basketball player of all time. He was a 14-time All-Star, and his teams won six NBA championships. But not until he failed to win a title in his first seven years.

Remember the story of Jonah? "The word came to Jonah . . . Go to the great city of Nineveh and preach against it" (Jonah 1:2). But Jonah ran the opposite direction. One giant fish later, "the word of the Lord came to Jonah a second time" (3:1).

We have a second-chance God. Have you failed? He's for you. Have you fallen? He's on your side. Have you relapsed? He's in your corner. So if you've fallen, get up. You serve the God of a second chance.

Recovery Step: Your past is no predictor of your future. No matter how far you have fallen, you can still get up. So get moving . . . you serve the God of a second chance.

All for One, One for All
June 30

John Dickerson, a Founding Father of the United States, spoke to the events of his day with the famous words, "United we stand, divided we fall," published in the *Boston Gazette* in July 1768.

French author Alexandre Dumas picked up on this theme in writing his most famous novel, *The Three Musketeers*, in 1844. The book recounts the adventures of a young man named Charles de Batz de Castelmore d'Artagnan, who left home to serve Louis XIV as captain of the Musketeers from 1632 to 1673. In a pact to remain loyal to one another through thick and thin, d'Artagnan and his fellow Musketeers adopted the following as their motto for life:

"All for one and one for all; united we stand, divided we fall."

The three Musketeers might have been the first recovery group. This kind of unity and mutual support is critical to lasting sobriety and daily victory. As John Maxwell says, "None of us is as strong as all of us."

Paul said it like this: "I appeal to you, brothers and sisters, in the name of our Lord Jesus Christ, that all of you agree with one another in what you say and that there be no divisions among you, but that you be perfectly united in mind and thought" (1 Corinthians 1:10).

The road to recovery is long and winding, with many hills and valleys, passing through treacherous lands unseen until they are conquered. It is foolish to tread such a road by oneself. You need to join with others for the walk.

Recovery Step: Say it with me: *"All for one and one for all; united we stand, divided we fall."* Identify a small recovery group and join them for the journey.

Rebound
July 1

One of the most fascinating subjects in the Bible is Samson. You can read his story in the Book of Judges. In many ways, Samson was a reflection of the people of Israel. God chose him for a specific reason – to be set apart and dedicated as a Nazirite. This meant living his life under a strict code, looking and acting differently from his peers.

But while Samson followed these laws in minute detail, his personal life was a wreck. He chased after women who were not of his faith, some who lived lives of ill repute. His life became infiltrated by idols and compromise. Eventually, he reached a breaking point.

With poor leadership comes poor followership. "Again the Israelites did evil in the eyes of the Lord, so the Lord delivered them into the hands of the Philistines for forty years" (Judges 13:1).

But like Samson, God's children eventually came home. Addiction and sin bring a price of judgment. But if we have sensitive hearts, out of the ditch we look to the Savior.

George Buttrick wrote, "If we walk by faith, every victory invests us with higher courage, and every failure flings us back on God."

It seems clear that Samson was a sex addict. This led him into a series of bad decisions. But he eventually flung himself back on God. You can do the same thing.

Recovery Step: Have you wandered from the God of your youth? There's still hope. Let your failures fling you back on God today.

It Worked for Ruth Graham
July 2

I love what Ruth Graham once said about her famous husband. "It's my job to love Billy. It's God's job to make him good."

The fact is, you can't make anybody good but yourself. And you can't even do that apart from the power of a supernatural God.

Jesus said, "You hypocrite, first take the plank out of your own eye, and then you will see clearly to remove the speck from your brother's eye" (Matthew 7:5).

Don't miss the order of speck removal. It starts with you.

This process of being made good is what theologians call *sanctification*. It means to be set apart. You have lived in your addiction long enough. It's time to be set apart. And if you're married to an addict, go light – on them and yourself. Remember, it's your job to love them and God's job to make them good.

Remember, no one works a perfect recovery plan. Deborah Day said it well: "Lighten up on yourself. No one is perfect. Gently accept your own humanness."

Recovery Step: Don't try to control anyone else. That's God's job. Focus on your own recovery. But in the process, gently accept your own humanness.

Amends
July 3

When working the 12 steps, many men and women hit the wall with steps eight and nine. These steps tell us to "make a list of all persons we have harmed and become willing to make amends to them all," and then to "make direct amends to such people wherever possible, except when to do so would injure them or others."

Many times, making amends is about keeping promises made years before. King David did this in regard to his friend Jonathan. David had made a covenant to bless Jonathan's family (1 Samuel 20:14-17) but failed to fulfill this promise. Years later, after the deaths of both Saul and his son Jonathan, David knew he needed to make amends for his failure to live up to his commitments. So he asked around, "Is anyone in Saul's family still alive – anyone to whom I can show kindness for Jonathan's sake?" (2 Samuel 9:1). He was directed to Mephibosheth, Jonathan's son.

David not only hosted Mephibosheth for a banquet at the king's table, where he would eat the king's food; he declared, "I will give you all the property that once belonged to your grandfather Saul" (9:3).

That's some serious amends making! So what about you? In your addiction, you have a past littered with broken promises. It is never too late to make amends, either directly to the person you have hurt, or, as in the case of Mephibosheth, to someone else.

Recovery Step: It's time to make amends, either directly or indirectly. Make that list and check it twice. Then go to work, blessing each person you have hurt, wherever possible.

The Great Conductor
July 4

Born in Budapest in 1897, George Szell was one of the most gifted pianists in the world. But no one remembers George Szell, the pianist. They remember George Szell, the conductor.

By age 20, Szell was conducting the Strasbourg Opera. By 27, he led the Berlin State Opera, and by 35, he had migrated to the United States and become lead conductor at the Metropolitan Opera House in New York City. For 25 years, Szell was recognized as the world's greatest conductor.

What was the key to Szell's success? One thing, he said. Early in life, "I decided to not focus on being the best pianist, but to help others be the best."

That is the definition of leadership – helping others. James defined religion as "visiting orphans and widows in their affliction, and to keep oneself unstained from the world" (James 1:27).

In recovery, we can only go so far if we don't pour our lives into others. The most sober people I know are the ones who do the most to sponsor newcomers, make calls, and give back. As we say in every 12-step meeting, "The measure we gave was the measure we got back."

Recovery Step: Look beyond yourself. Find someone this week who needs you and give them your time and your wisdom. You will discover that the best way to secure your own sobriety is by helping others secure theirs.

Three Shots
July 5

Two men went hunting in the woods. The game warden told them that if they got lost they should fire three shots in rapid succession to find help. Sure enough, they got lost.

While one of the men went in search of help, the other fired three shots, but no help came. So he tried it again, with the same result. After a while, his partner returned. He said, "I couldn't find anyone. We're still lost."

"What should we do?" asked the other hunter.

"I think you should fire three more shots," said his friend.

"It's too late," said the first. "I've run out of arrows."

The man had great intentions. But arrows are no substitute for the sound of a gun. And good intentions are no substitute for doing the right thing.

Jesus said, "Anyone who chooses to do the will of God will find out whether my teaching comes from God or whether I speak on my own" (John 7:17). In other words, getting it right matters more than *wanting* to get it right.

In recovery, sincerity is overrated. Put action behind your words. There are certain things you just have to do to be well. A well-intentioned misfire does no good.

Recovery Step: Go to meetings, make the calls, work with your sponsor. Do the things that work. Sincerity void of action gets you nowhere.

Two-by-Fours
July 6

The Bible says, "Therefore love the Lord your God and keep his commands" (Deuteronomy 11:1).

What God said in the Old Testament still applies today. We are to follow his plan for our lives with consistency and persistency. The key to lasting recovery is hard work – repeated over time.

Albert Einstein shared the key to his success. "It's not that I'm so smart, it's just that I stay at it longer."

Recovery is all about staying at it.

A man walked into a lumber yard and asked for some two-by-fours. The merchant wanted to make sure he cut the wood according to the customer's specifications, so he said, "Okay, two-by-fours. We can do that. But how long do you want them?"

The customer said, "A long time. I'm using them to build a house."

You need to put in place a recovery plan that will last for a long time. If you want your recovery to last, build it with enduring materials: go to meetings, pray the Serenity Prayer every day, and stay connected to others on the same path.

Recovery Step: Do things that make recovery last. It starts with obeying God's commands – over and over, day after day.

Fighting Failure
July 7

John Wooden said, "Success is never final, and failure is never fatal. It's courage that counts."

Failure won't kill you. Quitting will. If you have had a setback in your recovery, you aren't alone. The shortest distance between addiction and sobriety is never a straight line. But success will come if you stay in the game and trust the Head Coach.

Here's how it works. You can be "strengthened with all power according to his glorious might so that you may have great endurance and patience" (Colossians 1:11).

Thomas Edison stands as a great example of persistence. He invented hundreds of things but is best known for the light bulb. But did you know that before he succeeded, he failed over 1,000 times? I'm sure his buddies came by and asked, "Hey Tom, whatcha doin?"

Tom said, "I'm inventing the light bulb."

"What's that?" they asked.

Tom answered, "It will be easier to describe after I've created it."

Recovery is hard to describe. It can't be reduced to a pithy phrase or inscription on a coffee mug. Many people are like 'ol Tom. Before they get it right, they got it wrong – a thousand times.

Recovery Step: Have you failed? We all have. If you've fallen, get up. If you've slipped, stand up. It's what comes after you fall that will determine your destiny.

The Worst Curse
July 8

The Tartar tribes of central Asia spoke a certain curse against the enemy. They didn't call for their enemy's swords to rust or for their people to die of disease. Instead, they said, "May you stay in one place forever."

The best way to assure that you will never get better is by staying in one place forever. Standing still will get you nowhere.

Recovery is all about movement, making changes, and climbing the next hill. I know guys who have been in successful recovery for decades. "What did you do when you finished the twelve steps?" I asked one of them. "I started over" was his reply.

The Book of 2 Chronicles records the completion of King Solomon's temple and the split kingdom, with a focus on the Southern Kingdom of Judah. The writer chronicles (hence the name of the book) the activities of 19 kings, some good and some bad. One of those kings was Asa, who sought to be faithful to God when others around him were not.

God made this promise to the king: "But as for you, be strong and do not give up. Your work will be rewarded" (2 Chronicles 15:7).

In recovery, there is a temptation to look back, give up, or stand still. But it is only in moving forward that we get well and stay well.

Recovery Step: Keep moving. Take one step toward wholeness today.

Just As I Am
July 9

Charlotte Elliott, of Brighton, England, was an embittered woman. Her disability had hardened her heart.

"If God loved me," she muttered, "he would not have treated me this way."

Hoping to help her, a Swiss minister named Cesar Malan visited the Elliotts on May 9, 1822, seeking to calm Charlotte in the midst of her pain. She saw peace in him that she did not have.

"How do I find that peace?" she asked.

Malan said, "Give yourself to God just as you are."

She did. And years later, describing what had happened, she wrote a poem. "Just as I am, without one plea, but that thy blood was shed for me, and that thou bidd'st me come to thee, O Lamb of God, I come! I come!"

That famous hymn became the invitation song Billy Graham used for 60 years of crusades. It says it all. For those of us seeking to be made whole, the message is clear. We must come to God – not as we wish we were – but as we already are.

Jesus said, "Come to me, all you who are weary and burdened, and I will give you rest" (Matthew 11:28).

Recovery Step: Come to God today – just as you are. Give him your life, your heart, your everything.

Conquering Mountains
July 10

Edmund Hillary, the first man to scale Mount Everest in 1953, said, "It is not the mountain we conquer, but ourselves."

The greatest mountain you may ever climb is Mount Recovery. And Hillary is right. The challenge is not the mountain; the challenge is you.

One day, Jesus climbed a mountain. "Jesus took with him Peter, James, and John the brother of James, and led them up a high mountain by themselves" (Matthew 17:1).

From this simple verse, we learn quite a bit about climbing mountains. We learn that we cannot do it alone. We've all heard of Edmund Hillary. But you may have never heard the name, Tenzing Norgay. Mr. Norgay was Hillary's climbing partner. Even Jesus didn't climb the mountain by himself. If you are to scale Mount Recovery, you'll need others along the journey.

Every climb has a leader. Jesus didn't say, "There it is, boys, get after it!" He led them. In recovery, we need the help of experienced climbers. You need a mentor, someone who knows the way to the top.

Recovery Step: Mount Recovery is right in front of you. It's a tall climb, one whose end is beyond what you can see from below. But with the right Guide and support, it can be the most important climb of your life. It's time to get started.

The Ultimate Sign of Recovery
July 11

The year was 1919. A young man, recovering from World War I injuries, rented a small apartment in Chicago. He chose the location so he could be close to an author named Sherwood Anderson. He was an aspiring writer himself, so he spent as much time with Anderson as he could. For months, they talked every day. Anderson taught his mentee everything he knew about writing. The name of the young man was Ernest Hemingway.

John Maxwell says, "Great leaders produce other leaders."

And that is the sign of true recovery. Ultimately, your recovery is not about you, but those you will help. Nothing brings me more joy in my own recovery than to see a man I have sponsored become a sponsor to someone else.

There once lived a famous evangelist named Elijah. He did some pretty remarkable things in his career. But the time had come for a new man to replace him – a fellow named Elisha. Elisha wanted the blessing, power, and experience of his mentor. That hope was fulfilled. "The company of the prophets from Jericho, who were watching, said, 'The spirit of Elijah is now resting upon Elisha'" (2 Kings 2:15).

In recovery, you need someone to mentor you, and you need someone to mentor. Why? Because leading others into recovery is the ultimate sign that your own recovery is on track.

Recovery Step: Who helped you find recovery? Who are you helping now?

Seeing God
July 12

Isaiah has a book in the Bible that bears his name, but he was a common man. While he likely had wealth and was the most influential prophet of his time, he was a man of the people. Despite his achievements in ministry, he stood before God in fear. He recorded this experience.

"Then one of the seraphim flew to me with a live coal in his hand, which he had taken with tongs from the altar. With it, he touched my mouth and said, 'See, this has touched your lips; your guilt is taken away, and your sin atoned for'" (Isaiah 6:6-7).

Isaiah stood before the Lord in awe, unsure of what to do next. Then, when God called him to go minister among his people, he was ready. "Here I am. Send me!" (6:8).

Any true encounter with God changes what comes next. The same is true in recovery. The best medicine for the disease of addiction is an encounter with the God of the universe.

John Piper writes, "In the end, the heart longs not for any of God's good gifts, but for God himself. To see him and know him and be in his presence is the soul's final feast. Beyond this, there is no quest."

Try this for today. Rather than seeking recovery, seek God.

Recovery Step: Seek God today. Listen. Worship. Obey.

The Only Failure that Kills
July 13

There is failure, and there is failure. Buddha said, "The only real failure in life is to not be true to the best one knows."

Temporary failure is not failure, but a setback. If you have a slip or a relapse, that does not mean your recovery is done. It's only when you quit the battle that the enemy wins the war.

Muhammad Ali said, "My goal when I step into the ring is to get up more than I go down."

While we can question how a fighter gets up *more* than he goes down, Ali had a good point. No fighter in the history of boxing ever lost a fight because he got *knocked down*. He only lost because he *stayed down*.

One day Jesus told a parable about a man who doled out "talents" among his men. Two of the men put their talents to work and multiplied what they had been given. But the third man buried his talent out of fear.

"I was afraid and went out and hid your talent in the ground," he told his master (Matthew 25:25). The master responded by taking away what he had.

In recovery, you will lose what you have already attained if you bury it. Success is not about playing it safe. And sobriety is not about never going down. It's about what happens next.

Recovery Step: You've been knocked down. We all have. It's time to get up. The next move is yours.

Patting Birds
July 14

Linus, of *Peanuts* fame, was taking a lot of heat because of his newly found "calling." He liked to pat birds on their heads. Distressed little birds would approach him, lower their feathered pates to be patted, sigh deeply, and then walk away satisfied. This brought Linus indescribable joy.

Charlie Brown and Lucy asked him why he was doing this.

"What's wrong with patting birds on their heads?" Linus asked.

"Are you kidding me?" Charlie Brown asked. "What's wrong with it is that nobody else is doing it!"

Most men struggle with porn. What sets the man in recovery apart from the crowd is that he's doing something about it. Most people you know have a problem. They need recovery on some level. But that requires much of us, so most people aren't doing it.

Joshua was willing to stand up for God even when no one else was doing it. "But if serving the Lord seems undesirable to you, then choose for yourselves this day whom you will serve . . . but as for me and my household, we will serve the Lord" (Joshua 24:15).

If you are going to overcome your addiction to sex and porn, you need to take the steps of recovery – even if nobody else is doing it.

Recovery Step: Take the steps of recovery, whether anyone else does or not.

Wesley's Last Words
July 15

Not long ago, Beth and I watched a television show in which viewers were allowed to phone in their vote to determine how that episode would end. And that's how it is in life. We don't get to choose how we start, but we do get to choose how we end.

When John Wesley lay on his deathbed, he reflected on his life. Living from 1703 to 1791, Wesley traveled 250,000 miles by horseback and preached 40,000 sermons. On his last night on earth, he summoned his family to his bedside, where he spoke his final words.

"Best of all, God is with me. Best of all, God is with me."

You didn't choose the struggles of your life. And you can't do anything to go back and change the past. The fact is, you can't really change everything about the future. But you have this promise – no matter how hard the journey – you will not walk alone.

When the journey ends, Jesus said that some "will go away to eternal punishment, but the righteous to eternal life" (Matthew 25:46). The good news is that those paths will have long since been paved before that day comes.

You can't change yesterday, and you can't control tomorrow. The battles will not be easy, but one thing is sure. You need not walk alone.

Recovery Step: Settle your relationship with God today. Nothing matters more than his presence in your life. Wesley had it right. "Best of all, God is with me. Best of all, God is with me."

Lesson from Rocky Balboa
July 16

In the face of his greatest challenge, Rocky Balboa said, "All I wanna do is go the distance." He would go the distance against Apollo Creed, and he would win.

Recovery – like life – is about finishing what we start. There's an old saying in 12-step literature that goes like this: "I could stop, but I couldn't stay stopped."

Rosalyn Carter said, "You have to have confidence in your ability, and then be tough enough to follow through."

It's all about finishing strong.

Chuck Norris speaks for most of us when he admits, "I am a start-and-stop guy. I can never really follow through on anything that I start."

We make life more difficult than we should. The Bible keeps it simple. "If anyone, then, who knows the good they ought to do and doesn't do it, for them it is sin" (James 4:17).

The most important 24 hours of recovery are the next 24 hours. You can't finish what you don't start. But it can't end there. You must keep doing the things you know to do. God is looking for the man or woman willing to go the distance.

Recovery Step: Get in it for the long game. Get in recovery and stay in recovery. You can enjoy a lifetime of serenity – but only if you're willing to go the distance.

Joe DiMaggio
July 17

When World War II ended, Joe DiMaggio returned home. Not yet ready to resume his baseball career, he took his son, Joe, Jr., to a Yankees game. The Yankee legend wore sunglasses and a ball cap, hoping to go unnoticed.

Eventually, the Yankee Clipper was recognized by the fans. They stood and chanted, "Joe, Joe DiMaggio! Joe, Joe DiMaggio!"

Hearing the thunderous crowd, Joe, Jr. looked up at his dad and said, "See, Daddy, everyone here knows my name!"

Of course, the adulation was intended for Joe, Sr. That's where we get into trouble – when we take the glory intended for our Father. We can never take credit for the recovery that only God makes possible. We often refer to the "gift of sobriety" because that's what it is – a gift. And behind every gift is a giver.

Like Joe DiMaggio, Jr., we are made in the image of our Father. "God created mankind in his own image" (Genesis 1:27). We must be content to be in his image, in his shadow. It is when we define ourselves by what we have done instead of by whose we are that we get into trouble.

Recovery Step: Recovery starts where pride leaves off. When we realize who we are and who God is, we have just taken the first step in our recovery.

Look What Noah Did
July 18

I see it all the time. Addict admits he has a problem. Addict reaches out for help. Addict gets into recovery. Addict finds a short period of recovery. Addict gets overconfident. Addict drops out of recovery. Addict relapses into his old lifestyle.

If ever there was a story of rousing success, it is the story of the world's first great shipbuilder. His name was Noah. Talk about crazy success! He built a huge ship, rescued a zillion animals, lived in that boat for over a year, and lived to be 950 years old.

That's not a bad life. But unfortunately, there's more to his story.

One night Noah became intoxicated. "When he drank more wine, he became drunk and lay uncovered inside his tent. Ham, the father of Canaan, saw his father naked" (Genesis 9:21-22).

That's not an image any son should have to endure. Walking in on your naked, 900-year-old dad creates issues far beyond my level of training.

The lesson of Noah is a simple one. Years — even centuries — of unbridled success can be tossed in a second. Noah drank in too much alcohol, and his sons drank in too many images. Never forget this basic truth — we can lose what we have built for a lifetime. And it can happen so fast.

Recovery Step: Remain diligent. Don't let your guard down for one second.

Unfinished Business
July 19

The shortest book of the New Testament tells us the story of a runaway slave named Onesimus. While in prison, Paul led Onesimus to faith in Christ. But he soon discovered that the man had fled from his master, a man named Philemon. While Onesimus was a new man in Christ, and while slavery was abhorrent, Paul sent him back to his master to surrender himself to his authority – even though his actions were punishable by death.

Paul wrote a letter to Philemon, which he stuffed in Onesimus' pocket. Imagine the surprise that must have come over Philemon when the fugitive slave returned to his estate. And imagine what went through his mind when he read the letter from Paul, an old friend.

In that letter were these words: "Onesimus is no longer like a slave to you. He is more than a slave, for he is a beloved brother" (Philemon 16).

Philemon gave Onesimus a full pardon.

Here's the lesson: your past did not disappear the moment you came to Christ or found sobriety. If you hurt people in your past, you still have unfinished business. It's called making amends. It's called doing the right thing. It's called character. Oh – and another thing. It's also called recovery.

Recovery Step: Think of one person you hurt while you were still a slave to your addiction. Then go to this person and offer your most sincere amends.

Dry Bones
July 20

When Beth and I answered God's call to begin a sexual addiction recovery ministry, we knew the name had to include the word "hope." We have discovered that no matter how grim the situation or how dark the moment, *There's Still Hope*.

Shane Lopez wrote about hope in his best-seller, *Making Hope Happen*. He said, "Hope is created moment by moment by our deliberate choices."

Ezekiel 37 draws the ultimate picture of presumed hopelessness – a valley of dry bones. Where there had once been life, there was now death. God led Ezekiel to a stroll through this valley, to demonstrate God's ultimate "before and after."

God said, "This is what the Sovereign Lord says to these bones: I will make breath enter you, and you will come to life" (Ezekiel 37:5).

What God did for those dead, decaying, dry bones, he can do for you.

Randy Alcorn said it like this: "We should stretch our vision of what's in store for us. God's redemptive work is far greater than we imagine because God himself is far greater than we imagine."

Recovery Step: No matter your circumstances, *There's Still Hope*. No matter the odds stacked against you, *There's Still Hope*. But the next move is yours, because "hope is created moment by moment by our deliberate choices."

Brothers
July 21

In recovery, we all need a band of brothers. John wrote, "We know that we have passed from death to life because we love each other. Anyone who does not love remains in death" (1 John 3:14).

In the history of the Major Leagues, there have been an astounding 350 sets of brothers to play the game. The greatest set of baseball brothers was the famous DiMaggio trio: Vince, Dom, and a fellow named Joe. The threesome combined for 22 All-Star appearances. Dom once said, "Nothing is so sweet as doing it with your brother."

Another famous baseball player named Satchel Paige said, "Work like you don't need the money. Love like you've never been hurt. Dance like nobody's watching."

That's good advice, but here's the thing. Somebody is watching. You are not dancing alone.

Recovery is a team sport. You need your group, your inner circle, and your sponsor. I've seen it happen too many times. The man who runs alone fails to finish the race.

Recovery Step: To win, you must be a part of the team. Then, when you find successful recovery, you can credit God and your team. But if you fail to join a team – that's on you.

Banquet of Consequences
July 22

We hear it all the time. "Life isn't fair." But is that really true?

It's not fair that you were emotionally abandoned by your parents. Abuse isn't fair. Neglect, family history, maltreatment – none of them are fair.

The American Psychiatric Association states that three million children experience abuse in America each year. The World Health Organization says this abuse comes in four forms: physical, sexual, emotional, and psychological. It's all abuse, and none of it is fair.

But at some point, we are responsible for our own decisions. What happens to us is not our fault. But our destructive responses are.

The prophet said, "The day of the Lord is near for all nations. As you have done, it will be done to you; your deeds will return upon your own head" (Obadiah 15).

Robert Louis Stevenson said, "Sooner or later, everyone sits down to a banquet of consequences."

Your choices bring a banquet of consequences. You can blame your past, or you can change your future. Those are your two options.

Recovery Step: Which way will you go? You can blame your past, or you can change your future. The next step is yours.

Antidote to Anxiety
July 23

Paul gave the church only two options. "Do not be anxious about anything, but in everything by prayer and supplication make your requests known to God" (Philippians 4:6).

You can worry. Or you can pray. Pick one.

The Anxiety and Depression Association of America states, "Anxiety disorders are the most common mental illness in the U.S., affecting 40 million adults in the United States, or 18.1 percent of the population. Yet, only 36.9 percent of those suffering receive treatment."

But anxiety is not new. Famed 19th-century preacher Charles Spurgeon said of anxiety, "Anxiety does not empty tomorrow of its sorrows, but only empties today of its strength."

And 21st-century preacher Max Lucado offered this advice. "Become a worry-slapper. Treat frets like mosquitoes. Do you procrastinate when a bloodsucking bug lights on your skin? Of course, you don't! You give the critter the slap it deserves. Be equally decisive with anxiety."

The great worry-slapper is prayer. To find victory, you must turn your hurts, habits, hang-ups, and anxiety over to God.

Recovery Step: You can pray. Or you can worry. But you can't do both.

The Pain Will Pass
July 24

The doctor warned me, "This is gonna hurt." Then came the shot, followed by unmitigated screaming. But it was worth it. Before healing comes a little pain.

The same is true of recovery of every kind.

Peter said, "The God of all grace, who called you to his eternal glory in Christ, after you have suffered a little while, will himself restore you and make you strong, firm, and steadfast" (1 Peter 5:10).

Friedrich Nietzsche said, "To live is to suffer, to survive is to find some meaning in the suffering."

Whether your suffering and pain are the direct result of bad decisions or elements beyond your control, you have this promise: what is coming is better than what is in the past, and it will last longer. Peter said the suffering of today is only for "a little while." The Greek word used here is *oligos*, which means "small in amount of time" but also "small in number."

In other words, the rest of your life can be the best of your life. That is God's promise, and that is your hope.

Recovery Step: The pain will pass. Healing will come. The best is still in front of you.

Don't Trip
July 25

Charlie Brown had aspirations to play baseball in the big leagues, but he told Lucy he was afraid he'd never make it. "You've got to start small," Lucy told him. "See if you can walk out onto the mound without falling down."

That's a good place to start. Take the field of play – and life – without falling down.

In recovery, our ultimate goals are well beyond our reach. That's why we must do two things: (a) take it one day at a time, and (b) trust God to do for us what we could not do for ourselves.

That was a hard lesson for Israel to learn. Oppressed, the people feared they would never be strong and independent again. Then God showed up, just in time. God promised to let the armies of Moab, Edom, and Ammon escape his wrath – but not Egypt.

In the Old Testament, Egypt represented captivity for God's people. The prophet spoke on behalf of God: "He will extend his power over many countries; Egypt will not escape" (Daniel 11:42).

Just as Israel could not defeat Egypt in its own power, you cannot defeat your enemies. Your job is to surrender to the God who promises to do for you what you could not do for yourself – and then take the mound. Game on.

Recovery Step: God promises to do for you what you cannot do for yourself. But you have to get into the game – one day and one pitch at a time.

Escape
July 26

Have you heard of a book called *The Worst Case Survival Guide*? The author puts meticulous research to work, providing us a way out of the most common dilemmas we might find ourselves in. Chapters include "How to escape from a sinking car," "How to jump from a building into a dumpster," and "How to escape from a bear."

Missing are the chapters I need: "How to find your way home when Google Maps are down," "How to reset the clock on the microwave," and "How to restart your jet ski when it dies 300 yards from the beach and you see a four-foot long shark three feet from the ski."

How about this one: "How to escape the clutches of a personal addiction."

Actually, there already is a Survival Guide for that one. It is the same Guide that tells us how the Israelites escaped the Egyptian army, how Daniel escaped the lion's den, and how Peter escaped his prison cell.

In the darkness of the night, God opened the cell for which Peter had no key. "Then Peter came to himself and said, 'Now I know without a doubt that the Lord has sent his angel and rescued me from Herod's clutches'" (Acts 12:11).

You can escape the prison of your addiction. The key that unlocks the door is called surrender – it's about letting God do for you what you could not do for yourself. As for jumping into a dumpster – well, you're on your own for that one.

Recovery Step: The only escape from the prison of addiction is surrender. You must trust God to provide the way of escape you have failed to find on your own.

Greatness
July 27

No one remembers *good*. We remember *great*.

There is no clear definition of greatness, or we could agree on who is the greatest. Our greatest president was Abraham Lincoln, George Washington, or Franklin Roosevelt, depending on which list you believe. The greatest baseball player was Babe Ruth, Cy Young, or Willie Mays. The greatest singer was Frank Sinatra, Elvis Presley, or Michael Jackson. Our greatest actor? Jack Nicholson, Tom Hanks, or Marlon Brando. Maybe you have someone else on your list.

We know Muhammad Ali was the greatest boxer because he declared himself "The Greatest." But is there more to greatness than saying it?

In *The Godfather*, Mario Puzo said, "Great men are not born great, they grow great."

I agree. But how does this happen? How do we "grow great"? Jesus has the answer. When some of his followers asked him, "Who is the greatest in the kingdom of heaven?" (Matthew 18:1), Jesus said the answer was all about being a servant.

If you aspire to greatness, serve. There are many ways to do that. Serve others in your 12-step group. Serve at your church. Serve someone who has no means of repayment. Serve.

Recovery Step: We all aspire to greatness. And that's okay – as long as we remember what greatness is. The growth toward greatness is taken one servant step at a time.

Blindness
July 28

One of the first steps toward recovery is the recognition of one's problem. It is only when we see our addiction that we can address it. Sight is everything.

There once lived a prophet named Zephaniah. He wrote perhaps the most obscure book in the Bible, bearing his name. The theme of the book is "the day of the Lord," as it is a book about judgment. Zephaniah came along a generation after the Southern Kingdom had turned its back on its covenant obligations toward Yahweh, resulting in exile. Zephaniah's message to the people was to turn to God, or there would be no hope for their future.

In his message, Zephaniah pronounced God's harshest judgment. "I will bring such distress on all people that they will grope about like those who are blind, because they have sinned against the Lord" (1:17).

Did you catch that? God's judgment was not the destruction of their crops or economy; it was not a curse on their people or their livelihood. What was God's greatest threat?

Blindness.

There is nothing worse than the inability to see things as they are. And that is the hope of recovery. The blinders are lifted, the light comes on, and we see reality for the first time.

Recovery Step: Ask God to remove your blinders, to let you see yourself as you really are. Then respond by seeking the face of the One who can renew, repair, and restore.

The Antidote to Sexual Sin
July 29

Many seek recovery in a bottle. They chase after the right pill, drug, or drink to find relief and freedom. What they find, instead, is frustration. There is no silver bullet for recovery. There is no antidote for sexual sin.

Or is there?

Paul told the church, "Let the Holy Spirit guide your lives. Then you won't be doing what your sinful nature craves" (Galatians 5:16). The Holy Spirit is the antidote for sexual sin. Paul was clear. If we follow the Spirit, we will not give in to our natural temptations.

But how does this work, exactly? Andrew Murray explains, "When we pray for the Spirit's help, we will simply fall down at the Lord's feet in our weakness. There we will find the victory and power that comes from his love."

A.W. Tozer was right when he said, "The Spirit-filled life is not a special, deluxe edition of Christianity. It is part and parcel of the total plan of God for his people."

The antidote for sexual sin is submission to the leadership of God in our lives, through the person of the Holy Spirit. That requires a daily choice to follow when we'd rather lead, to bow when we'd rather stand.

Recovery Step: The antidote to sexual sin is following the Holy Spirit in our daily lives. For you, that can begin right here and right now.

You're So Vain
July 30

In her biggest hit, Carly Simon sang these words: "You're so vain, you probably think this song is about you. You're so vain, I'll bet you think this song is about you. Don't you? Don't you?" Those words, apparently aimed at former lover Warren Beatty and Mick Jagger, encapsulate the dilemma of man. We are so vain.

Throughout history, pride has been man's undoing. Greece said, "Be wise and know yourself." Rome said, "Be strong and discipline yourself." Religion says, "Be good and reform yourself." Epicureanism says, "Be resourceful and expand yourself." Psychology says, "Be confident and assert yourself." Materialism says, "Be possessive and please yourself." Asceticism says, "Be lowly and suppress yourself." Humanism says, "Be capable and believe in yourself." Pride says, "Be superior and promote yourself."

But Jesus says, "Be unselfish and humble yourself."

God has always promised blessings to the humble. We read in the Old Testament, "When the Lord saw that they humbled themselves, this word of the Lord came to Shemaiah: 'Since they have humbled themselves, I will not destroy them but will soon give them deliverance'" (2 Chronicles 12:7).

You will not come to the beginning of recovery until you come to the end of yourself. First, you must discover, this song really isn't about you.

Recovery Step: Come to the end of yourself so you can come to the beginning of recovery.

Darkness
July 31

Addiction thrives in darkness.

Jesus said, "This is the verdict: Light has come into the world, but people loved darkness instead of light because their deeds were evil. They refuse to go near the light for fear their sins will be exposed" (John 3:19).

Many of us avoid 12-step groups, therapy, and recovery materials for one simple reason – we are still walking in darkness. There are areas in our lives that we aren't ready to deal with. We aren't ready for them to see the light of day.

What is the answer? There is no answer until we are ready. Until we are ready for real change, darkness is our closest friend. Darkness is the chief ally of addiction.

But when we are ready to see the light, there is hope. Martin Luther King, Jr., said it well: "Darkness cannot drive out darkness; only light can do that."

When you are ready for your addiction to come to light, there will be hope. Until then, get used to the dark, because addiction thrives in darkness.

Recovery Step: When you get tired of living in the shadows, you can step into the light. And when you do that, you will discover a God who was waiting for you the whole time.

Channel Surfing
August 1

"David sent someone to find out about her [Bathsheba]" (2 Samuel 11:3).

Before David got into trouble with Bathsheba, he got into trouble with himself. At a time when other kings were off to war, David chose to stay back in his man cave.

It was just another spring night, and boredom set in. The couch made no demands and the remote fit snugly in his hand. David hit the channel button at random until an alluring flicker caught his eye. Reverse. Stop. Pause. He zoomed in to watch a tantalizing scene – an intimate candlelit spa. He could almost smell the candle wax and bath oil. Although the cool evening air caused a slight haze to rise from the water, the bather's physical attributes were unmistakable.

Long before channel surfing, King David knew about channel surfing. Bored, he became curious. Curious, he became enticed. Enticed, he became trapped. Then, within minutes, it seemed like hours. It was too late. The sin had been committed.

David got into trouble because he didn't get into anything else.

Anne Baxter said, "Idleness is a constant sin, and labor is a duty. Idleness is the devil's home for temptation and for unprofitable, distracting musings; while labor profits others and ourselves."

Recovery Step: We get into trouble because we aren't into anything else. When you let your mind channel surf, you're done. The rest is simply the inevitable result.

Storms
August 2

It is still known as the Great Storm 300 years later. The year was 1703. The place was southern England. The storm killed 8,000 people, blew over 400 windmills, and demolished 2,000 large chimneys in London while destroying the famed Eddystone Lighthouse.

I'm from Houston. I was there for Hurricanes Carla (1961), Alicia (1983), and Ike (2008). Storms are unpredictable, and they are deadly. And we all must go through them from time to time.

One day, the twelve disciples were riding out a great storm. Jesus was sleeping through it. "The disciples went and woke him, saying, 'Lord, save us! We're going to drown!'" (Matthew 8:25).

I think the disciples get a bad rap. Sure, they lacked faith. Sure, they should have followed the example of Christ and remained calm. But give them credit. When panic overtook them, they knew where to turn.

Albert Barnes said, "From these storms and billows – these dangerous seas and tempestuous voyages – we are brought at last safe to heaven."

Are you in a storm right now? Addiction does that. If panic has set in, do what the twelve disciples did. Turn to Jesus, and let him right your ship.

Recovery Step: If you are in panic mode, in the midst of a storm, look to Jesus. Let him deliver you safely to the other side.

Saturday
August 3

"When the Sabbath was over, Mary Magdalene, Mary the mother of James, and Salome bought spices so that they might go to anoint Jesus' body" (Mark 16:1).

Tony Campolo made famous a sermon, which he first preached in Philadelphia, then around the world: "It's Friday, but Sunday's Comin." Campolo contrasts how different the world looked on Friday – the day that Jesus died, as opposed to Sunday – the day of the great resurrection.

Campolo skipped one very important day in the story. We call it "Saturday." Though the other two days have earned a special place on the church calendar – Good Friday and Easter Sunday – it is Saturday where most of life is lived. Saturday represents the period after the death but before the resurrection.

Your darkest days are probably behind you, and your best days are still ahead. We can't live in the past or in the future. Life is lived today.

Andrew Murray prayed, "Father, teach us all how to wait."

Keep making good decisions day by day. Plant recovery seeds today and tomorrow will be fine. Friday has passed. Sunday will come in due time. Saturday is your gift for today. Accept it and live it.

Recovery Step: Move beyond your past and be willing to wait on your future. Life is lived on Saturday. So focus only on today.

Four Keys to Success
August 4

In the late 1980s, Stephen Covey wrote *The Seven Habits of Highly Effective People*. The book has sold over 10 million copies. We all want to experience success.

But a couple of years before Stephen Covey, there was this fellow named Moses. No last name required. Just Moses. And he knew a little about success, as well. As he paused near the end of his life, he shared a brief "How To" talk on success for those who would come after him.

He spoke to those "who are standing here with us today in the presence of the Lord our God but also with those who are not here today" (Deuteronomy 29:15). Moses identified four keys.

Remember – Moses reminded the people of all God had done in the past.

Obey – The people were told to live according to their promises.

Focus – Moses warned them to not fall into the customs of those around them.

Recall – Moses said when in trouble, reflect on how God had always been faithful.

Recovery Step: What worked for Moses will work for you. Stephen Covey did not have a corner on success. To remain steadfast, do these four things: remember, obey, focus, and recall. On the other side awaits your Promised Land of recovery.

Lift Your Eyes
August 5

The only route to a certain harbor in Italy leads through a narrow channel between dangerous rocks and shoals. Over the years many ships have crashed as crews have tried to navigate through the channel. To solve this problem authorities mounted three lights on three huge poles in the harbor to guide ships safely into port. When a ship's captain lines up the three lights and all three appear as one light, the ship can proceed safely up the narrow channel. Everything depends on the captain's eyes. If he sees two or three lights, he knows he's off course and in danger.

In the same way, the songwriter of Psalm 123 turned his eyes toward God. "I lift my eyes to you, to you who sit enthroned in heaven" (Psalm 123:1).

Guillaume de Saluste du Barta wrote, "The world is a stage where God's omnipotence, justice, knowledge, love, and providence do act the parts."

Everything in creation screams: "Look to God!" As you navigate the narrow channel of recovery, nothing is more important than lining up your focus. It is only when you lift your eyes to God that you can safely reach your intended destination.

Recovery Step: Lift your eyes to God today. When the channel is narrow, and the waters are choppy, that will be the only way you can stay on course.

The Enemy Will Find You
August 6

During a battle in the Civil War, one of General Longstreet's officers approached him to say that he couldn't obey Longstreet's order to bring up his men to the line of battle, as the enemy was too strong. Longstreet responded with sarcasm. "Very well. Never mind. Just let them stay where they are. The enemy will advance, and that will spare you the trouble."

If we are to maintain sobriety, we must engage the enemies of our recovery every day: temptation, fantasy, past failures, and — most of all — complacency.

An Alpine guide died on a mountainside in Europe. At that spot, a sign reads, "He died climbing." May that be said of each of us.

A.W. Tozer said, "Complacency is a deadly foe of all spiritual growth. Acute desire must be present, or there will be no manifestation of Christ to his people. He waits to be wanted."

Solomon was right: "Through laziness, the rafters sag; because of idle hands, the house leaks" (Ecclesiastes 10:18).

Engage the enemy or the enemy will engage you. Complacency is not an option. If your house is leaking, it's time to plug the hole.

Recovery Step: Your problem is not lack of knowledge, but lack of action. You know what to do. Now do what you know.

Give Up!
August 7

"No one cares about the win-loss record of the referee" (John H. Holcomb).

We cannot win the game of life from the sidelines. We must get in the game. And we must go all in. Jesus said it like this: "Those of you who do not give up everything you have cannot be my disciples" (Luke 14:33).

In a weak moment, I found myself watching a poker game on television. In dramatic fashion, one of the players suddenly shoved all of his chips to the center of the table. That was his way of saying, "I'm all in."

When Jesus said we must give up everything to follow him, he was saying we must go all in.

I love the way John Stott said it. "Every Christian should be both conservative and radical; conservative in preserving the faith and radical in applying it."

Are you ready to go all in? You know the basic principles of recovery. Are you prepared to become radical in applying them?

Recovery Step: It's time to go all in. Be conservative in preserving the faith and radical in applying it.

Running Man
August 8

In his autobiography, *Blessings in Disguise*, late actor Alec Guinness wrote that as he was walking up Kingsway in the middle of the afternoon, he had an impulse to start running. He ran until he reached a little church. He'd never been there before, but he caught his breath and knelt to pray. For the next ten minutes, he said he was "lost to the world."

The date was March 24, 1956. It was not long until the lifelong atheist had converted to Christianity. It all started with an unexpected run.

Paul wrote, "Do you not know that those who run in a race all run, but only one receives the prize? Run in such a way that you may win" (1 Corinthians 9:24-25).

Clearly, Alec Guinness won the prize.

Merle Haggard had a different experience with running. In his famous song, *The Running Kind*, he sang, "I know running's not the answer, but running's been my nature – and a part of me that keeps me moving on."

The fact is, we are all running – to something or from something. Running is a key ingredient to recovery, as long as we are running to something, or better yet, Someone.

Recovery Step: To find lasting recovery, you need to run from your sexual sin and to the Savior. Then do what Alec Guinness did. Bow before him in complete surrender.

Restitution
August 9

Restitution – it's something we don't talk about much, and we do it even less. But restitution is a key to recovery. Restitution is a biblical word for making amends. And the concept is rooted in the Law of Moses.

One of the earliest writings of the Law includes a passage on making restitution.

"They must confess the sin they have committed. They must make full restitution for the wrong they have done, add a fifth of the value to it and give it all to the person they have wronged" (Numbers 5:7).

God provided clear steps for those who have violated others. These steps include admitting the wrong things we have done and providing restitution wherever possible. If we follow these simple steps, we will make significant progress toward recovery.

There are three ways to make amends.

First, we can make direct amends – to the person we have offended, in an effort to make things right. Sometimes, it is not possible or wise to contact the offended party. In these cases, we can make indirect amends – doing things for someone else. Finally, we can make living amends – making a lifestyle change.

It's all about restitution. In recovery, we seek to make things right. In the process, God makes us right.

Recovery Step: Ask God to bring to mind a person with whom you need to make amends or restitution. Then pray about which kind of amends you need to make – direct, indirect, or living.

Slaves No More
August 10

Slavery is perhaps the greatest blight in American history, only abolished with the passage of the 13th Amendment.

Abraham Lincoln said, "If slavery is not wrong, nothing is wrong."

Harriet Tubman said, "Now that I'm free, I know what a dreadful condition slavery is. I have seen hundreds of escaped slaves, but I never saw one who was willing to go back and be a slave again."

Yet, that is exactly what addicts do. Despite the freedom offered in Christ and the tools of recovery that are abundantly available today, they remain a slave to their own passions. For them, slavery has become a choice.

We are reminded, "Christ has set us free. Stand firm, then, and do not let yourselves be burdened again by a yoke of slavery" (Galatians 5:1).

Freedom is a promise, but not a guarantee. We must choose to walk in freedom, taking the steps that secure our sobriety. Gandhi said it well: "The moment the slave resolves that he will no longer be a slave, his fetters fall. Freedom and slavery are mental states."

Recovery Step: You can be set free. But you must then choose to walk in that freedom, one day at a time.

The Best of Times
August 11

Charles Dickens began his iconic novel *A Tale of Two Cities* with this now famous phrase: "It was the best of times, it was the worst of times."

Those words describe the struggle for sobriety. Finding freedom from years of carnage can be an indescribably painful journey, while also providing strength and hope. If you are new in recovery, know this: you are about to face some of your darkest times, but you will never walk alone.

Hear some of David's most famous words: "Even though I walk through the darkest valley, I will fear no evil, for you are with me; your rod and your staff, they comfort me" (Psalm 23:4).

If you are the wounded spouse, you need to know that out of your pain will come healing.

In 1963, President Kennedy was killed. But that was also the year that Dr. Michael Debakey performed the first successful installation of an artificial heart pump – an invention that has saved thousands of lives.

Similarly, even in the darkest valley, there is hope. And on the other side of every valley is a mountain. So keep on walking. What may feel like the worst of times can become the best of times.

Recovery Step: For you, these may be the worst of times. But as you keep your eyes on Christ and keep walking in faith, recovery will come – the best of times.

Finding Nemo
August 12

Revelation 2:10 says, "Do not be afraid of what you are about to suffer. I tell you, the devil will put some of you in prison to test you, and you will suffer persecution for ten days. Be faithful, even to the point of death, and I will give you life as your victor's crown."

Paul wrote, "Do not be weary in well doing" (Galatians 6:9).

Nothing is more important to recovery than to keep doing what we know to do – over and over again. It's called persistence.

In that iconic movie *Finding Nemo*, Dory explained the key to success. "Just keep swimming. Just keep swimming. Just keep swimming, swimming, swimming. What do we do? We swim, swim, swim."

In my experience, the vast majority of those who fail in recovery fail, not for lack of knowledge, but for lack of follow through. Our problem is not that we don't know what to do, but that we don't do what we know. Success in life – and recovery – is all about persistence.

Recovery Step: You know what to do. It's time to do what you know.

Unintentional Sin
August 13

Is it possible to sin – unintentionally? The Bible says yes. In the Levitical Law we read, "Say to the Israelites, 'When anyone sins unintentionally and does what is forbidden in any of the Lord's commands, he must bring a young bull to the Lord'" (Leviticus 4:2).

Let's break that down. We see two things here. First, it is possible to cross some lines, break some commands, and commit some sins – without being aware of it at the time. Second, we must own the results. The fact that their mistakes might have been unintended did not exonerate God's children from the damage caused.

You may have hurt your spouse without even knowing it. An unintended glance, viewing an old friend's Facebook page, talking to the lady at church – you did none of these things from bad motives. But given the damage you have already brought upon your marriage, these actions brought pain.

Unintended actions have unintended consequences. But these are still consequences. And the pain is real.

Blaise Pascal said, "There are only two kinds of men: the righteous who think they are sinners and the sinners who think they are righteous." We all continue to make mistakes from time to time. That's not the issue. But we must atone for those mistakes – intended or not.

Recovery Step: You may have committed unintended sins against your husband or wife. It's time to own it and atone for what you've done.

How to Help
August 14

Two men in a restaurant noticed that another man kept falling off his stool. Apparently, he was so drunk that he couldn't sit on his stool. Being good Samaritans, they offered to drive him home. They dragged him to the door and placed him in their car. When they got the man to his house, he fell down four times on the way to the door. They finally made it to the porch and rang the doorbell. When his wife answered the door, they told her they had brought her husband home.

She said, "Great, but where's his wheelchair?"

Sometimes, we try to be helpful, but only make things worse. We can be sincere, but if we are sincerely wrong, we are still wrong.

We should all be committed to helping those who struggle. The Bible says, "Do not forget to do good and to share with others, for with such sacrifices God is pleased" (Hebrews 13:16). But we need to do it right.

Every addict needs a sponsor. None of us finds recovery on our own. If you want to receive, give. Help those early in their recovery. But first, learn from your sponsor and equip yourself with all the tools, in order that you might do it right.

Recovery Step: We help ourselves by helping others. So go ahead – lead a group, sponsor a newcomer, and help those who are hurting. But make sure you do it right.

Dare to Prepare
August 15

Let's play a game. How many times do you find the word "prepare" in these four statements?

"Moses my servant is dead. Now then, you and all these people, prepare to cross the Jordan River into the land I am about to give to them – to the Israelites" (Joshua 1:2).

"The will to succeed is important, but what's more important is the will to prepare" (Bobby Knight).

"It's better to look ahead and prepare than to look back and regret" (Jackie Joyner-Kersee).

"I will prepare, and someday my chance will come" (Abe Lincoln).

Every great task requires meticulous preparation. A pilot takes lessons, a basketball player practices jump shots, and a doctor goes to med school.

Recovery is no different. It doesn't just happen. If you want to be sober tomorrow, you must do the right things today. If you want a year of sobriety, you must take steps to prepare for that now. You can experience lasting recovery – but only if you do the things to prepare in advance.

Recovery Step: A call to recovery is a call to prepare. Tomorrow's sobriety is dependent on the things you do today.

Wheaties
August 16

In 1937, Wheaties sponsored baseball broadcasts on 95 radio stations around the country. They held a nationwide contest to find their "most popular announcer." The winner would receive a free trip to California. The winner was a minor league play-by-play announcer from Des Moines, Iowa. He cashed in on his trip to California, where he was spotted by Warner Brothers, where they were impressed with his voice and good looks, so they offered him a screen test.

His name was Ronald Reagan.

When asked the key to his success, young Reagan said, "Success is about being where you're supposed to be when you're supposed to be there."

Jesus said it like this: "Whoever can be trusted with little can be trusted with much" (Luke 16:19).

Recovery is about being faithful where you are in the moment. If you are faithful where you are today, tomorrow will bring greater challenges — and rewards. It's all about making the next right decision.

Recovery Step: Be faithful where you are, right now. Do the little things right, and greater challenges — and blessings — will come.

12 Stones
August 17

God's children had dreamed of reaching the Promised Land for generations. Finally, under the leadership of Joshua, that day came. And they were quick to commemorate the event. Joshua told the men to set stones in place as a memorial of the crossing of the Jordan River. And then he told them what to tell the next generation.

"Tell them that the flow of the Jordan was cut off before the ark of the covenant of the Lord. When it crossed the Jordan, the waters of the Jordan were cut off. These stones are to be a memorial to the people of Israel forever" (Joshua 4:7).

The children of God still had a long way to go, but this was a day to remember how far they had already come. They didn't have much, but they were headed in the right direction.

In recovery, it is important to remember what we have already achieved, with the help of God.

Charles Spurgeon said, "It is not how much we have, but how much we enjoy that makes us happy."

Sure, you still have a long way to go. But today, be thankful for how far you have already come.

Recovery Step: Be grateful for the Jordan Rivers you have crossed in your life. Take the time to look back and celebrate how far you have already come.

Unchained
August 18

Neil Armstrong said, "The important achievement of Apollo was demonstrating that humanity is not forever chained to this planet and our opportunities are unlimited."

Sam Cooke wrote these lyrics to his most famous song:

That's the sound of the men working on the chain gang.
That's the sound of the men working on the chain gang.
All day they work so hard
Till the sun is goin' down.
Working on the highways and byways
And wearing a frown.
You hear them moanin' their lives away,
Then you hear somebody say,
That's the sound of the men working on the chain gang.

Jesus met a man who was part of a chain gang. "This man lived in the tombs, and no one was able to bind him anymore, not even with a chain" (Mark 5:3). Then Jesus set him free.

Are you bound by chains today? Join the gang. But the chain gang is not one for which there is a permanent membership. What Neil Armstrong said of the Apollo space mission rings true for you. You can be freed from your chains, and the opportunities are unlimited.

Recovery Step: It's time to leave the chain gang. Only God can set you free. But he can do just that. If you are willing.

More than You Can Handle
August 19

"Under love's heavy burden do I sink." (Romeo)

One of the biggest myths ever told – and we repeat it every day – is that God won't give you more than you can handle. Tell that to the mother who just lost her son. Tell that to the man whose wife was just diagnosed with stage four cancer. Tell that to the child whose parents were killed in an automobile accident.

Here's the truth: Sometimes, God does give you more than *you* can handle. And that is by design.

From Paul's pen to your eyes: "We do not want you to be uninformed about the troubles we experienced in the province of Asia. We were under great pressure, far beyond our ability to endure, so that we despaired of life itself" (2 Corinthians 1:8).

Yes, sometimes God does give us more than we can handle. Why? I think the answer is actually pretty simple. God gives us more than we can handle so that we will realize the incredible depth and breadth of our need for him.

For example, your addiction is more than you can handle. So quit handling it! Turn your life and your will over to the care of God.

Recovery Step: You have more than you can handle. The only answer is to turn your addiction, your life, and your will over to the care of God.

How to Survive
August 20

Cheryl McGuiness kissed her husband Tom goodbye, then took her teenage kids to school that Tuesday morning, just like every other day. A while later, she got a call from a friend asking if Tom was at home. The date? September 11, 2001.

Cheryl's friend asked about Tom because she knew he was a pilot for American Airlines. And her friend had just heard that a plane had been hijacked and crashed into the World Trade Center.

Then things got worse. After an hour or so, a car pulled up in front of Cheryl's house. Out stepped an executive for the airlines. It was his task to tell Cheryl that Tom was the pilot on that plane. Everyone on board had perished.

Three years later, Cheryl wrote a book, *Beauty Beyond the Ashes*. In it, she said, "As unfair, unreasonable, and impossible as it seems, we must go on. Life pauses, but it does not stop."

If you have caught your spouse in an affair or addiction, your life has hit the pause button – big time. But your life did not stop. You must find a way to move on.

Romans 15:4 says, "For everything that was written in the past was written to teach us, so that through the endurance taught in the Scriptures and the encouragement they provide we might have hope."

Recovery Step: Perhaps your life has been put on pause. But it did not stop. Even in your toughest times, God is still there. And there's still hope.

From Distant Lands
August 21

God's children had lived prosperous lives, to the point of becoming overconfident. They thought they could not fall – and then they fell. The result was captivity. With every passing day, the dreams of the old country seemed like just that – dreams.

Then Amos brought a message of hope. The good old days could become good again. He proclaimed God's truth: "I will bring my people back from distant lands. They will rebuild the ruined cities and live in them. They will plant vineyards and drink their wine; they will make gardens and eat their fruit" (Amos 9:14).

When we fall to our greatest depths, in our addiction or our marriage, we find the wilderness an affront to the idea of a loving God. But in recovery, we discover that while we will never recapture the past, we can capture the future.

Ravi Zacharias said, "We all want Canaan without going through the wilderness." I like the way Edward Abbey wrote it: "The idea of wilderness needs no defense, it only needs defenders."

God is in the business of bringing people back from distant lands. For the couple whose marriage has been wrecked by sex and porn addiction, can the future be as good as life before the addiction? No – it can actually be better.

Recovery Step: Don't allow your past to rob your future. And if you are straying from God, know this – he is in the business of bringing people back from distant lands.

Take-Home Exams
August 22

Angelina Jolie said, "I don't see myself as beautiful, because I see a lot of flaws."

How do you see yourself? The old prophet wisely advised, "Now this is what the Lord Almighty says: 'Give careful thought to your ways'" (Haggai 1:5).

On the road to recovery, you must avoid two ditches. On one side of the road is the "I'm okay" ditch. We drive into this ditch when we refuse to acknowledge our struggles.

On the other side of the road is the "I'm a horrible human being" ditch. We drive into this ditch when we define ourselves by our shortcomings.

Haggai recommended driving in the middle lane. Step 4 of all 12-step programs says it like this: "We made a searching and fearless moral inventory of ourselves."

When was the last time you did that? Recovery calls for frequent take-home exams. It calls on us to take periodic moral inventories. We cannot define ourselves by our faults, nor must we run from them. Instead, we must grow from them.

Recovery Step: Take an honest, fearless, moral inventory of yourself. Don't define yourself by your faults and don't ignore them. Acknowledge them. Confess them. Then move on.

God's Voice
August 23

Years ago, one Christmas Eve, a man living in a posh California neighborhood set out with his wife and children to sing Christmas carols in a poor neighborhood. When they approached their first door and began to sing, a woman came out, complaining about the "noise." At several more stops, they got the same reaction. So the family went on down the road until they found a welcoming home.

The name of the scorned caroler was Bing Crosby. I'm sure that if any of the neighbors had recognized his voice, they would have been thrilled to have him on their porch.

That Bing Crosby's voice could go unrecognized is a travesty. But here's something worse.

Jesus said, "My sheep listen to my voice; I know them, and they follow me" (John 10:27).

Successful recovery is spiritual recovery. And that requires recognizing God's voice. Here's the key. The best way to get to know God's voice is to get to know God.

The neighbors did not recognize Bing Crosby's voice because they did not have a personal relationship with him. The same is true with God. Until you know him personally, you will not recognize his voice. As for recovery, you'll be on your own.

Recovery Step: You need to know God's voice. But first, you need to know God.

God Satisfies
August 24

Porn is not a bad problem; it's a bad solution. It's called looking for fulfillment in the wrong place when only God can truly satisfy.

The weeping prophet brought this message from God to his people: "I will bring Israel back to their own pasture, and they will graze on Carmel and Bashan; their appetite will be satisfied on the hills of Ephraim and Gilead" (Jeremiah 50:19).

Only God can truly satisfy. Sadly, most of us don't embrace this truth until we suffer a significant loss.

Terry Fox was 18 when cancer was discovered in his right leg, which had to be amputated six inches above the knee. After he was fitted for a prosthetic leg, he decided to run across Canada to raise funds for cancer research. He set out on his "Marathon of Hope" on April 12, 1980. His run ended 3,339 miles later, on September 1, 1980. After averaging a marathon per day, cancer returned. Fox died less than a year later.

But his legacy continues in the form of an annual "Terry Fox Run" in 52 countries. Nearly a half billion dollars have been raised.

In the final days of his bout with cancer, Fox celebrated the victory that had been won through his suffering. Terry Fox died a satisfied man.

Porn or sex addiction may have brought great misery to you and your family. It's time to look up. Bring your unmet needs to the Savior. Only he can satisfy your soul.

Recovery Step: If you are living in a dry land today, come to God. Only he can satisfy your thirst.

Mulligan
August 25

Have you heard of a mulligan? It's a free shot in golf, claimed by millions of hackers across the globe every day. In most friendly competitions, each golfer is given one mulligan per 18 holes. But did you know where the term "mulligan" came from?

About 90 years ago, a Canadian golfer named David Bernard Mulligan was playing with three buddies. On the first hole, Mulligan's tee shot missed the fairway badly, sailing into the woods. He did what every self-respecting golfer always does. He made excuses for the horrible shot. He claimed his hands were slick. His partners gave him a do-over. And the "mulligan" was born.

God is in the mulligan business. None of us would be here without taking more than our fair share of mulligans in life.

In the Old Testament, God's children had strayed off the fairway of life deep into the woods. And they suffered the consequences. But a loving God offered a mulligan.

"I will repay you for the years the locusts have eaten – the great locust and the young locust, the other locusts and the locust swarm – my great army that I sent among you" (Joel 2:25).

Gordon MacDonald wrote, "If our yesterdays are in a state of good repair, they provide strength for today. If not repaired, they create havoc."

You and I need to be repaired. We need a mulligan. We need God.

Recovery Step: If your tee shot has sailed out of bounds, claim a mulligan. Turn to the God of a second shot.

John Mark
August 26

A Book in the Bible bears his name. But Mark was far from a reliable disciple as a young adult. He accompanied Paul and Barnabas on their first missionary journey. But when the going got tough, Mark got going – home to his mother.

A few years later, it was time for Paul and Barnabas to embark on their second missionary journey. Barnabas wanted to bring Mark – his relative – along again. Paul balked. The Bible says it like this: "Barnabas wanted to take John, also called Mark with them, but Paul did not think it wise to take him, because he had deserted them in Pamphylia and had not continued with them in the work" (Acts 15:37-38).

Barnabas wasn't ready to give up on Mark. He so believed in him that he chose Mark over Paul, and he took his mentee on their own missionary journey where they enjoyed God's favor and great success. The day would come when Paul would lament his earlier decision and recognize the change that had come to Mark's life.

All Mark needed was a little encouragement. Because someone believed in him, he could believe in himself.

God wants to use you that same way. Find someone who is early in recovery and encourage him or her. Ralph Waldo Emerson said, "The purpose of life is not to be happy, but to be useful."

Recovery Step: Find someone who is down and lift him or her up. Be an encourager. Be a Barnabas. Make a difference.

Excuses
August 27

In Latin, "human being" means "one who makes excuses." We are born into it. Making excuses is a trait of humanity. It needs no training or practice. It comes naturally.

Did you ever hear of the kid who failed to do his homework, and explained to his parents, "I was going to do it, but video games are more fun"? Nope. We all make excuses. It's a gift.

Clubhouse Magazine held a contest for kids. They asked for the best excuse for not doing one's homework. The winner said, "I went on a hot air balloon ride, and we were going to crash because there was too much weight in the basket. So I threw my homework out to lighten the load, and it saved our lives."

In our addictive behaviors, we learned to make excuses in our earliest years.

The opposite of excuses is recovery. And responsibility. Mitt Romney said, "Leadership is about taking responsibility, not making excuses."

We will all stand before God one day. The Bible says, "For we must all appear before the judgment seat of Christ, so that each of us may receive what is due for the things done while in the body, whether good or bad" (2 Corinthians 5:10).

Recovery Step: You cannot come to the start of recovery until you come to the end of excuses. Own your addiction. Own your recovery. Period – no more excuses.

Process
August 28

"I am the Lord your God, who brought you out of Egypt so that you would no longer be slaves to the Egyptians; I broke the bars of your yoke and enabled you to walk with heads held high" (Leviticus 26:13).

Recovery is about learning to walk with your head held high.

As with the Israelites' sojourn to Egypt, the wilderness, and eventually the Promised Land, recovery is a long, winding journey.

The Transtheoretical Model of Change (TTM) offers five stages of recovery: pre-contemplation, contemplation, preparation, action, and maintenance.

Let me simplify that. We think about thinking about it, we think about it, we prepare for it, we take steps toward recovery, and we maintain the ground we have gained.

Where are you in the recovery process? Chances are you are somewhere between thinking about thinking about it and maintaining total success. You aren't where you're gonna be, but you aren't where you used to be, either.

And that is a good place to be. So thank God for the process. Then take the next right step – one day at a time.

Recovery Step: You aren't where you're gonna be, and you aren't where you used to be. Celebrate the progress you have already made. And keep moving forward. Your Promised Land awaits.

Keep It Simple
August 29

Confucius said, "Life is really simple, but we insist on making it complicated."

Paul said, "For I resolved to know nothing while I was with you except Jesus Christ and him crucified" (1 Corinthians 2:2).

Paul kept things simple. We must do the same.

One day Lucy explained life to Charlie Brown. "Life is a lot like a deck chair. Some place it so they can see where they are going. Others place it so they can see where they have been. And some place it so they can see where they are now. Where do you place your chair, Charlie Brown?"

Charlie sighed, then said, "I can't even get my chair unfolded!"

Perhaps you are a visionary – you like to look forward. Maybe you face backward because you like to reminisce. Life is lived better in the present. But first, you have to unfold your chair. And God can help you with that.

It is important in life – and recovery – to not make things complicated. Live in the present. Live for today, because it's the only day you are promised.

Recovery Step: Keep things simple. Stay focused on the little things. And leave your deck chair to Someone Else.

All the Rage
August 30

Most addicts have anger issues. Some of us have a history of rage, so we try to stifle our feelings. Others stuff their feelings of anger, pretending they don't exist. Why? We were never allowed to express these feelings in the past. Evaluating our anger and how to deal with it appropriately is an important part of our recovery.

We are warned in Scripture, "In your anger, do not sin" (Ephesians 4:26).

Why is this important in recovery? Because anger leads to bitterness, and bitterness leads to falling. Our anger hurts those around us, but it mostly hurts us.

Ralph Waldo Emerson wrote, "For every minute you remain angry, you give up sixty seconds of peace of mind."

That's sixty seconds you cannot afford to give up.

Early in my recovery, I was angry toward those who contributed to my childhood isolation. I was angry toward family, neighbors, friends – and God. Especially God. But through therapy and growth, I learned to deal with my anger. It's not that anger ever really goes away, but it can be managed. Let's rephrase that. *It must be managed.*

Recovery Step: Do you have anger issues? Then you have recovery issues. You must learn to control your anger before you anger controls you.

One Is the Loneliest Number
August 31

Those great theologians, Three Dog Night, sang, "One is the loneliest number." And they were right.

Solomon wrote, "Two are better than one, because they have a good return for their labor; if either of them falls down, the other can help them up" (Ecclesiastes 4:9-10).

You will never go far in life – especially in recovery – on your own. You need someone to whom you can be accountable.

A football player named Tom Brady knows a little about teamwork. He said of his coach, "Coach Belichick holds us accountable every day. We appreciate when he's tough on us. He gets the best out of us."

And basketball coach Lenny Wilkins said, "The most important quality I look for in a player is accountability."

In *Five Values for the Workplace*, Robert Dilenschneider identified the following keys to success on any team: integrity, accountability, diligence, perseverance, and discipline.

There's that word again – *accountability*. Successful recovery cannot be achieved alone. You need a sponsor, a counselor, and a group. You need accountability – because in recovery one is the loneliest number.

Recovery Step: You need accountability. That means building relationships with others in recovery. That way, when you fall down, "the other can help you up."

The Golden Rule
September 1

In 2014, the Centers for Disease Control and the Department of Education released the first federal uniform definition for bullying. They found that 30 percent of children in middle school have experienced bullying. The effects of bullying include depression and anxiety, both of which feed the addiction to sex.

Most addicts were bullied on some level as children. It may have been physical abuse or a form of emotional abuse that went undetected. As adults, we become that bully. It's all we know. We do unto others as has been done unto us.

Jesus prescribed a better medicine. "In everything, do to others what you would have them do to you, for this sums up the Law and the Prophets" (Matthew 7:12).

Tony Campolo is right when he suggests, "Each of us comes into the world with a predisposition to live in such a way as to inflict pain on those who love us most, and to offend the God who cares for us infinitely."

Our recovery is largely dependent upon how we treat others. When the bullied becomes the bully, the unhealthy cycle continues. But it can stop with you. Now.

Recovery Step: Determine to be a blessing to others today – even those who have hurt you the most.

Living with Purpose
September 2

We need to live lives of purpose. David said, "The Lord will vindicate me; your love, Lord, endures forever. Do not abandon the works of your hands" (Psalm 138:8).

No one lived a purposeful life better than Teddy Roosevelt. He was a cowboy, explorer, and big game hunter. He rode as a cavalry officer in the Spanish-American War. As a vice presidential candidate, he gave 673 speeches and traveled 20,000 miles. Years after his presidency, he was shot in the chest just before a scheduled speech in Milwaukee. He gave the one-hour speech anyway, then went to the hospital.

Asked the key to success, Roosevelt said, "Spend yourself on a worthy cause."

You can't do that if you are mired in addiction. Make recovery your "worthy cause." Everything else can be built on that solid foundation.

Coretta Scott King said, "My story is a freedom song of struggle. It's about finding one's purpose, how to overcome fear and to stand up for causes bigger than one's self."

There you have it – from King David, President Roosevelt, and Coretta Scott King. Live life with purpose. Set your eye on the prize, then order your steps in that direction.

Recovery Step: God's purpose for your life is that you make a difference in the lives of others. You can't do that unless you are sober.

Justin Timberlake
September 3

They are the trifecta of historic hymn writers: Charles Wesley, Fanny Crosby, and Justin Timberlake. Okay, so Timberlake isn't as well known for his Christian melodies as the other two, but he wrote one particular song with a poignant message for today – *Losing My Way*. It tells the story of a man whose search for meaning has come up short:

Now you gotta understand I was a family man
I would have done anything for my own –
But I couldn't get a grip on my new found itch
So I ended up all alone.
Losing my way, I keep losing my way,
Can you help me find my way?
Keep losing my way, keep losing my way –
Can you help me find my way?

Many of us have lost our way because of this "new found itch" we call sex addiction. But there is hope. Paul states it clearly: "Continue in your faith, established and firm, and do not move from the hope held out in the gospel. This is the gospel that you heard and that has been proclaimed to every creature under heaven, and of which I, Paul, have become a servant" (Colossians 1:23).

Recovery Step: Have you lost your way? There is a way home. Continue in your faith and walk in your hope. Let the Holy Spirit help you find your way.

Lots-of-Stuff
September 4

There once lived a man in a faraway place. It had so much stuff that they called it Stuffland. And this man had more stuff than anyone else. So they called him Lots-of-Stuff. He earned his stuff the old-fashioned way – through self-reliance and hard work. Then he heard about a new place with even more stuff. They called it New Stuffland. Lots-of-Stuff had to see it for himself, so he traveled to New Stuffland. And sure enough, he saw more stuff than he ever imagined.

Then a stranger approached, offering Lots-of-Stuff more stuff than he had ever seen. But he could only keep it on one condition. He had to give it away. And miraculously, the more stuff Lots-of-Stuff gave away, the more he got back.

The stranger in this parable is Jesus Christ. The "stuff" represents sobriety, and Lots-of-Stuff is you and me.

Recovery is not a reward for hard work and brilliance; it is a gift. But you cannot receive this gift until you meet the Giver – and commit to giving it away to others.

Jesus came to "seek and to save that which was lost" (Luke 19:10). He came for you and for me. He offers the gift of sobriety you could not earn on your own. The next step is yours.

Recovery Step: You may have lots of stuff. You may even have lots of sobriety. But if you want the lasting gift of recovery, you must do two things: you must meet the Giver and share the gift with others.

It's Not Your Fight!
September 5

In the Civil War, 620,000 lives were lost, equal to all other American wars combined. The carnage ended on April 9, 1865, at Appomattox, Virginia, when Gen. Robert E. Lee surrendered his 28,000 troops. Then it was up to President Lincoln to decide the fate of the soldiers from both sides. Lincoln chose peace and reconciliation. He did for the South what they could not do for themselves.

There was a king in the Bible named Jehoshaphat. His army faced a formidable enemy, one he knew they could not conquer. The king turned to God, who issued a promise for the ages.

"You will not have to fight this battle" (2 Chronicles 20:17).

Andrew Murray said it like this: "God is ready to assume full responsibility for the life wholly yielded to him."

The battle for purity is not your battle to win. Victory is found only through surrender to your Higher Power who has all strength. Jehoshaphat prayed something like this: "Lord, I know you're in charge. So I choose to recognize this trouble as your problem, not just mine."

Pray that prayer of surrender. Then rejoice in the fact that while you are in the battle of your life, "You will not have to fight this battle."

Recovery Step: Surrender to the only one strong enough to win the battle.

Love vs. Lust
September 6

Bill and Steve were discussing the possibility of love. "I thought I was in love three times," said Bill.

Steve responded, "You *thought* it was love? What do you mean?"

Bill explained, "Three years ago, I cared deeply for a woman who wanted nothing to do with me. That's called obsession. Two years ago, I cared deeply for an attractive woman who didn't understand me. That was lust. Then, last year, I met a woman while I was on a cruise. She was gorgeous, intelligent, a great conversationalist, and had a super sense of humor. Everywhere I followed her on that ship, I'd get a strange sensation in the pit of my stomach."

Steve said, "I get it. *That* was true love."

"No," said Bill. "That was motion sickness."

We often confuse love with other things. Danielle Steel said, "Lust is temporary, romance can be nice, but love is the most important thing of all because, without love, lust and romance will be short-lived."

Jesus defined authentic love. "Greater love has no one than this: to lay down one's life for one's friends" (John 15:13).

In any relationship, especially marriage, that must be the definition of love – sacrifice. Everything else is just motion sickness.

Recovery Step: Ask God to deepen your love for your spouse and make it authentic. Then let your emotions follow your actions rather than the other way around.

Lesson from LifeCall
September 7

In 1989 a company called LifeCall burst onto the American conscience with a series of television commercials featuring senior citizens who were armed with their medical alarm device designed to notify designated family and friends in the event of a fall. The message was simple: "I've fallen and I can't get up."

That could be the mantra for addicts in early recovery. We have fallen – and on our own, we can't get up.

Paul addressed those who had fallen in his second letter to Corinth. "If anyone has caused grief, he has not so much grieved me as he has grieved all of you to some extent – not to put it too severely. The punishment inflicted on him by the majority is sufficient. Now instead, you ought to forgive and comfort him, so that he will not be overwhelmed by excessive sorrow. I urge you, therefore, to reaffirm your love for him" (2 Corinthians 2:5-8).

Paul was telling the church to lift those who have fallen, rather than assigning blame. Do you know someone who has fallen and can't get up? The next move is yours.

Recovery Step: If you have fallen and can't get up, *find* a good church. If you know someone else who has fallen, *be* a good church.

A Better Man
September 8

In the 1997 movie *As Good As It Gets*, Melvin Udall (Jack Nicholson) turns to Carol Connelly (Helen Hunt), his wife, and says, "You make me want to be a better man."

A good marriage does that. Guys, your wife should make you want to be a better man.

Martin Luther said, "There is no more lovely, friendly, and charming relationship, communion, or company than a good marriage."

Winston Churchill said, "My most brilliant achievement was my ability to be able to persuade my wife to marry me."

So where does this motivation to be a better man come from? Paul addressed the men of the church with these words: "For husbands, this means love your wives, just as Christ loved the church. He gave himself up for her" (Ephesians 5:25).

We become the kind of men that stay true to our marriage vows when we commit to loving our wives and giving ourselves for them.

Recovery Step: Commit to loving your wife and giving yourself to her – 100 percent.

Delilah
September 9

In a moment, the world's strongest man threw it all away.

"Samson said to Delilah, 'A razor has never come upon my head, for I have been a Nazirite to God from my mother's womb. If my head is shaved, then my strength will leave me, and I shall become weak and be like any other man'" (Judges 16:17).

Samson's weakness was in how he related to women. He was especially blinded to Delilah. His enemies paid her to discover the secret of his strength. Three times she begged Samson to tell her his secret. Each time she set him up and tried to hand him over to the enemy. Three times, Samson evaded her attempts and was able to escape. But each time he got closer to telling her the truth. Finally, Samson revealed his secret, was taken captive and died a slave in enemy hands. Samson's real problem can be found in the lies he told himself. He had convinced himself that he could be strong without the help of his Higher Power. By not admitting his powerlessness, he remained blind to the danger of the foreign woman.

It didn't have to end this way. If Samson had decided what to do before the temptation hit, he would have survived. That's how it is in life. That's why you need a battle plan to be firmly in place *before it is needed*. The world is full of Delilahs, whose conniving ways may cost you everything. If you wait until the crisis hits to decide how you will respond, it will be too late.

Recovery Step: Delilahs come in many forms. When you meet your own Delilah, you better be ready – *before the encounter*.

Paid in Full
September 10

Kierkegaard wrote, "In the understanding of the moment, never has anyone accomplished so little by the sacrifice of a consecrated life as did Jesus Christ. And yet in this same instant, eternally understood, he had accomplished all, and on that account said, 'It is finished.'"

Peter said that Jesus died to secure "the genuineness of our faith" (1 Peter 1:7).

Jesus' death was not primarily for the history books. It is more personal than that. Because Jesus died for our shortcomings, we can find victory. Freedom is not based on what we can do, but on what he has already done.

In the nineteenth century, Elvina Hall understood this when she became the first to perform a new hymn, at the Monument Street Methodist Church in Baltimore. This is the first stanza of that hymn. Perhaps you've heard of it.

I heard the Savior say, thy strength indeed is small.
Child of weakness, watch and pray, find in me thine all in all.
Jesus paid it all, all to him I owe;
Sin had left a crimson stain, he washed it white as snow.

Recovery Step: Jesus paid it all, then said, "It is finished." That means we can live *from* victory, not *for* victory. Rest in the one who has already secured your freedom.

No Fear
September 11

In the second grade, I was bullied by a classmate who would steal my lunch money and tear up my homework. I had finally had enough, so I asked her to stop.

Many of us are paralyzed by fear – of acting out, the next temptation, being betrayed, or being alone. The Bible offers the antidote for fear. God said "Fear not" 365 times in Scripture – once for every day of the year.

One of those verses is Isaiah 40:31, which reads, "Do not fear, for I am with you; do not be dismayed, for I am your God. I will strengthen you and help you."

There are three reasons we need to overcome fear. First, fear makes you *frail*. Doctors report that almost all chronic patients are gripped by fear. Second, fear makes you *frantic*. And third, fear makes you *foolish*.

It is in our foolishness that we do dumb things. While we may never move beyond our fear, we can move forward in the midst of our fear.

Nelson Mandela said, "I learned that courage was not the absence of fear, but the triumph over it."

Recovery Step: Tell God about your fears. Then ask him to give you the courage to keep moving forward anyway. That's the only way to do recovery successfully.

Nyctophobia
September 12

John played six years of professional football. He was an offensive lineman and one of the strongest men in the NFL. He snapped the ball to such greats as Joe Montana. After football, he joined Team Impact, traveling the world preaching the Gospel – and performing insane feats of strength. Now he is one of America's most successful Student Pastors.

Several years ago, John was on my church staff, where I was the senior pastor. The staff went off to a ranch for an overnight retreat. After a planning session, it was time to walk from the guest cabin to the main house, where John would spend the night. But there was just one problem. It was dark, and John suffered from nyctophobia.

Big John was afraid of the dark.

Millions suffer from this phobia. In addiction, darkness represents secrecy. It is in that secrecy that the addiction thrives – and the addict becomes desperately scared and lost.

John found his way out of the darkness with the aid of a flashlight and a few friends. God offers the same to you.

"For God has rescued us from the dominion of darkness and brought us into the kingdom of the Son he loves" (Colossians 1:13).

Are you afraid of the dark? You should be. But there is an Answer. It's called the Light.

Recovery Step: Walk out of the darkness into hope and joy. You can't find your way on your own. That's okay. It just means it is time to follow the Light.

The Best Is Yet to Come
September 13

"I've lost everything."

The call from a man I had never met had a familiar message. A good man, successful by all measures, had served his churches with distinction. "Bob" had been a senior pastor for over 30 years. But now he had lost it all – his church, his ministry, and even his wife. His porn habit had been discovered. I recognized true remorse and repentance in his voice – and loss.

What do you tell a man like Bob? You tell him to read the Book of Job. If anyone could relate to losing everything, it was Job. He literally lost the farm, and worse yet, his family.

We are all too familiar with how the Book of Job begins. But we forget how it ends.

"The Lord blessed the latter part of Job's life more than the former part. He had 14,000 sheep, 6,000 camels, 1,000 yoke of oxen, and 1,000 donkeys" (Job 42:12).

Did you catch that? "The Lord blessed the latter part of Job's life more than the former part."

Dale Carnegie observed, "Most of the important things in the world have been accomplished by people who have kept on trying when there seemed to be no hope at all."

For Bob there is hope. For you there is hope. Even if you've lost everything, the Lord can bless the latter part of your life more than the former part.

Recovery Step: Have you lost everything? Take heart, for we have a God who can do in your future more than he had done in your past. The best is yet to come.

No More Secrets
September 14

George Orwell said, "If you want to keep a secret, you must hide it from yourself."

Secrets kill.

Isaiah 29:15 reads, "Woe to those who go to great depths to hide their plans from the Lord, who do their work in darkness and think, 'Who sees us? Who will know?'"

Secrets kill.

Andre Malraux said, "Man is not what he thinks he is; he is what he hides."

Secrets kill.

Dr. Michael Slepian wrote a paper in *Journal of Personality and Social Psychology*. Slepian said of secrets: "One problem with keeping secrets is that your goal becomes keeping secrets. Then your motivational system is centered on fulfilling this goal, which fixes your mind on that which has become your secret, and this leads to relapse. You keep thinking about the secret you are trying to protect."

Even your darkest, most intimate secrets must come to light. Why? Because secrets kill.

Recovery Step: It is critical to get your secrets out. In 12-step work, this is called "working the First Step." You must let go of your secrets – because secrets kill.

Fear of Falling
September 15

I have a tremendous fear of heights. Yet, I have no problem flying on a plane. How does this make sense? A private aircraft pilot explained it to me. "You don't really have a fear of heights," he said. "You have a fear of falling."

For a guy committed to a lifetime of recovery, that's a pretty healthy fear. Regardless of how much sobriety you have, you can only be sober one day at a time. Long ago, I made a decision – and I repeat it every day. "I'm not saying I'll never fall again. But I am saying it won't happen today." I awaken every day to a fear of falling.

Here's what I've learned from flying. I trust the pilot to do what I can't do. I wear a seatbelt because it keeps me steady through the turbulence. And I put my tray in its upright and locked position before landing. (While I'll admit I've never heard of a passenger surviving a crash because he put his tray in an upright position, I still do it because that's what the pilot says.)

Not all recovery activities will make sense to you. But you need to do them. You need to trust your pilot – Higher Power, sponsor, therapist. But you probably won't – until you develop a healthy fear of falling.

The Bible warns, "There is not a righteous person on earth who never sins" (Ecclesiastes 7:20).

Recovery Step: If you don't already have a fear of falling, get one. And commit to sobriety – just for today.

Follow Through
September 16

Successful recovery is a full-time enterprise. We must go all in.

A construction crew was putting a drain line in a building. A power cable was directly in the path of their work. Construction stopped while an electrician was called, who declared that there was no electrical power to the cable.

The foreman asked the electrician, "Are you sure the power is dead to the cable, and there is no danger?"

The electrician said, "Absolutely. It's safe to cut the line."

The foreman said, "Then *you* cut the line!"

The electrician countered, "Well, I'm not *that* sure!"

When there are ten squirrels sitting on a branch, and five decide to jump off, ten squirrels remain on the branch. Why? Because *deciding* to do something is not the same thing as *doing* it.

Consider Isaiah 43:18-19. "Forget the former things; do not dwell on the past. See, I am doing a new thing!"

Recovery is not about right decisions, but right actions. It's about going all in.

Recovery Step: What actions do you need to take in your recovery? Quit making decisions about it. It's time for follow-through. It's time to go all in.

The $1 Bike Ride
September 17

"Great job!" my granddad said as he handed me a dollar.

In one ten-minute session, my granddad taught me how to do something my dad had been trying to teach me for over a year – ride a bike without the aid of training wheels. How did he do it? He offered me a dollar. And for a 24-year-old man, that was all the motivation necessary.

Actually, I was about five. But the lesson is there either way. A reward at the end of the journey enhances the chance that journey will end well.

The same is true of recovery. While the journey itself is rewarding enough, the thought of hearing my Master say, "Well done, thou good and faithful servant" (Matthew 25:23) motivates me. But so does the thought of going to bed tonight absent guilt and shame.

Before I made it around the block the first time, I fell a few times. The result was skinned knees and a bruised ego. But I kept at it because the reward of success was worth it.

The same is true in recovery. If you've fallen, get back up. Stay at it, and your progress will lead to victory – and a good reward at the end of the journey, as well as at the end of today.

Recovery Step: If you've fallen, get back up. Your ride to recovery may include a few falls at first, but you'll eventually make it if you don't give up. And great rewards await.

The Sinking Feeling
September 18

That sinking feeling.

Peter knew it well. In an instant, he went from hero to goat, from walking on water to nearly drowning.

"Peter got down out of the boat, walked on water and came toward Jesus. But when he saw the wind, he was afraid and, beginning to sink, cried out, 'Lord, save me!' Immediately Jesus reached out his hand and caught him" (Matthew 14:29-31).

Like Peter, many of us walked on top of it all. But our addictions caught up to us. We began to sink. But Jesus majors in catching those who sink.

In 1912, in Saugatuck, Connecticut, James Rowe read this passage about Peter, then jotted down a few words on paper, writing from his personal experience as the impoverished son of a copper miner.

I was sinking deep in sin, far from the peaceful shore,
Very deeply stained within, sinking to rise no more;
But the Master of the sea heard my despairing cry,
From the waters lifted me, now safe am I.
Love lifted me, love lifted me!
When nothing else could help, love lifted me!

Recovery Step: Do you know that sinking feeling? Turn to Christ. He majors in rescuing those who are sinking deep in sin, far from the peaceful shore.

The Wounded Spouse
September 19

If you are the wounded spouse, one of the toughest mountains you will ever climb will be Mt. Forgiveness. In forgiving your mate, you relinquish all rights to retribution and payback. You accept him or her as though they had never abandoned you for the selfishness of their addiction.

Forgiveness may not seem fair. But it is necessary. Absolutely necessary – for your own healing.

Ephesians 4:31 says, "Get rid of all bitterness, rage and anger, brawling and slander, along with every form of malice."

In other words, forgive the one who has hurt you the most. Bryant McGill was right when he said, "There is no love without forgiveness, and there is no forgiveness without love."

Legendary wrestler Lex Lugar has a lot of regrets. But he has found hope in Christ. A few years ago, he reflected on his life. "Many times, the decisions we make affect and hurt our closest friends and family the most. I have a lot of regrets in that regard. But God has forgiven me, which I am very grateful for. It has enabled me to forgive myself and move forward one day at a time."

Has your spouse wounded you? You need to forgive him or her. Don't do it for them. Do it for you.

Recovery Step: Forgive the one who has hurt you the most. Otherwise, they win.

End Game
September 20

You are going to die. But don't feel singled out. That applies to pretty much everyone.

Jesus said, "You must be ready, because the Son of Man will come at an hour when you do not expect him" (Luke 12:40).

Elton Trueblood said, "Our life is a gift *from* God. What we do with that life is our gift *to* God."

What have you done with your life? If you had just one week to live, how would you spend it? Would you try to fulfill a lifelong dream? Would you make sure you said your goodbyes to loved ones? Or would you indulge in all kinds of pleasures, expecting to make your life right with God in some sort of "deathbed conversion" at the last possible moment?

I just read an article by Kimberly Hiss titled, *16 Things Smart People Do to Prepare for Death.*

Amos had only one: "Prepare to meet thy God" (Amos 4:12).

I'm with Amos on this one. We need to keep it simple. Prepare to meet God. Let that inform every decision you make about recovery.

Recovery Step: Prepare to meet God because it could happen at any moment. I'd tell you what that means about your acting out, but I'm pretty sure you already know.

Mired in the Weeds
September 21

The date was October 13, 1960. Andy Jerke was just like every other boy growing up in Pittsburgh. He loved baseball, and especially the Pirates. On this day, the Pirates were hosting the vaunted New York Yankees for Game 7 of the World Series. The game came down to the bottom of the ninth inning. The score was tied. And Andy was there, at Forbes Field.

Then he remembered he had promised his mother to be home by 4:30 to help with dinner. So he left the game in the bottom of the ninth, to walk home.

As he was walking across the lot beyond the outfield wall, a baseball landed near his feet. Andy picked up the ball, and a security man informed him that Bill Mazeroski had just hit that ball for a game-winning home run. And now the ball belonged to Andy.

Andy played with the ball a year later and lost it in a field. He looked for it for ten minutes, then gave up. What happened to the ball? It got mired in the weeds.

Jesus said, "As the weeds are pulled up and burned in the fire, so it will be at the end of the age" (Matthew 13:40).

Dale Carnegie warned, "Our fatigue is caused by worry, frustration, and resentment." In other words, we tend to get mired in the weeds. In recovery, we must never lose focus. We must keep moving forward, not sidetracked by worry, frustration, or resentment.

Recovery Step: Watch out for the little things that can trip you up. Don't get mired in the weeds.

It's What's Wrong with Us
September 22

It's the malady of every addict. They want what they shouldn't have, then don't want it once they have it. Exhibit A – David (and Bathsheba). Exhibit B – The Israelites (and Egypt). Exhibit C – Every person who was ever addicted to pornography.

The problem isn't that we want too much. It's that we look in the wrong places.

Life Coach Lukas Schwekendick said it well. "People do not feel satisfied with what they have because they believe that they can still find happiness from something outside themselves."

The children of God wanted the benefits of the Promised Land, but they didn't want the work it would take to get there. They wanted it, then didn't want it. They were confused because they thought that joy would come from *where* they were instead of from *who* they were. The Bible records their story.

"And they spread among the Israelites a bad report about the land they had explored. They said, 'The land we explored devours those living in it. All the people we saw there are of great size'" (Numbers 13:32).

And therein lies the problem – looking for life's fulfillment in the wrong place. It's what's wrong with us.

Recovery Step: You will never be satisfied by what you crave the most. It will never be enough. And when you get it, you will want to let it go. So quit chasing after the wrong dreams.

All Alone
September 23

Dr. Shahram Heshmat wrote an excellent article, *Addiction as a Disease of Isolation.* He makes a case for isolation as a leading contributor to addiction.

He writes, "Since insecurely attached individuals doubt the availability and support of others, they use other tactics to mitigate and control negative effect. One compensatory strategy is attachment to non-human targets (for example, objects and materialism). In other words, they substitute relationships with objects for relationships with people."

Heshmat is suggesting that in our addiction we avoid personal connections. We isolate. And that never ends well. Consider the prophet Elijah, for example.

"The Israelites have rejected your covenant, torn down your altars, and put your prophets to death with the sword. I am the only one left, and now they are trying to kill me, too" (1 Kings 19:10).

Elijah actually had 7,000 others ready to stand by his side. But in the face of difficulty, he retreated into isolation and depression. The fact is, isolation is a choice. You are only alone if you choose to be. Be aware – your isolation feeds your addiction. And that never ends well.

Recovery Step: Dr. Heshmat is right. Sex addicts treat women as objects in order to avoid personal connections. That leads to isolation, and that never ends well.

Involuntary Slavery
September 24

"Jesus said, 'Very truly I tell you, everyone who sins is a slave to sin'" (John 8:34).

Ancient philosophy taught that those who are devoted to their lusts are subject to the most degrading kind of slavery. You own your addiction, then your addiction owns you.

The word Jesus used for "slave" is *doulos*. It refers to an involuntary state. We do not volunteer to become slaves to our addictions. The physiology of sex addiction confirms this.

After the sex act, addicts quickly slide into despair, their dopamine receptors left hungry for more sex. This craving is set up biologically and physiologically. Quick fixes provide a state of ecstasy and nirvana. But it doesn't last. The addict is rendered emptier, distressed, and fragmented. To quell these painful feelings, he is compelled to resume his pursuit of the next fix.

In the SA (Sexaholics Anonymous) White Book, it says, "The only way we knew to be free of it was to do it."

Calvin nailed it when he said, "Men are destitute of freedom unless they find it in Christ."

Recovery Step: Addicts are slaves to their drug of choice. For the sex addict, this leads him or her down a cruel journey of isolation and despair. That is why successful recovery is a spiritual recovery. It cannot be done apart from the One who sets us free.

Special Delivery
September 25

"Then the Lord said to Joshua, 'See, I have delivered Jericho into your hands, along with its king and its fighting men'" (Joshua 6:2).

God is in the delivery business. And the same God who delivered Jericho can deliver you – from your fears, resentments, and addictions. God is the master of accomplishing the unattainable.

Wilbur Howard wrote, "The future belongs to those who set their sights on what is humanly unattainable."

Let me illustrate.

When the World's Fair came to Canada in 1986, Henry Blackaby saw an opportunity to reach more than 22 million people with the message of the gospel. There was just one problem. The association of churches Blackaby served in Vancouver had just 2,000 members and a budget of less than $9,000 a year. Still, convinced of God's leading, Blackaby set a budget of $202,000, prayed and trusted God to do the rest. God didn't disappoint. By the end of the year, more than $264,000 had come in from all over the world, and some 20,000 people began personal relationships with Christ through the efforts of a small but faithful band of believers.

It may feel like you will never be able to quit your porn habit, affairs, or self-stimulation. But the God who delivered the entire city of Jericho stands ready to deliver you – if you let him.

Recovery Step: Surrender to the God who is in the delivery business. The next miracle can be yours.

Pushing Trains
September 26

Do you ever tire of straining to stay sober, of trying to do the right things? Perhaps you can relate to the rural pastor.

The pastor was spotted sitting by the train track each morning. A church member asked him what he was doing. "Why do you sit here watching the train each day?" she asked him.

"It's simple," replied the pastor. "I enjoy watching something move that I don't have to push."

Life is most effective when we leave the pushing to God. The psalmist wrote, "The Lord is my strength and my shield; my heart trusts in him, and he helps me. My heart leaps for joy, and with my song I praise him" (Psalm 28:7).

J.I. Packer said it well with these now-famous words: "Our high and privileged calling is to do the will of God in the power of God for the glory of God."

It is natural to want to do all the pushing ourselves. But it doesn't work. We need to learn to let go and let the Conductor take over.

Recovery Step: Quit pushing. Relax. Turn control of your train – and your life – over to God.

It's Not About Actions
September 27

Marcus Aurelius said, "The happiness of your life depends upon the quality of your thoughts; therefore, guard accordingly, and take care that you entertain no notions unsuitable to virtue and reasonable nature."

Thoughts lead to acts, which lead to habits, which lead to character, which leads to destiny. It all starts in the head.

Many addicts put too much stock in how they *act*, as opposed to how they *think*. Sobriety is not the absence of acting out; it is a progressive victory over lust. And you can lust a thousand times a day and never act out again. But Jesus said that when we lust after someone, we have already crossed the line.

So what is the answer? It is found in one of Jesus' last teachings. "Watch and pray so that you will not fall into temptation. The spirit is willing, but the flesh is weak" (Matthew 26:41).

Whatever your triggers may be, the dual response is the same: watch and pray. First, be on the *watch* for temptations and intrusive thoughts. Second, when an image catches your eye, or a fantasy invades your thoughts, do the "double p" – *pop and pray*.

Recovery Step: Marcus Aurelius had it right. "The happiness of your life depends upon the quality of your thoughts." Recovery does not begin with right actions; it ends there. The beginning of recovery is the next thought you choose to entertain.

Lesson from Camden Yards
September 28

It was on my bucket list. A lover of the traditions of baseball, I had wanted to visit Baltimore's Camden Yards since the ballpark opened in 1992. In Baltimore for a meeting, I had one day to take in the significant sites of the Baltimore/Washington, D.C. area. I narrowed my options to the Lincoln Memorial, the White House, and Camden Yards. In choosing baseball over politics, I was reminded of the Babe Ruth quote of the 1920s. When asked to defend the fact that his salary eclipsed that of President Calvin Coolidge, Ruth explained, "I'm having a better year than he is."

The lessons from baseball to recovery are infinite. Let me cite one.

Baseball is a team sport.

The great Nolan Ryan once posted an ERA below 2.00 – and had a losing record. "How was this possible?" he was asked. "It's simple," said Ryan. "I'm not a very good hitter."

Even Nolan Ryan could not win unless others on the team scored some runs. In recovery, you cannot make it by yourself. And this is the point where I see most fail. You need a group, a sponsor, and accountability. You need a team.

Jesus prayed that we would be one (John 17:21). Why? Because he knew that we cannot make it without a team.

Recovery Step: Babe Ruth and Nolan Ryan needed a team. So do you.

Hiding Place
September 29

When I was a child, I loved to play "hide and seek." Somehow, no matter how well I thought I had hid, my father could always find me. Perhaps it was my feet sticking out from under the curtains or my giggling from under the bed covers that gave me away. But I always thought that if I couldn't see my father, he probably couldn't see me.

The good news for every believer is that even when we can't see our Father, he still sees us. King David went through this kind of struggle often – sometimes of his own doing, but not always. He was often overcome with hopelessness and despair.

And then he looked up. And he said this: "The Lord is my rock, my fortress, and my deliverer" (2 Samuel 22:2). And then David found the God who had already found him.

In the past, we used our addiction as our hiding place when life became overwhelming. Now that we are in recovery, life can at times feel even more overwhelming. We need a new place of refuge to escape the storms and find protection.

Philip Yancey wrote, "A God wise enough to create me and the world I live in is wise enough to watch out for me."

Turn to God as the one who delights in watching out for you. You've played "hide and seek" long enough. You lost. God won. And that's a good thing.

Recovery Step: Rest in God as your hiding place.

Death March
September 30

Memorize this truth – addiction will take you further than you want to go, keep you longer than you want to stay, and cost you more than you want to pay.

Solomon described the plight of the man who seeks a prostitute. "All at once he followed her like an ox going to the slaughter, like a deer stepping into a noose" (Proverbs 7:22).

It is a death march. We follow our passions blindly – into a trap. What starts as a moment of pleasure ends in a lifetime of shame. We lose our reputation, family, health, and our minds. But we still do it. Such is the cunning and baffling nature of this disease.

Here's the process, as described by Thomas A. Kempis: "Sin is first a simple suggestion, then a strong imagination, then delight, then assent."

Satan tempted Adam with a suggestion. He tempted Jesus the same way. That's his M.O. Suggestion leads to imagination, which leads to brief pleasure. And then it's all over.

So what's the solution? It's simple. Don't negotiate with the enemy. By even entering into the discussion, you have gone too far. The rest is predictable. And sad.

Recovery Step: Don't give an ear to the temptations that surround you. What you consider, you imagine. And what you imagine, you do. And what you do rewrites your destiny.

Only the Lonely
October 1

I heard it said once, "Recovery is always lived in the twelfth step." In other words, from the very beginning of our recovery journey, we need to give back and help others. Part of that is telling our stories. But know this – you will not always be well received.

Peter wrote, "They are surprised that you do not join them in their reckless, wild living, and they heap abuse on you" (1 Peter 4:4).

Not everyone will embrace your road to recovery. It is the road less traveled. At times you will feel like you are in this thing alone.

Perhaps you can identify with the 1961 hit by Roy Orbison, *Only the Lonely*.

"Only the lonely know the way I feel tonight.
Only the lonely know this feeling ain't right.
There goes my baby. There goes my heart.
They're gone forever. So far apart.
But only the lonely know why I cry.
Only the lonely."

Yes, the road can be lonely at times. That's okay; your recovery will never be dependent on how you are treated by others, but by how they are treated by you. So stay at it. Tell your story, help others, and remain focused – whether you sometimes feel alone or not.

Recovery Step: When you find yourself walking alone, keep walking. And keep helping others.

All My Children
October 2

We know that sex addiction runs in the family. If you or your spouse are addicted to porn, there is likely a history of addiction that goes back two or three generations. Or your family history may be characterized by isolation, intimacy disorders, or tightly held secrets.

The Bible confirms this trend. "The Lord is slow to anger, abounding in love and forgiving sin and rebellion. Yet he does not leave the guilty unpunished; he punishes the children for the sin of the parents to the third and fourth generation" (Numbers 14:18).

Clearly, there is a thread that runs from one generation to the next within addicted families. Often, these startling episodes and conditions do not present themselves to the next generation easily. But the seeds have been planted; the damage has been done.

Mark Twain said that he spent a large sum of money to trace his family tree and then spent twice as much trying to keep his ancestry a secret.

But think about it. Even if you could change your ancestry, would it matter? Spend your time where you have the most influence, with your family. The seeds you plant today will bear fruit tomorrow.

Recovery Step: Learn from your family history. Then commit to being the one who charts a new course – for yourself, your children, and the generations that follow. Remember, the seeds you plant today will bear fruit tomorrow.

Waterloo
October 3

The Battle of Waterloo was fought on June 18, 1815, near the city of Waterloo in present-day Belgium. All of England knew that the Duke of Wellington was leading the British forces against the French Emperor, Napoleon Bonaparte, in this epic battle. A ship signaled news of the outcome of the battle to a man on top of Winchester Cathedral. The message consisted of three words: "Wellington defeated Napoleon."

But the fog rolled in before the man at the Cathedral saw the third word. So the message that went out across England was, "Wellington defeated." The British thought they had lost the decisive battle, which they had actually won.

Sometimes we get mixed messages. In recovery, we often feel defeated – until we realize this battle is not our own. Our Higher Power has already defeated the enemy. We don't live *for* that victory but *from* it.

Sun Tzu had it right: "The supreme art of war is to subdue the enemy without fighting."

Because the battle has already been won, we can say, "Give glory to him who is able to keep you from falling and to present you before his glorious presence without fault and with joy" (Jude 24).

Yes, the enemy is strong. But you must hear the full message. The enemy was defeated.

Recovery Step: Claim the victory that has been secured on the cross.

True Confession
October 4

Confession is good for the soul.

Pablo Diaz wrote, in *The Power of Confession*, "By confessing our sins to God we decide to punish ourselves no longer."

The ancient Jews had to confront their sins. The Bible says there came a time when "those of Israeli descent had separated themselves from all foreigners. They stood in their places and confessed their sins and the sins of their ancestors" (Nehemiah 9:2).

Notice, the Jews who returned from exile *confessed their own sins*. This speaks volumes. It is important to understand the meaning of confession in that time. Confession was a three-step process: owning it, bemoaning it, and discarding it.

Admitting your addiction to porn or sex is not confession – unless you own it, bemoan it, and discard it. It is only when you do all three that the healing begins.

Recovery Step: Confession is not simply admitting you were wrong. You must own what you have done, endure a period of deep regret, then set that sin aside. When you do that, your recovery can begin.

Double Life
October 5

Chad worked hard and usually came straight home after work. But once a month, he stopped by a massage parlor on the way home. Sue taught a children's dance class. There, she met Jeff, the father of one of her students, and a six-month affair ensued. Sam traveled to Chicago once every few weeks on business. There, he met a prostitute, whom he paid for sex for three years.

Bill W., one of the founders of AA, said, "More than most people, the addict lives a double life. He is very much the actor."

I've never met an addict who didn't live a double life. In fact, I'm not sure I've ever met *anyone* who didn't live a double life on some level. Who we are on stage rarely matches who we are backstage.

And that gets us into trouble. James said, "A person with divided loyalty is as unsettled as a wave of the sea that is blown and tossed by the wind" (James 1:7).

The essence of recovery is bringing these two lives into alignment. And one of the best places to do that is in a recovery group. Okay, I'm thinking it, so I'll say it. I find more honesty in an SA group than I do in a Sunday school group. It is there that the double life is exposed, not hidden. And the healing begins.

Recovery Step: Are you living a double life? Does the person you present on stage match who you are backstage? If not, it's time to get real, be honest, and surround yourself with others committed to the same ideals.

The Fly
October 6

The other day, I was in a room listening to the desperate sounds of a life-or-death struggle just a few feet away. There was a small fly burning out the last of its short life's energies in a futile attempt to fly through the glass of a windowpane. The whining wings tell the poignant story of the fly's strategy: try harder. But it's not working.

The frenzied effort offers no hope for survival. In fact, the struggle is part of the trap. It is impossible for the fly to try hard enough to succeed at breaking through the glass. Meanwhile, across the room, the door is wide open. Five seconds of flying time and the tiny creature could reach the outside world it seeks. With only a fraction of the effort now being wasted, it could be free of this self-imposed trap. The breakthrough possibility is there. It would be so easy.

Yet, the fly remained locked in this prison of self-effort, a prison in which he would die.

In his famous song, *God Will Make a Way*, Don Moen penned, "God will make a way where there seems to be no way. He works in ways we cannot see. He will make a way for me."

God's servant prayed, "Teach me, and I will be quiet; show me where I have been wrong" (Job 6:24).

Your prison of addiction has a way out. It is when you come to the point of least persistence and accept God's direction that you will be set free.

Recovery Step: Quit banging your head against the glass and seek God's way out.

The One You Need to Forgive the Most
October 7

In the movie *Spider-Man 3*, Peter Parker spoke this famous line: "You want forgiveness? Get religion."

The fact is, we all want forgiveness. The sad thing is that we are more prone to offer our forgiveness to others than we are to accept our forgiveness for ourselves. The answer? Stay at it.

Paul said, "We glory in our sufferings, because we know that suffering produces perseverance" (Romans 5:3).

Forgiveness of self is the picture of perseverance. We grow impatient with ourselves as we continue to commit the same sins over and over. We relapse. We slip. We vow, "Never again!" And then it happens. Again and again – it happens.

Jesus said to forgive 490 times (Matthew 18:22). I suggest that if this is to be our mindset toward others, it should be our mindset toward ourselves, first. After all, we are told to love others *as we love ourselves* (Matthew 22:39).

Slips do not need to lead to shame. A relapse is not the end, but a beginning. And that beginning starts by forgiving yourself, just as God already has.

Recovery Step: Okay, so you've slipped. Call it a full relapse, perhaps. But the more important word is not *slip* or *relapse*. It is *forgiveness*. So forgive yourself. Then enjoy your new beginning.

The Great Philosopher
October 8

That great philosopher Willie Nelson said, "When I started counting my blessings, my whole life turned around."

I'll say something I rarely say. Willie makes sense. The fact is, the people who have received the most blessings, who have been healed of the greatest addictions, should be the most grateful for their new lease on life.

Case in point – Mary Magdalene.

Mary was a shining example of gratitude. Once possessed by seven demons, she had been set free by Christ. And she responded with unparalleled gratitude and loyalty. When Jesus was crucified on the cross, she was there. When Jesus needed a tomb for burial, she was there. And when he rose the third day, she was there. She had come to the tomb to offer a sacrifice of rare perfume.

The Bible says, "When Jesus rose early on the first day of the week, he appeared first to Mary Magdalene, out of whom he had driven seven demons" (Mark 16:9). People full of gratitude find themselves in the right place at the right time.

Recovery Step: What can you offer God today, in gratitude for the healing he has brought to your life?

The Saw
October 9

A man had a firewood factory that employed hundreds of men. He paid them well and gave them specific directions on what to do. But their work was slow and unproductive. Eventually, he had no choice. He fired the men and purchased a circular saw powered by a gas engine. In one hour, the new saw accomplished more than the men had done in a week.

The man talked to his new saw. "How can you turn out so much work? Are you sharper than the saws my men were using before?"

The saw responded, "No, I am not sharper than the other saws. The difference is the gas engine. I have a stronger power behind me. I am productive because of the power that is working through me, not because my blade is stronger."

The man or woman who finds successful recovery doesn't do so because he or she has a better saw. It's all about the power within. The Bible calls that power the Holy Spirit.

Jesus promised his earliest followers, "You will receive power when the Holy Spirit comes on you" (Acts 1:8).

That's the secret. It's not the sharpness of the saw, but the presence of the Spirit.

Recovery Step: Ask God to empower your saw through the filling and power of the Holy Spirit.

The Patient Patient
October 10

Be patient, and recovery will come.

Solomon promised, "It is good to wait quietly for the salvation of the Lord" (Lamentations 3:26).

Martin Lloyd Jones said, "There is nothing which so certifies the genuineness of a man's faith as his patient endurance, his keeping on steadily in spite of everything."

We all want to recover as quickly as possible. It's hard to be patient as we wait for the process to work. Sure, we realize that we didn't get to the difficult spot we are in overnight. We understand that we cannot undo a lifetime of damage in just a few moments. But still, it is a challenge to wait patiently. But every part of the recovery process requires time and patience.

The key to tomorrow's sobriety is today's work. Attend a meeting. Call someone in the program. Read a chapter of recovery material. Pray the 3rd Step Prayer. Do the little things you can do today, and God will bring a great miracle tomorrow.

Recovery Step: Pray the 3rd Step Prayer – *"God, I offer myself to you, to build with me and do with me as you will. Take away my difficulties, that victory over them would bear witness to those I would help of your power, your love, and your way of life."*

Princess Diana
October 11

Proverbs 24:16 says, "For though the righteous fall seven times, they rise again, but the wicked stumble when calamity strikes."

Few people in modern history epitomize the power of overcoming as did Princess Diana. Marrying into the Royal Family gave her a platform of influence known to a precious few. But her divorce from Prince Charles in 1996 did not change that. Such was her impact through her support of AIDS research, leprosy cures, and a ban on landmines that when Diana died in 1997 at the age of 36, her funeral was carried in 44 languages and viewed by 2.5 billion people.

There's a line in *Braveheart*, the 1995 war film about William Wallace, a 13th-century Scottish warrior who led the Scots in the First War of Scottish Independence against King Edward I of England. Wallace, played by Mel Gibson, said, "Every man dies, but not every man really lives."

Addiction brings a form of death – to the addict, his reputation, his family. Upon his discovery, his habit may end the life he once knew. But there is still time to pick up the pieces and really live, perhaps for the first time.

Recovery Step: The question is not whether you have fallen. You have. We all have. The question is what you will do next. It's what comes after you fall that will determine your ultimate destiny.

Apollo 13
October 12

The day was Monday, April 13, 1970. The crew of Apollo 13 found themselves marooned 200,000 miles from Earth. During a routine maintenance task, one of the spacecraft's four oxygen tanks exploded. For the next four days, astronauts Jim Lovell, Jack Swigert, and Fred Haise worked against all odds to bring their wounded ship back to Earth.

People around the world prayed for the trio's safe return. Each time the engineers at NASA solved one problem, another took its place. But a little faith and a lot of sweat eventually worked wonders. After four long days, Apollo 13's parachutes opened. The craft lowered safely into the Pacific Ocean.

Perhaps your "spaceship" is out of orbit, spiraling out of control. As with Apollo 13, the answer is not hard work or prayer. The answer is hard work *and* prayer.

St. Augustine said, "Pray as though everything depends on God, then work as though everything depends on you."

Solomon said it like this: "Commit to the Lord whatever you do, and he will establish your plans" (Proverbs 16:3).

You may have battled porn and sex addiction for years. Don't give up! If you work hard *and* pray hard, your ship can still have a safe landing.

Recovery Step: If your spacecraft is out of control, do what only you can do. Then trust God to do what only he can do.

Taking the 4th Step
October 13

Jason Wahler, the founder of Widespread Recovery, states, "The addiction is but a symptom of a spiritual disease. The real problem is in character flaws that need to be faced and overcome. This requires one thing – total honesty."

Therein lies the rub – total honesty. This is what the 4th step is all about. This is what recovery is all about. Most of us wished we could have avoided taking a personal inventory. It's normal to hide from personal examination. But in our hearts, we knew that day would come when we would have to face the truth about ourselves.

The Bible warns of a day when no man can hide. "And I saw the dead, great and small, standing before the throne, and books were opened. Another book was opened, which is the book of life. The dead were judged according to what they had done as recorded in the books" (Revelation 20:12).

It is best to do our inventory now so we will be ready for the big one to come. The 4th step is just nine words: "Made a searching and fearless moral inventory of ourselves." But those are nine powerful words. To get well, you have to get honest – about your past, your struggles, and most of all – your character defects. You're going to have to come clean eventually; you might as well do it now.

Recovery Step: If you haven't already done so, under the guidance of your sponsor, you need to work the 4th step.

Allota Warmheart
October 14

The year was 1985. When Beth and I stepped out of the elevator at the Fairmont Hotel in San Francisco, we were greeted by the sound of clicking cameras. Why? Because Elizabeth Taylor was staying at the same hotel. And she was expected to come down the same elevator to the lobby below. The media knew she was there because the woman who appeared on the cover of *Life Magazine* more than any other person always traveled under her own name.

Contrast that with Allota Warmheart. Allota would be as famous to her generation as Elizabeth Taylor was to hers. But unlike Ms. Taylor, Allota doesn't travel under her real name, because she prefers her anonymity.

The Bible says, "I praise you because I am fearfully and wonderfully made; your works are wonderful, I know that full well" (Psalm 139:14).

Tim Keller has written, "To be loved but not known is comforting but superficial. To be known and not loved is our greatest fear. But to be fully known *and* truly loved is, well, a lot like being loved by God. It is what we need more than anything. It liberates us from pretense, humbles us out of our self-righteousness, and fortifies us for any difficulty life can throw at us."

There is nothing so liberating as being fully known. And as for Allota Warmheart, you may know her better as Britney Spears.

Recovery Step: You need to be fully known – by God and someone else. So find a way to tell your story. It will bring freedom to your heart and hope to the hearts of others.

Impossible!
October 15

One day in the late 1800s a religious leader was asked his opinion on the possibility of flight. "Nonsense!" he said. "We'll never fly!"

The name of the religious leader was Bishop Wright. The names of his two boys were Orville and Wilbur. Perhaps you've heard of them.

What seems impossible is often made possible.

An angel told Mary – still a virgin – that she would give birth to a really important son. When she questioned the plausibility of such an occurrence, the angel assured her, "Nothing shall be impossible with God" (Luke 1:37).

What seems impossible is often made possible.

I love the words of Lincoln Brewster's song, *God of the Impossible*. He wrote, "You are who you are – the God of the impossible."

What does this mean for recovery? Everything. When it seems there is no way you can maintain sobriety and find lasting recovery, pause and remember . . .

What seems impossible is often made possible.

Recovery Step: Stop right now and say it with me. What seems impossible is often made possible.

Shelter
October 16

Jonah was us – each of us. He ran *from God* (chapter 1), *to God* (chapter 2), *with God* (chapter 3), then *ahead of God* (chapter 4). We have all done the same. Toward the end of the story, Jonah isolated. He went off by himself in the depths of depression, where he sat under a tree, which became his choice of shelter. And then we read this:

"At dawn the next day God provided a worm, which chewed the plant so that it withered. When the sun rose, God provided a scorching east wind, and the sun blazed on Jonah's head so that he grew faint. He wanted to die, and said, 'It would be better for me to die than to live'" (Jonah 4:7-8).

The tree became Jonah's crutch. He had come to rely on it for comfort and protection in the midst of his pain. As with Jonah, our addictions function as a shelter from our pain. And as with Jonah, when that crutch is removed, it reveals deep wounds. For Jonah, it was anger. He was angry that God didn't do things the way he wanted, and that his life had not turned out according to his plan.

Sound familiar?

In 1719, Isaac Watts penned these words: *"Our God, our help in ages past, our hope for years to come, our shelter from the stormy blast, and our eternal home."*

Your life has not turned out exactly as you had hoped. No one's does. That leaves you two choices: get better or get bitter. You get better by trusting in the true shelter . . . starting today.

Recovery Step: Allow God to cut away all that you have put in his place, all that you have come to trust in for your comfort. Quit isolating and trust in him.

Out of this World
October 17

A Russian Soyuz spacecraft with two Americans and one Russian on board lifted off from Kazakhstan. One of the Americans was computer game zillionaire, Richard Garriott. Why did he want to go for the ride?

"It's simple," he said. "I have everything there is in this world, but it's not enough."

So off he went, chasing new worlds.

The psalmist wrote, "You make known to me the path of life; you will fill me with joy in your presence, with eternal pleasures at your right hand" (Psalm 16:11).

One reason addicts pursue their fantasies is to escape the world they know. It's a two-fold thing. They are running *to something* by running *from something* – often themselves. But at the end of every rainbow is fool's gold. That elusive thing called *happiness* is always within reach but never reached.

And so the search continues . . . until they find God.

C.S. Lewis said, "God cannot give us a happiness and peace apart from himself, because it is not there. There is no such thing."

Recovery Step: You will never find the peace you covet by escaping your world. It cannot be found apart from God. So seek him today.

Inventory
October 18

When I was about ten, my dad gave my brother and me a summer job. For a few hours a week, we went to his office to count inventory. Dad owned his own company, where he worked as a sales rep. He sold electronics components from major factories to companies all over the country. He also stocked some parts at his office, to fill smaller jobs.

These capacitors and reed relays were stored in small boxes. And they had to be counted from time to time. That's where Jim and I came in.

Dad paid us $1 per box that we counted. But I made the most money. While Jim would count the boxes with dozens of tangled small parts, I'd open the boxes, and if there were a lot of parts inside, I'd close them back up. I only counted the boxes that had one or two parts.

That's how most of us do our personal inventory. We count empty boxes. When we look inside ourselves and find the complexity of tangled parts, we quickly shut the box and move on.

Paul said, "Examine yourselves" (2 Corinthians 13:5).

We all need to take an honest inventory of ourselves from time to time. Patrick Henry said it brilliantly: "Whatever anguish of spirit it may cost, I am willing to know the whole truth, to know the worst and to provide for it."

It is when you open the box and begin to untangle the worst parts that you find truth, freedom, and lasting recovery.

Recovery Step: It's time to open the box and untangle the mixed-up parts.

Restitution
October 19

Dr. George Simon is a leading expert on manipulators and the author of *In Sheep's Clothing*. He cites four marks of true change: acknowledgment of a wrong, the willingness to confess it, the willingness to abandon it, and the willingness to make restitution.

Did you catch that last one – restitution?

When Zacchaeus – who turned government tax fraud into a sport – came to faith in Christ, it changed everything. Zacchaeus quickly raced through the first three steps. He acknowledged that he had been robbing people of their taxes. He confessed it openly. And he committed to never doing it again. But then came the difference-maker.

"Zacchaeus stood up and said to the Lord, 'Look, Lord! Here and now I give half of my possessions to the poor, and if I have cheated anybody out of anything, I will pay back four times the amount'" (Luke 19:8).

We know we have become sober because we have quit acting out. And we know we are in recovery because we make restitution. It's called *making amends*. It's the 9th step in 12-step work. But it doesn't have to wait. Like Zacchaeus, you can start right away.

Recovery Step: In your addiction, you have trampled on the hearts of those you love the most. Today, find one small way to offer restitution. Make things right – one day at a time.

How to Treat a Woman
October 20

The Old Testament Book of Esther tells the story of a powerful man who easily became enraged. King Xerxes wanted what he wanted when he wanted it – how he wanted it. One day, he called for the Queen, Vashti, to come to him at the snap of his fingers. His reason was one of selfishness. In a drunken state, the king wanted to show off her physical beauty to those in his inner circle.

Queen Vashti refused the king's orders. Therefore, to prove he was in control, the king had her vanquished. There had to be a replacement.

We read, "Now the king was attracted to Esther more than he was to any of the other women, and she won his favor and approval more than any of the other virgins. So he set a royal crown on her head and made her queen instead of Vashti" (Esther 2:17).

According to the traditions of the day, the king's request of Queen Vashti was highly inappropriate. This was a case of a man objectifying his wife. While casual readers of the Book of Esther are intrigued by the story of Esther, we must not miss the first two chapters. Sadly, we never hear from the vanquished queen again.

There may be someone in your past whom you discarded – perhaps a former wife or girlfriend. While you probably can't (and shouldn't) go back to them, you can confess the sins of your past and pray for those you have hurt.

Recovery Step: Is there someone you have hurt in the past? It's never too late to make things right. The best thing you can do for that person is to pray for them.

Vengeance
October 21

Two little brothers, Harry and Jimmy, had finished supper and were playing until bedtime. Somehow, Harry hit Jimmy with a stick, and tears and bitter words followed. Charges and accusations were still being exchanged as Mother prepared them for bed. She said, "Now, Jimmy, before you go to bed you're going to have to forgive your brother."

Jimmy was thoughtful, and then replied, "Well, okay, I'll forgive him tonight, but if I don't die before I wake up, he'd better look out in the morning."

It is natural to seek revenge on those who have hurt us – but it is never healthy.

Rodney King said, "I'm a religious person. I remember my mom told me, 'Vengeance belongs to God. It's up to him to wreak vengeance.' It's hard for me to get to that point, but that's the work of God."

You are the product of the harms done to you by others. You can't help what has been done to you. But you are responsible for how you respond.

1 Peter 3:9 says, "Do not repay evil with evil or insult with insult. On the contrary, repay evil with blessings, because to this you were called so that you may inherit a blessing."

Recovery Step: Think of one person who has hurt you. Then make the decision to forgive him or her. Release that person to God.

Instant Gratification
October 22

Living in our addiction is all about instant gratification. We trade what we want *more* for what we want *now*. We choose that which will kill us tomorrow because it satisfies us today.

God says, "See, I set before you today life and prosperity, death and destruction" (Deuteronomy 30:15).

Eric Hoffer said it like this: "People will cling to an unsatisfactory way of life rather than change in order to get something better, for fear of getting something worse."

Instant gratification has swallowed up an entire generation. It makes us do things that violate our conscience, values, and faith. But we do it – repeatedly – because instant gratification has really become our god.

Darren Hardy wrote a great little book on the subject of instant gratification, *The Compound Effect.* Hardy wrote, "We understand that scarfing pop tarts won't slenderize our waistlines. We realize that logging three hours a night watching *Dancing with the Stars* and *Bachelorette* leaves us with three less hours to read a book, walk a dog, or pray a prayer. So why are we so irrationally enslaved by so many bad habits? It's because our desire for instant gratification can turn us into the most reactive, non-thinking animals on earth."

Instant gratification. Or lasting gratification. Pick one.

Recovery Step: You have to choose. It's either that which you want now or that which you want more. Instant gratification or lasting gratification. Pick one.

American Idol
October 23

One of the most popular shows of the last two decades is *American Idol*. It is in our nature to seek idols. I grew up idolizing Willie Mays. In my teen years, everyone I knew had posters on their walls, representing their personal idols, such as Patrick Swayze from *Dirty Dancing* or the best-selling poster of all time, the 1976 *Life* magazine cover featuring Farrah Fawcett.

John Calvin said, "Every one of us, even from his mother's womb, is a master craftsman of idols."

It's in our nature.

The Bible warns us, "Dear children, keep yourselves from idols" (1 John 5:21). It's one of the Ten Commandments. Repeatedly, the Bible warns us to avoid idols.

An idol is something we can see, but it never fulfills. The list of examples is endless: money, fame, success, another person. Or how about this one – sex. Every addict has made an idol out of his obsession. The problem is that it never fulfills.

You have crafted idols in your own head. They are elusive. And just when you think you have finally captured your idol – you discover your idol has captured you.

Recovery Step: Identify your idol. If it is sex, porn, or a relationship, know this. What you idolize today, you worship tomorrow. And then it owns you.

It's All about Grace
October 24

Jesus preached one sermon. We call it the Sermon on the Mount. We read in the first Gospel, "When Jesus saw the crowds, he went up on a mountainside and sat down. His disciples came to him, and he began to teach them" (Matthew 5:1-2).

Jesus touched on a lot of things in his great sermon. But underneath it all is the subject of grace. I like Philip Yancey's commentary on this sermon: "God has set the performance bar so high that no one can get over it, and he has set the bar of grace so low that no one is too low for it."

There can be no recovery apart from grace.

My friend Jonathan Daugherty has written a great book titled *Grace-Based Recovery.* He writes, "Grace does not teach us to say no to temptation in order to receive more grace. What grace teaches us is that because we are already accepted and loved, we are free to say no to sin."

Don't miss that! *You are already accepted and loved.* God is not waiting for you to get it all together in order to accept you. So quit trying to be good enough for God, and celebrate the fact that he is good enough for you.

Recovery Step: You are already accepted and loved. It's called grace. Quit trying to earn what has already been given.

Don't Settle
October 25

Addiction is about settling. We settle for pleasure over peace and sex over serenity. Saying yes to porn is another way of saying no to God. It is a matter of trading what satisfies for something that does not. And it's a bad trade every time.

The Old Testament tells the story of such a man. His name was Samson. The guy had it all – power, strength, and anything he asked for. And while Samson had it all, he didn't have enough. He coveted the "big fix." And he thought he had found it in the person of a beautiful woman. But it was a trap.

When Samson directed his parents to bring him this woman, "Samson's father and mother said, 'Isn't there an acceptable woman among your relatives or among our people? Must you go to the uncircumcised Philistines to get a wife?' But Samson said to his father, 'Get her for me. She's the right one for me'" (Judges 14:3).

Israelites were forbidden to marry Philistines, who were outside of their faith and worshiped other gods (Exodus 34:12).

Worldwide, 50 million people seek romantic hook-ups online every day. Since the days of Samson, we really haven't changed. We trade what we want most for what we want now.

Recovery Step: Make a determination today that you will no longer seek pleasure in the wrong place – or person. Determine that you won't settle.

Hypocrisy
October 26

Hamlet said to Ophelia, "God has given you one face, and you make yourself another."

Addicts are hypocrites. They have to be in order to maintain the ruse. Addicts live the normal life in front of the audience they know while living a different life backstage.

Those in church leadership are not immune. Paul wrote of such in his letter to Titus. "They claim to know God, but by their actions they deny him. They are detestable, disobedient, and unfit for doing anything good" (Titus 1:16).

That's strong language!

George Harrison said, "It is better to be an outspoken atheist than a hypocrite."

If you are in church leadership, or simply a Christ-follower, know this. You are being watched. The question the world is asking is this: Is the person they see really the person you are? It is only when we get real that we get right. Today is a pretty good time to start.

Recovery Step: It's time to start living the life you say you live. You have a God of second chances. So come clean with someone this week. And know this – there is nothing you have ever done that has made God love you less.

The Silver Bullet
October 27

Is there a silver bullet to sobriety? Is there one key, one thing that will bring recovery? Is there a simple fix?

The answer is yes, but you aren't going to like what it is. It's called *discipline*.

Paul told young Timothy how to win in life. "Fight the good fight of the faith" (1 Timothy 6:12).

I've seen boxers fight and I've seen them train. The fight is determined by the training. It is the miles of roadwork and hundreds of rounds in the gym that create the successful fighter. It is what is done when no one is watching that makes the fighter great.

In your addiction, you have found your strongest opponent. He will come at you with everything that he's got. And he keeps getting up, no matter how many rounds you have won. He is relentless in his attack and unyielding in his efforts. And even though you may be ahead on points, he can still take you out with a single punch in the final round.

Unless you are diligent in your preparation and disciplined in your defense. Jim Rohn was right: "Discipline is the bridge between goals and accomplishment."

Recovery Step: If you are committed to your sobriety, you must embrace the discipline that precedes each battle – discipline to go to meetings, make calls, and never give up.

Your Wedding Day
October 28

Do you remember your wedding day? The Bible tells us of the wedding of a king.

"Come out and look, you daughters of Zion. Look on King Solomon wearing a crown, the crown with which his mother crowned him on the day of his wedding, the day his heart rejoiced" (Song of Solomon 3:11).

One of the things you can do to secure your sobriety is to remember the joy of your wedding day. Reflect on the love that brought you and your spouse together.

A married couple, both aged 60, were celebrating their 35th wedding anniversary. During their party, a fairy appeared to congratulate them and grant them each one wish. The wife wanted to travel around the world. The fairy waved her wand and poof – the wife had tickets in her hand for a world cruise. Next, the fairy asked the husband what he wanted. He said, "I wish I had a wife 30 years younger than me." So the fairy picked up her wand and poof – the husband was 90.

When it comes to our youth, we can't *go* back, but we can *think* back. Remembering the promises and celebration of your wedding day can feed your recovery.

Prince Philip said, "When a man opens a car door for his wife, it's either a new car or a new wife." That may be true for most, but it doesn't need to be your story.

So look back. Celebrate your marriage vows. Celebrate your spouse. Celebrate recovery.

Recovery Step: Remember your wedding day. Remember your vows. Now, live them out for the rest of your life.

"Rabbit"
October 29

"Rabbit" Maranville was a 5'3" baseball player, born in 1891. He made it to the big leagues when he was 21. Though just a career .258 hitter, "Rabbit" stuck for 23 years. While bouncing among five teams – the Braves, Pirates, Cubs, Dodgers, and Cardinals – "Rabbit" could do one thing well. He could run. And he ran faster than anyone else.

But alcohol nearly ended his life as a young player. Then one night in 1927, "Rabbit" gave his life to his Higher Power. Christ changed his life, and "Rabbit" never took another drink.

But choices have consequences. In 1954, "Rabbit" died from the effects of years of alcohol abuse. Two weeks later, he was elected to the Baseball Hall of Fame.

Choices have consequences. Paul said it like this: "The wages of sin is death" (Romans 6:23).

In the movie *The Number 23*, Jim Carrey's character said, "There's no such thing as destiny. There are only different choices. And that's what defines us."

Recovery Step: Tomorrow's destiny is in your hands today. You can't see your destiny, but you can create it – one choice at a time.

Hammers and Nails
October 30

A lot of men and women who are new to recovery like to play "Chase" with their sponsors. They feel a sense of entitlement and get frustrated when their sponsor doesn't pick up every call or chase after them when they miss meetings. But a good sponsor doesn't chase after a sponsee. As you get into recovery, it is your responsibility to make the calls and set up the meetings. This means getting over yourself and your pride.

The Bible says, "Do not be like the horse or the mule, which have no understanding but must be controlled by bit and bridle or they will not come to you" (Psalm 32:9). In other words, you must take ownership of your recovery. When you attend your next SA or SAA meeting, check your pride at the door.

Will Smith starred in a movie titled *Focus*. In the movie, his character described life: "There are two kinds of people in the world. There are hammers, and there are nails. You decide which one you want to be."

For the purpose of recovery, you need to become a nail at times. Your own best efforts got you in this mess. Now it is time to fall under the authority of a hammer (sponsor). This is part of what we call "letting go." The AA "Big Book" says, "If we still cling to something, we must let go and ask God to help us to be willing" (p. 76).

Recovery Step: If you don't have a sponsor, get one. If you aren't following his lead, start now. You've tried being the hammer. Now you need to be the nail for a while.

Collect Calls
October 31

2 Corinthians 10:5 tells us to "take captive every thought to make it obedient to Christ."

I encourage people to practice what I call the "3-second rule." When your eyes are triggered, or an intrusive thought or memory invades your mind, move away from it within three seconds. Say a prayer, read a verse, make a call.

Let me illustrate. Back in the day, we had this thing in our house we called a land line. It was a precursor to the modern cell phone. We called it a telephone. When someone wanted to contact us, they dialed our number, and this thing would ring. We'd pick up the receiver. And sometimes, it would be what we called a "long distance call." This one cost money. We'd hear the voice of the "operator," who would ask us if we were willing to "accept" a call that was made "collect." In other words, once we knew who was trying to call us, we had about three seconds to decide if we were willing to pay to hear what they had to say.

Lustful thoughts make collect calls. They will enter our minds at times. That is reality. It's what we do with those thoughts that matters. When we accept the call, it will cost us – mightily.

Aristotle said it like this. "It is the mark of an educated mind to be able to entertain a thought without accepting it."

Temptations always call collect. You will recognize the voice. And when you do, don't negotiate the price or ask what he/she wants. Just hang up – fast!

Recovery Step: The tempter has your number. He or she will come calling. And if you stay on the line, you will pay for that call, and it will cost you more than you can afford. So reject the call. Know when to hang up.

Buy Ducks
November 1

There was a chicken farmer whose land was flooded every spring. He didn't want to give up his farm, but when the water backed up onto his land and flooded his chicken coops, it was always a struggle to get his chickens to higher ground. Some years he couldn't move fast enough, and hundreds of his chickens drowned.

After his worst spring ever, and having lost his entire flock, he came into his farmhouse and said to his wife, "I've had it. I can't afford to buy another place. I can't sell this one. I don't know what to do."

His wife offered the obvious: "Buy ducks."

Author Neale Donald Walsh asserted, "Life begins at the end of your comfort zone."

Perhaps you've been through a few floods in your life. The good news for the farmer is that he had his wife. And she told him to make something great from what seemed to be a disaster. God does the same for you. From the floods can come great victory. But only if you don't try to go it alone.

Moses encountered his share of difficulties. He offered this promise: "He [God] is the one who goes before you. He will be with you. He will not leave you or forsake you. Do not be afraid" (Deuteronomy 31:8).

Recovery Step: When tough times come, keep moving forward. But don't do it alone.

Driving Out Your Demons
November 2

The second Gospel tells the story of a boy possessed by demons. His father brought him to Jesus' disciples in the hope that they would cast out the demons. But they failed to do so. So the man brought his son to Jesus, who cast out the demons. The disciples asked Jesus why they had failed in their efforts. Jesus offered a simple answer. "This kind can come out only by prayer" (Mark 9:29).

"Only by prayer," Jesus said.

Perhaps you can identify with the boy in this story. You feel like there is something inside of you that has a craving for which there is no answer. You have tried to overcome your addiction in many ways. At first, you ignored it. Then you downplayed it. Eventually, you came to recognize it as the adversary that it is. But you still didn't understand that this is a spiritual battle.

It's time to do what the disciples did. It's time to call in reinforcements, because "this kind can come out only by prayer." But the power isn't actually in the prayer; it's in the One to whom you pray.

Charles Spurgeon defined prayer like this: "True prayer is neither a mere mental exercise nor a vocal performance. It is far deeper than that – it is a spiritual transaction with the Creator of Heaven and Earth."

If you recognize the nature of the opposition, you are ready to get well. It's time to pray.

Recovery Step: You have worked as though it all depended upon you. Now pray as though it all depends upon God. Because it does.

Harry Callahan
November 3

Harry Callahan spoke the words that have been repeated for decades since. It was 1983. The movie was *Sudden Impact*. Harry Callahan, played by Clint Eastwood, said, "Go ahead, make my day."

The brother of Jesus said it like this: "Anyone who listens to the word but does not do what it says is like someone who looks at his face in the mirror and, after looking at himself, goes away and immediately forgets what he looks like" (James 1:23-24).

In recovery, it is not enough to acknowledge the problem. Recovery requires action. Just as it would be foolish to look in the mirror and not respond, it is foolish to see the road to recovery and not take it. There comes a time when we need to do what Harry said and "go ahead."

Sam was hired to rid a mill of muskrats. The first thing he did was to buy a gun. A year later, his buddy saw him looking over a dam when a muskrat ran out in full view. Sam just watched. His buddy said, "Shoot him!" But Sam didn't budge. "Why didn't you shoot him?" asked his friend. Sam replied, "Do you think I want to lose my job?"

Too often, we respond to a call to action with inactivity. Sam was afraid that if he got rid of all the muskrats, the sawmill wouldn't need him anymore. But recovery isn't like muskrats. The task is never complete.

Recovery Step: Knowing what to do is no good unless you follow through with what you know. So take one step forward in your recovery today. Go ahead. Make God's day.

Bottom's Up
November 4

The enemy had attacked and demolished the walls around Jerusalem. The children of God had been taken captive. Fast forward a few hundred years. Their descendants had returned to the homeland. But nothing was as it had been. The people were truly desperate, and the wall had to be rebuilt.

After they viewed the carnage, they prayed. After they prayed, they planned. But now it was time to go to work. Then the Bible says, "The people said, 'Let us start rebuilding.' So they began this good work'" (Nehemiah 2:18).

J.K. Rowling said, "Rock bottom became the solid foundation on which I rebuilt my life."

Rock bottom is a good place to be. In fact, I always worry about anyone who seeks recovery before his addiction has cost him something. Until our lives lie in ruins, we rarely rebuild them.

What does the rebuilding process require? I suggest one thing, in particular. You must do what Nehemiah did, and eliminate anything in your life that causes stress. Nehemiah discarded those who competed for his attention – Sanballat and Tobiah. He maintained his focus.

After you hit bottom, you can rebuild. But in the process, maintain your focus. Steer clear of circumstances – and people – who compete for your recovery. You have a lot of work to do. Don't let anything stop you.

Recovery Step: Have you hit bottom? Good! Now it's time to rebuild. And maintain your focus along the way.

Emancipation
November 5

It is listed in legislative history as "Proclamation 95." It was an executive order that changed the lives of 3.5 million Americans in a single day. That day was January 1, 1863. The executive order is better remembered as the Emancipation Proclamation. And with that order, President Lincoln freed every slave who lived in the South. But they could not realize that freedom as long as the Civil War continued – unless they found their way to the North.

Jesus has declared your freedom. That's what "It is finished" was all about. But you still have to do the work of recovery to find the Promised Land.

Scripture tells us that "people are slaves to whatever has mastered them" (2 Peter 2:19).

If you want to know who or what has mastered you, I suggest you look in two places: your calendar and your checkbook. It is where we spend our time and money that becomes our master.

But God has a better way. John MacArthur said it simply: "To be a Christian is to be a slave of Christ."

The fact is, you are a slave to something. If you spend an inordinate amount of time and money on sex, that is your master. The good news is that you have been emancipated. Now it's time to do the work necessary to fully enjoy the blessing of that glorious freedom.

Recovery Step: Look at your calendar and checkbook. Who owns you? Christ came to set you free. The next move is yours.

The Farmhouse
November 6

There was a preacher who saved up enough money to buy some cheap land. On it stood a dilapidated farmhouse. For a year, the preacher refurbished the house on his days off. Once the work was complete, a neighbor came over and said, "Well, preacher, I have to hand it to you. It looks like you and the Lord have done a pretty good job with this place."

Wiping the sweat from his brow, the preacher said, "Yeah, I suppose we have. But you should have seen the place when the Lord had it all to himself."

The Bible says, "We are God's fellow workers" (1 Corinthians 3:9).

There is an old statement we say in recovery work. "Without God, I can't. Without me, God won't."

Recovery is like any other great undertaking. To be successful, there must be a partnership. God could make us right without our participation, but he won't. And we could get right on our own except for one thing – we really can't.

Michael Jordan famously said, "Talent wins games, but teamwork wins championships."

You can experience a lifetime of recovery from porn and sex addiction – and every other addiction you may have. But it won't happen until you partner with the God of the universe.

Recovery Step: Are you ready to get well? The only limit to the success of your recovery will be your resistance to partner with God to make it happen.

Fully Accountable
November 7

One of the great examples of an accountability relationship is found in the Bible. It involved two unlikely friends, David and Jonathan. Theirs was an unlikely relationship because it was Jonathan's father who tried to have David killed – repeatedly.

This is their story: "After David had finished talking with Saul, Jonathan became one in spirit with David . . . and Jonathan made a covenant with David" (1 Samuel 18:1, 3).

David accomplished amazing things as long as he maintained accountability in his life. And the same can be true for you. But what makes accountability work? I suggest five things.

Accountability will accelerate your progress.
Accountability provides a clear measure of your work.
Accountability will keep you engaged and on track.
Accountability will hold you responsible.
Accountability will validate your direction.

Nothing great can be done by one person. And there is nothing greater that you will ever achieve than lasting recovery. So connect with your sponsor or someone else in recovery and become accountable to them. That will provide your best chance of success.

Recovery Step: Find one person to whom you can be accountable. This may be a 12-step sponsor, a member of a men's small group or a ladies' group. Then initiate contact with this person and prayerfully pursue a relationship of accountability.

The Key to the Key
November 8

The key to a fresh start is forgiveness. And the key to forgiveness is confession. Bruce Lee said it like this: "Mistakes are always forgivable if one has the courage to admit them."

One day, children were lined up in the cafeteria of a Christian school, waiting to buy lunch. At the end of the line was a large pile of apples. Someone had written a note and placed it by the apples. It read, "Take only one. God is watching."

Beyond the apples was a small table with three plates of chocolate chip cookies. One of the boys wrote his own note and placed it by the cookies. It read, "Take all you want. God is watching the apples."

That's how a lot of us do life. We do what we think we can get away with. But in recovery, we must come clean. We need the forgiveness that only God can supply. But that only comes when we admit our mistakes.

Those who confess their sins to God have this promise. "God does not punish us for all our sins; he does not deal harshly with us, as we deserve. For his unfailing love toward those who fear him is as great as the height of the heavens above the earth. He has removed our sins as far from us as the east is from the west" (Psalm 103:10-12).

The same God who is watching the apples is watching you. And he sees your mistakes. But when you confess them to him, he will see them no more.

Recovery Step: God sees you, and he sees your sin. But he offers forgiveness – if you come clean. Confession – it's the key to the key.

Do It for the Children
November 9

Stephen Curry is one of the greatest players in the NBA. His father was also an NBA star. I have met Steph, as chaplain for the Houston Rockets. He never missed chapel when the Warriors were in town. Curry is a follower of Jesus Christ. To what does he attribute his faith? In his own words, "My parents had us in church every Sunday and every Wednesday. It was more of a tradition at that point; I didn't have a personal relationship with the Lord until I went to the altar call one Sunday, and the youth pastor told us to make a decision for ourselves."

The importance of a spiritual connection to recovery cannot be overstated.

Step 11 states, "We sought through prayer and meditation to improve our conscious contact with God as we understood him, praying only for knowledge of his will for us and the power to carry that out."

As with the example of Steph Curry, that spiritual connection is often passed down through the example of our parents. So here's my question. Given that a spiritual connection is foundational to sobriety, what are you doing to provide that for your children?

Paul warned, "Fathers, do not embitter your children, or they will become discouraged" (Colossians 3:21).

In a world filled with temptation and sensuality, your kids need a connection with God, but also with you. It is your responsibility to encourage them on their journey to purity. Are you honestly committed to that process?

Recovery Step: Your example will play a huge role in the sobriety of your children. Will you commit to maintaining a connection with God and your kids? What will you do to make that happen?

The Desperation Cycle
November 10

Buried deep in the historic writings of the Old Testament is the story of King Jehoahaz. His reign over Israel lasted for 17 years. In his early years, the king "did what was evil in the Lord's sight" (2 Kings 13:2). His rebellion against God resulted in judgment, as the army of Aram defeated Israel on multiple battlefields. "Then Jehoahaz prayed for the Lord's help, and the Lord heard his prayer" (13:4). Now, "Israel lived in safety again as they had in former days" (13:5).

Then the people did what so many do. When times were good once again, they returned to their old ways. "They continued to sin, and the king of Aram trampled them like dust under his feet" (13:6-7).

King Jehoahaz is a case study on addiction. Notice the cycle: (a) wrong actions, (b) price to pay, (c) remorse and repentance, (d) God's restoration, (e) return to the old ways.

I see it all the time. In recovery literature, it's what we call "half measures." They avail us nothing.

Jim Carrey nailed it. "I don't think human beings learn anything without desperation. Desperation is a necessary ingredient to learning anything."

Where are you in the desperation cycle? It's time to get off the crazy train. When God forgives and restores, you can follow the example of Jehoahaz and return to your own ways. But you don't have to.

Recovery Step: God has restored you. Determine right now, to never go back to your old ways.

Veterans Day
November 11

Today is Veteran's Day, established as an official holiday in 1954. Here's the brief history.

Today's holiday honors military veterans of the United States Armed Forces. It coincides with other holidays, including Armistice Day and Remembrance Day, celebrated in other countries that mark the anniversary of the end of World War I. Major hostilities of that war ended at the 11th hour of the 11th day of the 11th month of 1918 when the Armistice with Germany went into effect. This is why Veterans Day is celebrated on November 11.

So today is the day to remember those whose sacrifice has provided for our freedom.

Thucydides said, "The secret to happiness is freedom."

The Bible declares, "Now the Lord is the Spirit, and where the Spirit of the Lord is, there is freedom" (2 Corinthians 3:17).

Freedom is the theme of Veterans Day, and it is the theme of recovery. Whether you have struggled in addiction for one year, ten years, or for decades, freedom can be yours. It is because of those who offered their very lives that America is free today. And it is because of the one who offered his life 2,000 years ago that you can be set free from your addiction.

Recovery Step: Celebrate freedom today – in your country, but also in your heart. Jesus died to set you free. Claim that freedom today.

Stay at It
November 12

Charles Schultz debuted his first-ever Peanuts comic strip on October 2, 1950, in nine newspapers around America. Over the next six decades, Schultz produced 18,000 more comic strips. The wisdom of Charlie Brown, Lucy, Linus, and the whole gang has guided many of us through the challenges of life.

One of those challenges – especially for those of us in recovery – is to stay at the hard work necessary to find success. We give up too early.

Lucy has the answer. "If no one answers the phone, dial louder."

Paul said it like this. "To those who by persistence in doing good seek glory, honor and immortality, he will give eternal life" (Romans 2:7).

One day a young lady was driving with her dad in the passenger seat. They encountered a bad storm. She noticed that several cars had pulled over because of the severity of the storm. She asked, "Should I pull over?" Her dad said to keep driving. The storm got worse, and more cars pulled over. "Should I pull over now?" asked the young driver. "No, keep driving," said her dad. Eventually, they emerged from the storm. "Now pull over," said the father. "Why now?" asked his daughter. "So you can look back at all the people who gave up and are still in the storm."

The fact is, the road to recovery will encounter many storms. The answer is not to pull over, but to keep driving. It's about persistence. It's about determination. Don't believe me; ask a veteran.

Recovery Step: As you encounter trials and temptations, keep moving forward. That is the only way out of the storm.

Emotional Regulation
November 13

Don Clay, national marketing consultant for March & McLennan Companies, wrote a report called "The Happiness Halo." His conclusion: "Appeal to customers' reason and they're yours for a day. Appeal to their emotions and they're yours for a lifetime."

The Bible – and modern psychology – confirm the role of emotions in setting the course of a person's life.

Paul acknowledged that we will face good days and bad days emotionally. "Rejoice with those who rejoice, weep with those who weep" (Romans 12:15).

In an article titled *The Psychological Causes of Addiction*, published on August 26, 2013, Dr. Tom Horvath wrote, "Related to psychopathology is the concept of an addictive personality. Certain personality characteristics might be the underlying factors in all addictive personalities. These may include problems with emotional regulation."

Your addictive struggles are not just spiritual or cognitive. They have an emotional component, as well. You were created that way. God actually *wants* you to be an emotional person.

In recovery, there will be periods of laughter and times of loss. And that's okay. Accept it. Your emotions are a part of who you are, but they don't have to dictate what you do.

Recovery Step: Accept your emotions. But don't let them dictate your behavior.

A Single Punch
November 14

On November 5, 1994, Michael Moorer, the undefeated heavyweight champion of the world, stepped into the ring against 45-year-old George Foreman, who had not won a meaningful fight in nearly 20 years. Moorer led on all three judges' cards entering the final round. Then Foreman landed a single, devastating punch. Moorer went down. He would not get up.

Like Michael Moorer, in recovery, you can be ahead on points, and still go down with a single blow.

Jesus' close friend Peter serves as an astounding example.

"They took Jesus away, and Peter followed at a distance. When they had kindled a fire in the middle of the courtyard and sat down together, Peter sat down among them. Then a servant girl, seeing him as he sat in the light and looking closely at him, said, 'This man also was with him.' But Peter denied it, saying, 'Woman, I do not know him'" (Luke 22:54-57).

No matter how close you are to Jesus, a single sin can bring you down. That is why the great baseball player turned preacher Billy Sunday said, "I'm against sin. I'll kick it as long as I've got a foot, and I'll fight it as long as I've got a fist. I'll butt it as long as I've got a head, and I'll bite it as long as I've got a tooth. And when I'm old and fistless and footless and toothless, I'll gum it till I go home to glory and it goes home to perdition!"

May each of us resist the temptations of sin with the same conviction!

Recovery Step: Sexual sin can bring you down with a single punch. So with every tool available and with every ounce of energy you have, fight the fight until the final bell rings.

Toe Stubs
November 15

Charles Kettering, CEO at General Motors, observed, "You never stub your toe when you are standing still."

The wisest man of the Old Testament was never one to stand still. Solomon was an advocate for taking risks and moving forward when all signs point the other way.

Solomon wrote, "He who observes the wind will not sow and he who regards the clouds will not reap" (Ecclesiastes 11:4).

The king's message was profound. If we only run when the wind is at our backs, we will die standing still.

Recovery will *always* demand a sprint into the wind. As Seneca said, "It's not because things are difficult that we dare not venture. It's because we dare not venture that they are difficult."

The task of recovery is hard, but the cost of failure is greater.

If you are to maintain sobriety, you will have to attend meetings when you don't feel like it, pray when you are exhausted, and reject invasive thoughts when you are in your weakest moments.

Recovery Step: It is time to take the risk. Go further in your recovery work than you ever thought possible. Will you stub your toe? Sure you will. But it's better than standing still.

Mack Robinson
November 16

In recovery, you cannot afford to fail. And the good news is that with God on your side, you don't have to.

The Scripture promises, "What then shall we say to these things? If God is for us, who can be against us?" (Romans 8:31).

History reminds us of the legendary Olympics of 1936. Among the four gold medals won by Jesse Owens was the one awarded for the 200-meter run on August 5. Owens set a new world record that day. But there is more to the story.

The world record that Owens set that day broke the "old" record, set just one day earlier by a 22-year-old runner named Mack Robinson. Like Owens, Robinson was a black American, running before an audience that included Adolf Hitler. Robinson was the second fastest man in the world, having just set the world record on August 4, which Owens would break the next day. Owens credited Robinson with making him better. "With Mack on my team, I knew I never had to run alone," he said.

Jesse Owens was better because Mack Robinson was on his team. And though you may have never heard of Mack Robinson, you may have heard of his younger brother, a baseball player named Jackie. Yes – Jackie Robinson.

In your race for sobriety, know this – you will never have to run alone.

Recovery Step: You are running the race of your life – for sobriety and recovery. But keep running, no matter what. And know this – you will never have to run alone.

The Hardest Command
November 17

Late in the winter of 1569, Dirk Willems found himself running from the Dutch authorities. Although no one today would see his beliefs about baptism as radical or threatening, leaders at the time regarded them as heretical and illegal.

Fleeing for his life, Willems came to a pond covered with thin ice. After safely making his way across, he discovered that his pursuer hadn't been so fortunate. Responding to the officer's cry for help, Willems ran back, pulled him out of the frigid water, and dragged him safely to shore. The guard then seized Willems and escorted him to prison. Soon thereafter, authorities burned Willems at the stake.

For Dirk Willems, Luke 6:27 was personal. "Love your enemies, do good to those who hate you."

Recovery is not measured by how you treat those who bless you, but by how you treat those who have hurt you. Among this group, there may be a parent, sibling, family friend, or even a total stranger.

Through their abuse – on any level – they exercised control over you. You can take control back. But to do so requires forgiveness. More than that, it requires *active* forgiveness.

Recovery Step: Think of someone who has hurt you. Now, identify one way to bless them, not because they deserve your forgiveness, but because you deserve to be free.

Your Funeral
November 18

In his best-seller, *The Seven Habits of Highly Effective People*, Stephen Covey recommends the following exercise. Imagine that you've died and four people will speak at your funeral, each representing a specific aspect of your life. The four speakers will include a relative, fellow church member, business colleague, and someone from your neighborhood.

Covey poses this question: What would each person honestly say about you?

While it is not easy to imagine one's own funeral and the eulogies that might be offered, this exercise provides perspective. There is nothing quite like the end of a person's life to gain that perspective.

The fact is, you are writing your own eulogy with the way you live your life every day. And the good news is that your story is not yet finished. While you can't go back and write a new beginning, you can still write a new ending.

NFL great Troy Polamalu said, "No matter how many times I've been hurt, I've learned from each injury and come back even more humble."

Solomon said, "Better is the end of a thing than its beginning" (Ecclesiastes 7:8).

You have been injured, and you have injured others. God's promise is that you can come back stronger. Commit to sobriety and the rest of your life will be the best of your life. And then you will be ready for your funeral, no matter who speaks.

Recovery Step: Start fresh today. Live 24 hours of sobriety. From this day forward, write a whole new ending.

Time to Come Out
November 19

Mike Genung has identified 11 steps to breaking free from sexual addiction, in *The Road to Grace: Finding True Freedom from the Bondage of Sexual Addiction*. He says the first step to freedom is to come out of isolation.

Isolation is depicted brilliantly in the movie *Burnt*, in which Bradley Cooper plays the role of Adam, a chef who battles a trio of addictions: women, drugs, and alcohol. Adam's road is a rocky one. On that road, he learns how to ask for help and how to quit isolating from family, colleagues, and friends. He discovers the strength that comes from needing others.

If you are to get well – and stay well – you must learn the lesson that Adam learned. You cannot do this on your own. You can have recovery or isolation, but you can't have both.

The psalmist wrote, "Though my father and mother forsake me, the Lord will receive me" (Psalm 27:10).

The first relationship that breaks through the wall of isolation is a spiritual one. Whether driven to isolation by parents, family members, or friends, you don't have to stay there. When you are all alone, you are not all alone. And no matter what you have done, the Lord will receive you.

Recovery Step: Break down the wall of isolation by connecting with God. Seek to find that connection today.

Not Fair!
November 20

Life is not fair. And the fact is, sometimes, we don't want life to be fair. Let me explain with a story about the greatest Little League baseball player of all time.

When my son was playing Little League baseball, I was the worst coach and best fan – at the same time. One time, when David was at bat, I stood behind the backstop. With a full 3-2 count, David took the next pitch, which was clearly a strike. But the umpire called it a "ball," and David was awarded first base.

Do you think for one second that I shouted at the umpire, "Not fair! That was a strike! My son was out! Get your eyes examined!"

No, I turned to another dad and bragged on my son's great eye as he took first base.

You have a sexual addiction. That probably resulted – at least in part – from childhood trauma, abuse, and isolation. Is that fair? No, it's not. But it's also not fair to your family that you didn't get help sooner, or that you have not paid a higher price for your sins.

The Bible says, "God is fair" (Psalm 25:8). But it also says, "Let us fall into the hands of the Lord, for his mercy is great" (2 Samuel 24:14).

So how do we respond in an unfair world? By moving our focus beyond *fair* to *mercy*. No, life is not fair. And that's a good thing.

Recovery Step: Quit chasing *fair* and celebrate *mercy*.

Bad Signs
November 21

I love funny signs. Let's consider a few examples.

In a London department store: "Bargain basement upstairs."

On the wall above the toilet in a public restroom: "This toilet out of order. Please use floor below."

Message on a leaflet: "If you cannot read this, please ask for assistance."

Message on a shop door: "We can repair anything. Knock on the door, as the bell does not work."

Those are bad signs. Let me suggest some other bad signs. You haven't been to a 12-step meeting in two weeks. You have quit working the steps. You haven't called your sponsor in a while. You missed your morning devotions for the last three days.

The Bible says a lot about reading signs of things to come. Each time, we are told to respond to that sign. Jesus said, "When you see these things, recognize that he is near" (Matthew 24:33).

Signs point to a larger reality. If you see signs of slippage in your recovery, do something about it today.

Recovery Step: What signs can others see that indicate you are serious about your recovery? Read the signs. Then respond accordingly.

Knowing God
November 22

In 1973, J.I. Packer wrote, in *Knowing God*, "Once you become aware that the main business that you are here for is to know God, most of life's problems fall into place of their own accord. What makes life worthwhile is having a big enough objective, something which catches our imagination and lays hold of our allegiance; and this the Christian has in a way that no other person has. For what higher, more exalted, and more compelling goal can there be than to know God?"

Step 11 says that in recovery we "seek through prayer and meditation to improve our conscious contact with God." Successful recovery is a spiritual process, and at the heart of that process is knowing God.

Paul said that his greatest desire was "that I may know him and the power of his resurrection" (Philippians 3:10).

Jim Elliot said it like this: "Oh, the fullness, pleasure, sheer excitement of knowing God on earth!"

One of the lessons of recovery is that when we seek answers, we find frustration. But when we seek God, the answers find us.

So don't make recovery your greatest pursuit. Save that one for knowing God.

Recovery Step: Celebrate recovery, but seek God.

The Last Thing Charley Did
November 23

A terrible explosion rocked a gunpowder factory. After the mess was cleaned up, the inquiry began. One of the survivors was pulled into the investigator's office and asked, "Okay, Simpson. You were near the scene, so tell me what happened!"

"Well, it was like this, sir. Old Charley Higgins was in the mixing room, and I saw him pull a cigarette from his pocket and light it up."

The investigator responded, "Are you telling me Higgins was smoking in the mixing room? How long had he been with the company?"

"About 20 years, sir."

"Well, he should have known better! You'd think lighting a cigarette in the mixing room would have been the last thing he would do."

"It was, sir."

Here's the lesson. In recovery, our problem is not a lack of knowledge. We are seldom at a loss for what we should avoid in life. Paul wrote, "The acts of the flesh are obvious: sexual immorality, impurity, and debauchery" (Galatians 5:19).

Learn from old Charley Higgins. It's not what you know that matters, but what you do with what you know.

Recovery Step: You know the things to do and the things to avoid. Recovery is the alignment of right knowledge and right actions. The next move is yours.

The Wedding Ring
November 24

Ravi Zacharias tells the story of a woman whose husband died. Shortly after his funeral, she lost her wedding ring. She searched everywhere, but never found it. Fifteen years later, she was working in her garden. While digging in the soil, she struck a small object buried several inches into the dirt. When she dug her hands deeper into the soil, she grabbed this piece of metal and pulled it out. To her amazement, she was holding her wedding ring in her fingers. It had been lost for a decade and a half.

Suddenly, a flood of memories overcame the widow. The ring represented a tie to her happier days. She was overcome with joy as she remembered what life had been before.

Do you remember what life was like before? Do you remember a time when you had not yet plunged into the full depths of your addiction before you had destroyed several lives – including your own?

Let those memories serve to remind you of what life can still be like – apart from porn and sex addiction.

Isaiah spoke of a time when "the former things will not be remembered or come to mind" (Isaiah 65:17).

It's time to bury your past while unearthing your future.

Recovery Step: Ask God to help you bury the past and guide you into a future you never thought was even possible.

Expectations
November 25

Rainer Maria Bilke said it well: "The only journey is the one within." In other words, what happens in your head today will set your course for tomorrow. This journey requires two decisions.

Decision #1: Decide who and what you want to be.

If you are to be in a better place in the future, you need to define that place in the present. Ralph Waldo Emerson was right. "The only person you are destined to become is the person you decide to be." So get about the business of defining a better future – one free of addictive behaviors and sexual fantasy.

Decision #2: Reject the expectations of others.

Michael Jordan said, "If you accept the expectations of others, especially negative ones, you will never change the outcome." Nothing will restrict your growth quite like listening to the wrong voices.

The Bible tells you to "set your heart on things above" (Colossians 3:1). That is how you win the "battle within." That is how you make the two decisions that will change everything. And that is how you find lasting recovery.

Recovery Step: Decide who and what you want to be. Reject the expectations of others. Then get about the work of recovery.

How to Talk to Your Addict Spouse
November 26

King Jeroboam pulled his wife into his problem. Their son Abijah was sick. Jeroboam sought to bribe the prophet Ahijah into promising his son's healing. But he wanted to do so secretly. So Jeroboam sent his wife in disguise. He told her, "Take Ahijah a gift of ten loaves of bread, some cakes, and a jar of honey, and ask him what will happen to the boy" (1 Kings 14:3). Rather than stand up to her husband, Jeroboam's wife went along. The results were disastrous.

Perhaps you have a husband or wife who is carrying on their porn habit in secret. You have a decision to make. When do you stand up for yourself? How do you confront your spouse? Polly Scott, editor-in-chief of the Addo Blog, suggests five lies women tell themselves about their husband's porn addiction.

1. Everyone uses porn.
2. His porn use doesn't affect our relationship.
3. If I looked better, he would stop using porn.
4. If we have sex every day, he will quit using porn.
5. It's my fault.

If you are thinking about confronting your spouse about his or her porn habit, let me make two observations. First, confronting him will likely cause conflict, but it's worth it. And second, confronting the situation won't heal your spouse, but it will help you.

Does your spouse have a problem? What he does about it is beyond your control. But how you respond is not.

Recovery Step: If you are married to an addict, stand up for yourself. Don't try to take ownership of his problem. You can only own your personal recovery.

Stay Close
November 27

It had been a great day. They were eyewitnesses to the feeding of the 5,000. Now the disciples of Christ were riding high, and they'd never look back, right? Wrong. We read, "That evening Jesus' disciples went down to the shore to wait for Jesus. But as darkness fell and Jesus still hadn't come back, they got into the boat and headed across the lake toward Capernaum. Soon a gale swept down upon them, and the sea grew very rough" (John 6:16-18).

We learn two lessons here. First, yesterday's victory is no guarantee of tomorrow's success. They had just witnessed an amazing miracle. Surely, they'd stay on track now. But their newfound faith stayed with them for about two hours.

Second, it is important to wait on God. At the first sign of darkness and pending storms, the disciples left Jesus and went out on their own. They were willing to walk with him as long as they could do it on their own terms.

As a consequence, the disciples would have never made it to the other side of the lake, had Jesus not saved them – again. Henry Ford was right when he said, "Those who walk with God always reach their destination."

In recovery, life will be like that of the disciples. In the same day, they witnessed a great miracle and then encountered a harrowing storm. The key to survival is to never walk away from Christ.

Recovery Step: When times are good, walk with Jesus. When times are bad, walk with Jesus. At all times – walk with Jesus.

Short Memories
November 28

One of our biggest problems is that we have short memories. We are like the guy whose wife made him dinner every night for their entire 50 years of marriage. The next day, he asked her, "Who's cooking dinner tonight?"

God has been cooking your dinner for a long time. He has proven his faithfulness over and over. But too often, you have pulled a Rehoboam. The Bible says of the young king, "After Rehoboam's position as king was established and he had become strong, he and all Israel with him abandoned the law of the Lord" (2 Chronicles 12:1).

G.K. Chesterton recorded the following dialogue.

Father Brown: "There is one great spiritual disease."

Flambeau: "And what is the one great spiritual disease?"

Father Brown: "Thinking one is quite well."

I love the words of the old 18th-century hymn, written by Isaac Watts. "When I survey the wondrous cross, on which the Prince of glory died, my richest gain I count but loss, and pour contempt on all my pride."

One of the keys to lasting recovery is to take nothing for granted. Watch out for pride. Never forget the danger of thinking you are quite well.

Recovery Step: Today's step is to remember yesterday's victory. But then beware of the fine line between confidence and overconfidence.

Self-Improvement
November 29

James Allen said, "People are anxious to improve their circumstances, but they aren't anxious to improve themselves."

Let's talk about how to improve ourselves. It's not easy, but it is simple. You must be intentional.

That great scholar Charlie Brown said it like this: "I've discovered the secret of life. Hang around until you get used to it."

Bruce Springsteen offered a better plan. "A time comes when you need to stop waiting around for the man you want to become and start being the man you want to be."

This involves intentionality. But you will never find recovery by good intentions alone. You must have good follow-through.

Most likely, you don't suffer in your addiction because of a lack of knowledge. It is the daily choices you make that have you in this mess.

One of the most misinterpreted verses in Scripture is 2 Corinthians 5:17. "If any man be in Christ he is a new creation. Old things have passed away; all things are become new."

The original text reads, "All things are *becoming new*." That is all about daily choices. You can enjoy a new life, filled with sobriety. But you have to go all in.

Recovery Step: You can find lasting recovery. But it won't come by simply *thinking* the right things. You must actually *do* the right things.

Holy God's
November 30

Christians all over the world sing the words of Chris Tomlin every hour of every day. One of his most popular songs of this generation includes this chorus:

"We fall down, we lay our crowns – at the feet of Jesus. The greatness of mercy and love – at the feet of Jesus. And we cry holy, holy, holy. And we cry holy, holy, holy. And we cry holy, holy, holy is the Lamb."

God calls us to holiness. "Even before he made the world, God loved us and chose us in Christ to be holy and without fault in his eyes" (Ephesians 1:4).

Indeed, God's primary goal is to make us holy – that is, to form his character in us. Looking through the eyes of love, he already sees us as we will be when his work is done. Then he works out his goals for us in the arena of everyday life.

Holiness is the undesired pursuit of recovery. Rarely has a man sought holiness because it was fun, easy, or quickly rewarding. Spurgeon was right when he said, "Revenge, lust, ambition, pride, and self-will are too often exalted as the gods of man's idolatry; while holiness, peace, contentment, and humility are viewed as unworthy of serious thought."

Holiness. It's time we started giving it serious thought.

Recovery Step: If you wish to grasp this slippery thing we call sobriety, you must value the virtue of holiness above all else.

Trauma
December 1

Patrick Carnes' study in 1992 found that 97 percent of addicts were at some point in their past emotionally abused, 87 percent were at some point physically abused, and 82 percent were sexually abused.

Dr. Gabor Mate has written extensively on the role of trauma in sex addiction, with a focus on how trauma relates to the brain and nervous systems and as a catalyst for addiction. He writes, "Not all addictions are rooted in abuse or trauma, but I do believe they can all be traced to a painful experience. A hurt is at the center of all addictive behaviors."

I agree that trauma plays a huge role in the development of addiction, both from my research and my personal experience. The question is not whether trauma is at the root of addiction, but how the addict should respond.

Authors at HelpGuide.org have offered several suggestions. Foremost is the insistence that we not isolate.

At this point, the psalmist gives us hope. "He will cover you with his pinions, and under his wings you will find refuge; his faithfulness is a shield and buckler. You will not fear the terror of the night, nor the arrow that flies by day, nor the pestilence that stalks in darkness, nor the destruction that wastes at noonday" (Psalm 81:4-6).

If you are an addict, you have trauma in your background – that is *almost a certainty*. And if you are an addict, you can find refuge in Christ – that is an *absolute certainty*.

Recovery Step: Bring your trauma to God. Find a refuge in him that cannot be found anywhere else.

Confession of a Sex Addict
December 2

My friend Tom Ryan has given us his story in *Ashamed No More*. It is the written confession of a sex addict. He writes, "It might seem highly incongruous to some people that a person can be a growing, earnest Christian – especially a spiritual leader like a minister, priest, or pastor – and also struggle with compulsive sexual behaviors. For years I was sure I was the only person in my church, in my clergy associations and among my Christian friends who did."

That begs the question, why do good people do bad stuff?

I affirm the words of Supreme Court Justice Sonia Sotomayor: "Good people can do bad things and make bad decisions. It doesn't make them bad people."

It all boils down to this. Are we to be judged according to what we do or who we are? The fact is, most of the sex addicts I know – and there are a bunch of them – are very spiritual, God-fearing, church-going men and women. That they have this struggle is not as much a testament to their character as to the cunning, baffling nature of the disease. But it does not define them.

Debbie Ford explains the dilemma well, in *Why Good People Do Bad Things*. She writes, "There are within each of us two voices fighting to be heard."

The confession of a sex addict is this – we try to do the right thing, but sometimes we fail. Add to that the confession of a follower of the Lord – "He is able to be to you a restorer of life and a sustainer in your old age" (Ruth 4:15).

Recovery Step: The confession of a sex addict is that the struggle is hard. But God brings good news. He will redeem and restore you.

The Price of Recovery
December 3

The choir had finished singing and it was time for the pastor to speak. But when he went too long, one member could no longer stay focused. So Elvina Hall began to doodle. She had no paper, so she grabbed a hymnal in the choir loft. Thinking about the redemption offered in Christ, she wrote on a page these words.

"I hear the Savior say, 'Thy strength indeed is small;
Child of weakness, watch and pray. Find in Me thine all in all.'
Jesus paid it all, all to Him I owe;
Sin had left a crimson stain, He washed it white as snow."

What Elvina Hall wrote in 1865 was reminiscent of what Peter said two thousand years ago.

"He himself bore our sins in his body on the cross so that we might die to sins and live for righteousness" (1 Peter 2:24).

Early in recovery, many addicts complain that their recovery seems to cost too much. And it's true – real recovery comes at a price. It will cost you time (meetings), money (therapy), and reputation (disclosure). But keep in mind – it cost Jesus everything.

You can afford the price of recovery because Jesus paid it all. Not some. Not most. *All*.

Recovery Step: Recovery is expensive. In fact, you can't afford it. But that's okay because Jesus paid the ultimate price.

The Great Stain Remover
December 4

God can take your worst mistake and redeem it. Remember that fellow in the Bible named David? He became the king of Israel at a young age, with all the rights and privileges that came with the throne. Then, one night, he went where he should not have gone. As a result, he saw what he should not have seen. And then he did what he should not have done. Within minutes, the king had begun an adulterous relationship, which would come at a great price. He would eventually marry the woman, but his sexual sin would cost him the life of his son.

But God didn't write David off. Out of the pain came hope. The Scriptures say, "Then David comforted his wife Bathsheba, and he went to her and made love to her. She gave birth to a son, and they named him Solomon. And the Lord loved him" (2 Samuel 12:24).

The amazing thing about God is not that he rescues you from unintended crises, but that he lifts you from the mess of your own making, the hole of your own digging, and he places you on mountains you could have never climbed yourself.

Journalist Germany Kent writes, "God will fight your battles if you just keep still. He is able to carry you through. Trust him. Keep standing, keep believing, and keep hoping."

In the book, *Blessing Out of Pain*, Rick Warren writes, "If we can surrender our will to his, through our pain God can deepen our faith, heal our heart, and restore our soul."

In your addiction, your pain has become your stain. But as with King David, God is the great stain remover. From death comes life, and from despair comes hope.

Recovery Step: Bring to God the mess of your past and receive the miracle of his blessing – starting right now – one day at a time.

Dreams
December 5

We all have dreams. We have dreams for our future, our family, and our faith. We dream of a fat wallet and a thin waist, more stuff and less debt. We all have dreams.

Unfortunately, too many of us leave it there – dreams. We dream, but we don't do.

One day, a passerby saw St. Francis tending a garden. He said, "You must have prayed very hard, Francis, for things to grow so well." Francis replied, "Yes, and every time I prayed, I picked up my hoe."

The Bible says it like this: "Whatever you do, work at it with all your heart, as working for the Lord, not for human masters" (Colossians 3:23).

Recovery is hard work. We can't say that too much. It's about going to meetings, lots of prayer, working with one's sponsor, working out, doing readings, daily exercise, and going to more meetings. If recovery was easy, everybody would do it.

Recovery begins with a dream. But it doesn't end there.

Colin Powell said of dreams, "A dream doesn't become reality through magic; it takes sweat, determination, and hard work."

Will you find lasting recovery in your life? Follow the example of St. Francis. Pray hard. Then pick up a hoe.

Recovery Step: Dreams are good. So dream big. Then pick up the hoe.

Predicting Your Long-Term Sobriety
December 6

How far will you go in your sobriety? Will you find solid recovery for a lifetime? There is a way to measure such things. It's called *honesty*. Only those who are completely honest remain on track.

Professors James Kouzes and Barry Posner have spent more than 30 years surveying leaders in virtually every type of organization. They ask, "What values, personal traits, or characteristics do you look for and admire the most in a leader?"

Over these years, Kouzes and Posner have administered a survey questionnaire called *Characteristics of Admired Leaders* to more than 75,000 people on six continents. They report, "The results have been striking in their regularity over the years, and they do not vary by demographical, organizational, or cultural differences."

What is the quality that consistently tops the list?

Honesty.

The same is true in recovery. Until you come clean – completely clean – and are 100 percent known, you will be stuck on an island without a way off.

Wise Solomon said it like this: "Better the poor whose walk is blameless than a fool whose walk is perverse" (Proverbs 19:1).

Recovery Step: You can get sober – but only after you get honest. Determine a time and place to come clean – with your spouse, therapist, or sponsor. It's the only way off the island.

The Hardest Nine Words You'll Ever Say
December 7

It didn't come out of my mouth easily. In fact, I attended dozens of counseling sessions and half a dozen 12-step meetings before I could bring myself to say it. The words came from a trembling basket of emotion.

"My name is Mark, and I'm a sex addict."

And that's when the healing began.

Nothing is more difficult for a Type-A personality than saying "I'm wrong. I have a problem, and I can't solve it myself."

I knew I had a problem for years before anyone else did. Like most of us, I struggled with my conscience, trying to make peace within my heart. I lived in denial of what I had done and who I was. I minimized it. I worked hard to "be good," treated others well, served God, and gave a tenth of my income to the church. I read my Bible and prayed daily. But still, I had this problem.

I was born with a built-in alarm clock that went off every time I had a relapse. It was God's way of holding me accountable. It was his way of breathing Romans 2:15 into my heart all over again: "Their own conscience and thoughts either accuse them or tell them they are doing right."

Recovery can only come when we admit that our issues actually run a lot deeper than right vs. wrong. Carl Jung said, "The pendulum of the mind alternates between sense and nonsense, not between right and wrong."

Like the prodigal, I had to come to my senses and admit it. "I am a sex addict."

Recovery Step: Admit what you know – to God and another person – but mostly, to yourself.

God Uses the Bad
December 8

"And we know that in all things God works for the good of those who love him, who have been called according to his purpose" (Romans 8:28).

This verse played out for Nathaniel and Sophia.

One day, Nathaniel hated to come home. He had just been dismissed from his job and couldn't stand the thought of facing his wife. But he had to do it. And her response blew him away.

"Praise God!" said Sophia. "Now you have time to write your book!"

Nathaniel had always wanted to write a book but never had the time. His response was predictable. "I've always wanted to write a book, but how will we survive financially while I am writing it?"

Sophia opened a drawer in the back bedroom. She pulled out an envelope from the back. Inside was thousands of dollars. She had been setting a little bit of money aside every week – for years – in anticipation of such a moment.

"This is enough to live on for a year," she said.

So Nathaniel went to work on his book. Perhaps you've heard of it – *The Scarlet Letter*. The author's name? Nathaniel Hawthorne.

Yes, God uses all things – good and bad. The same is true of your addiction. What God has allowed in your past, he will use in your future.

Recovery Step: Thank God for your past, because that is the foundation on which he is about to build a marvelous cathedral.

The Refuge of God
December 9

The words of the old hymn were written in Scotland in 1650.

"God is our refuge and our strength, our ever present aid.
And, therefore, though the earth remove, we will not be afraid.
The Lord of Hosts is on our side, our safety is secure;
The God of Jacob is for us, a refuge strong and sure."

Nahum 1:7 says, "The Lord is good, a strong refuge when trouble comes. He is close to those who trust him."

Recovery is a very difficult road to walk. Many abandon the journey out of fear, loneliness, or isolation. But when we feel deserted by others, we need to remember that we will never be deserted by God. He is for us, with us, and in us.

Writing *The True Christian Life*, John Calvin said, "Warned by such evidences of their spiritual illness, believers profit by their humiliations. Robbed of their foolish confidence in the flesh, they take refuge in the grace of God. And when they have done so, they experience the nearness of the divine protection which is to them a strong fortress."

I love Calvin's imagery. Addicts "profit by their humiliations" and "take refuge in the grace of God."

You have been humiliated by your addiction. But take heart. Better yet, take refuge – in the grace of the God who loves you still.

Recovery Step: In the depths of your addiction, take refuge in God.

Slow! God at Work!
December 10

A chicken and an elephant were locked in a cage together. The chicken turned to the elephant and said, "We need to set a few ground rules. First, let's not step on each other."

The chicken was looking at it from his point of view. Our chicken point of view affects our relationships with others. Our tendency is to want to straighten people out for our own benefit. This is especially true for those married to addicts.

If you think straightening people out is your job, I suggest you become a funeral director. That way, when you straighten them out, they will stay straightened out.

Only God can straighten people out. He is the great construction supervisor. Have you ever seen a sign that read, "Slow! Men at Work"?

These signs are usually accompanied by a dozen guys sitting around eating sandwiches. I have a suggestion for you. The next time you see someone who needs fixing, imagine a sign posted beside them: "Slow! God at Work!"

And there may be another sign: "Keep Out!"

You see, you don't always see. God is at work, whether you see it or not. Sure, your husband, wife, child, parent, or friend needs recovery. But only God can do that. So stay out!

May we follow the advice of Paul. "Bear with one another and forgive one another if any of you has a grievance against someone. Forgive as the Lord forgives you" (Colossians 3:13).

Recovery Step: Let up on those around you. You may be married to an addict. And while there is no excuse for his continued behavior (if he is not in recovery), you can't fix him. Only God is in the construction business.

Strength in Weakness
December 11

One thing that may make it hard to believe in God is that life often seems unfair to us. We didn't ask to be born into a dysfunctional family. We didn't have any say over the abuses and injustices we have suffered. We didn't choose our predisposition toward addiction. And yet we are held accountable for things we can't control on our own. This makes it hard to initially turn to God as the Power to restore our sanity. He seems unreasonable in his demands.

Job understood these feelings. In the midst of his suffering, he said, "How frail is humanity! How short is life, how full of trouble! We blossom like a flower and then wither. Like a passing shadow, we quickly disappear. Must you keep an eye on such a frail creature and demand an accounting from me? Who can bring purity out of an impure person?" (Job 14:1-4).

The good news is found in the answers to Job's questions.

Question #1 – Must you keep an eye on such a frail creature? *Yes!*

Question #2 – Who can bring purity out of an impure person? *God!*

Thomas Edison said, "Our greatest weakness lies in giving up. The most certain way to succeed is always to try just one more time."

Zig Ziglar added, "Try to look at your weakness and convert it into your strength. That's success."

Yes, you are frail. Actually, you are helpless in your own power. So quit trying to find victory in your own power. Recovery only comes to those who submit their wills to God.

Recovery Step: Admit your frailty to God and surrender to him today.

Broken Sexuality
December 12

We know why Jesus came to earth – to die for our sins, redeem us to God, and restore us to sanity. Let's focus on that last one, as it affects our sexuality.

We are the creation of God. The Bible says, "The Lord formed me from the beginning, before he created anything else" (Proverbs 8:22).

By definition of creating man, God also created his sexuality. Dr. Juli Slattery has written a book, *Rethinking Sexuality: God's Design and Why It Matters.* Dr. Slattery asserts directly, "Jesus came to redeem broken sexuality."

Let's talk about that. "Jesus came to redeem broken sexuality."

In the Christian community, we love to speak of the redemption of God. He has redeemed our hearts, souls, and eternity. But our sexuality?

Yes, our sexuality. That means that no matter how dysfunctional your sexual behaviors may have been, God can bring sanity to your mind and sanctity to your bedroom. God wants you to enjoy a healthy sex life within the bounds of marriage. Getting there may require therapy, but it will be worth it.

The truth is, we are all broken men and women. That means we all have experienced broken sexuality on some level. But the good news is that God offers hope and redemption.

Recovery Step: Bring your broken sexuality to God. And keep in mind, this will likely mean bringing your broken sexuality to a therapist, as well.

15 Rounds
December 13

The third Ali-Frazier fight was one for the ages. The "Thrilla in Manila" was a brutal contest, fought in 1975, toward the end of each fighter's career. Ali emerged the winner when Frazier was unable to answer the bell for the 15th round.

Like that epic battle, to win in recovery you must be able to go the distance. And the only way to do that is to have a spiritual connection with the God of the universe, who said, "I live in a high and holy place" (Isaiah 57:15).

J.C. Ryle summed it up perfectly. "There is no holiness without warfare."

Are you willing to step into the ring against the strongest foe you will ever face – your addiction? If you are willing to enter the ring, there is good news – you will have the best corner man ever. God will be there with you, through every round, every punch to the gut, and every knockdown. But you must be willing to go the distance.

Make no mistake, recovery is war. And the only ones who win are those willing to stay in the ring when they feel like quitting. They discover that by surviving each round, they find the strength to keep on going.

Benjamin Alire Saenz said of addictions, "If you can quit for a day, you can quit for a lifetime." He is right. The victory can be yours, one day – and one round – at a time.

Recovery Step: When you sign on for recovery, you step into life's toughest battle. But it is a battle you can win, one round at a time.

Surrendering Your Past
December 14

One of the titanic struggles in finding lasting sobriety is moving beyond our past. We know that the God who forgives our sin also forgets our sin. The problem is, we have memories that are hard to tune out. And most of us have people in our lives who are more than happy to remind us of every slip, sin, struggle, and stumble. We are haunted by our past. We remember the broken promises, false starts, and painful relapses.

As hard as it is, every person who wishes to move beyond his or her addiction, or the pain caused by another person's addiction, must learn to leave his or her past right there – in the past.

I once heard some solid advice: "When your past calls, let it go to voicemail. It has nothing to say."

Ralph Waldo Emerson framed it like this: "What lies behind us and what lies ahead of us are tiny matters compared to what lies within us."

The Apostle Paul had a checkered past, to say the least. He discovered the formula for success, in "forgetting what is behind and straining toward what is ahead" (Philippians 3:13).

You have a past. We all do. So let me say it like this. The key to a better future is to quit trying to have a better past.

You can find an incredible victory. But you must learn to live in the moment. I'm not saying you can forget the past. But you can surrender it, one day at a time.

Recovery Step: Surrender your past to God today.

Overcoming Stupid
December 15

William Shatner said, "I'm gonna reveal something to you that's going to come as a shock. If you're a stupid young man, you usually become a stupid old man. Most people, including myself, keep repeating the same mistakes."

Solomon said it like this: "As a dog returns to its vomit, so a fool repeats his foolishness" (Proverbs 26:11).

As addicts, we almost invariably repeat the patterns of the past; our old problems revisit us again and again. It is easy to slip back into our addiction; that is why we need to be diligent in the recovery process. When we relax in our recovery program, we are setting ourselves up for a relapse into our old lifestyle. Only through perseverance will we be able to overcome our dependency.

Legendary University of Texas Coach Darrell Royal said, "The measure of success is in not making the same mistakes today that you made yesterday."

What is the difference between a dog who returns to its vomit and an addict who returns to his habit? Answer: the dog's actions make more sense.

I have yet to meet to a man who said, "You know, I acted out for years. And I thought about getting the necessary help to end my destructive behaviors. But I decided to live the rest of my life in my addiction, and I'm sure glad that I did!"

Recovery Step: Get off the crazy cycle of addiction. Take the necessary steps of recovery, one day at a time, starting today.

Your Wedding Day
December 16

February 26, 1983. I remember it as if it was yesterday. It was my wedding day. I'll never forget the sheer ecstasy I felt when Beth entered from the back of the church sanctuary – the very same room where we first met nearly four years earlier.

I can relate to King Solomon on his wedding day. The Scripture says, "Come out and look, you daughters of Zion. Look on King Solomon wearing a crown, the crown with which his mother crowned him on the day of his wedding, *the day his heart rejoiced*" (Song of Solomon 3:11).

Nothing brings more joy to a man than his wedding day. And I can't think of anything that brings more pain than to break the sacred vows repeated there – to his wife in the presence of God and family.

The fact is, all marriages have challenges. Anyone who tells you otherwise is smoking something that is illegal in most states.

I love the way journalist Mignon McLaughlin said it. "A successful marriage requires falling in love many times, always with the same person."

Success in marriage is the same as success in recovery. It must be intentional. Serious reflection on the sanctity of marriage brought Martin Luther to this conclusion: "Let the wife make the husband glad to come home, and let him make her sorry to see him leave."

Husbands, do you remember the joy of your wedding day? Think about that the next time you are tempted to act out.

Recovery Step: Reflect on your wedding day and let the joy of that moment sink in. Bring those memories to mind the next time you think about viewing porn.

Not in a Vacuum
December 17

There is a great book for those serious about sponsoring others in the 12-step process. It's called *The Steps We Took*. Within its pages, the book identifies the source of addiction. "Most of our troubles stem from spiritual sickness, and this spiritual sickness is nothing more or less than being blocked off from God by some fear, resentment, guilt, or remorse caused by self-will."

Indeed, we have a spiritual problem, for which there must be a spiritual solution.

So what's the answer? The answer is not to merely rid ourselves of our addictive behaviors. We must put in their place those things that honor God and spur a dynamic relationship with him.

Paul told Titus of God's work to "train us to renounce ungodliness and worldly passions, and to live self-controlled, upright, and godly lives in the present age" (Titus 2:12).

In other words, we cannot just stop bad behaviors; we must replace them with good ones.

A 14th-century mystic named Meister Eckhart wrote, "It is said that nature abhors a vacuum; I tell you God abhors a vacuum and cannot abide in a vacuum anywhere on earth. So, empty yourself of self, and you automatically fill with God."

You can serve God, but not in a vacuum. You will not find him there. Your job is to ask him to empty you of self; then he can fill you with himself. And that is where life really gets fun!

Recovery Step: Empty yourself of self. Fill yourself with God.

Life Change
December 18

Rarely does life change occur void of brokenness.

John Calvin said, "Only those who have learned well to be earnestly dissatisfied with themselves, and to be confounded with shame at their wickedness truly understand the Christian Gospel."

Rarely does life change occur void of brokenness.

When God's children refused to bow to him, he pronounced a plague of locusts. But being the God that he is, he also said that if they repented of their ways and committed to true life change, there was hope beyond what they deserved. God said, "Even now, return to me with all your heart, with fasting and weeping and mourning" (Joel 2:12).

Rarely does life change occur void of brokenness.

John Newton said it like this: "My grand point in preaching is to break the hard heart, and to heal the broken one."

Rarely does life change occur void of brokenness.

Recovery Step: Let the damage of your addiction sink in. Take a moment to consider the cost it has brought to your life and to others. Let the pain of your actions bring brokenness to your heart. Why? Because rarely does life change occur void of such brokenness.

The Long Run
December 19

Czechoslovakian runner Emil Zatopek, winner of three gold medals at the 1952 Summer Olympics in Helsinki, said, "If you want to run, run a mile. If you want to experience a different life, run a marathon."

Recovery is a journey, not a destination.

Luke 11:9 says, "And so I tell you, keep on asking, and you will receive what you ask for. Keep on seeking, and you will find. Keep on knocking, and the door will be opened to you. For everyone who asks, receives. Everyone who seeks, finds. And to everyone who knocks, the door will be opened."

We must be willing to ask for help. And we can't ask for help just once and be done with it. We must be persistent and ask repeatedly as the needs arise. When we practice Step Seven in this way, we can be assured that our loving heavenly Father will respond by giving us good gifts and removing our shortcomings.

Recovery is a journey, not a destination.

Anyone can find sobriety for a few hours or days, even weeks or months. It's called "white knuckling it." But true recovery is a marathon. So keep asking for recovery. Keep seeking recovery. Keep knocking on God's door. Answers will come if you don't drop out of the race.

Recovery Step: Recovery is all about persistence. Stay in the race, and you will win.

You Need Friends
December 20

Dr. Susan Whitbourne wrote a wonderful book on relationships titled *15 Reasons You Need Friends*. Her premise is simple. She writes, "You are a product of your friends."

Think about that – you are a product of your friends. Many of us have spent thousands of dollars on our education. Some commit countless hours to the gym. Others are meticulous about their diets. Many define themselves by their job, their income, or their house, car, or boat. They spend money they don't have to buy things they don't need to impress people they don't like.

But the real difference maker – in life and recovery – is friendships.

Chuck Swindoll likes to say, "There are two things that will determine the difference between where you are today and where you will be one year from now – the books you read and the people you spend time with."

Establishing friendships that will help you navigate successful recovery does not happen by accident. Real friendships are intentional.

The old prophet Amos asked, "Do two men walk together unless they have made an appointment?" (Amos 3:3).

You need to make an appointment with people who will feed your recovery. Pray for God to direct you to such people. You may find them at church, in a small group, or in a 12-step meeting. Wherever you find them, find them! Why? Because you are a product of your friends.

Recovery Step: Ask God to direct you to a few friends who will help feed your recovery.

A New Perspective
December 21

Dr. Michael Barta has offered a new perspective with his groundbreaking book, *TINSA*. Barta's treatment for sex addiction recovery is the subject of this book. TINSA stands for Trauma Induced Sexual Addiction. Barta writes, "I later learned that long-term substantial recovery from addiction was not possible without finding and resolving the root cause of my addictive behaviors."

Dr. Michael Herkov agrees: "The most difficult issue involves facing the guilt, shame, and depression associated with this illness."

Barta and Herkov argue that any treatment of sex addiction must heavily consider the deep-seated emotions of abandonment, isolation, shame, and depression. Successful treatment cannot be based on condemnation or judgment.

Jack Morin, in his book, *Erotic Mind*, wrote, "If you go to war with your sexuality you will lose and cause more chaos than you started."

Let's summarize. God is for sex. And God is for you. Your sexuality is not your problem; the trauma and emotions that shaped you are.

But know this – there is hope. Paul, no stranger to emotional trauma himself, wrote, "Do not lose heart, but though our outer man is decaying, yet our inner man is being renewed day by day" (2 Corinthians 4:16).

So what's the answer? Bring your shame, your guilt, your trauma, and your greatest, most painful hurts to your God. He stands ready to receive, renew, and restore.

Recovery Step: Whatever the pain, bring it to the God who cares.

What God Allows
December 22

Behind every great success story is a history of failure. The only person who has not failed their God and hurt those around them is the person you've never met. We have all failed. But failure does not define us. It never has. We are defined, not by failure, but by our *reaction* to failure.

Soichiro Honda, the founder of Honda Motor Company, wrote, "Success is 99 percent failure."

Few of us get recovery right the first time. It's like riding a bike. Until you have fallen a few times, you don't really learn how to do it.

The prophet said, "This is what the Lord says: You know if a man falls down, he gets up again. And if a man goes the wrong way, he turns around and comes back" (Jeremiah 8:4).

Unfortunately, some seem to have to fall harder than others in order to rebound. I am thankful we serve a God who is willing to let us step in it in order to recognize our need for help.

As Joni Eareckson Tada said, "God allows what he hates in order to accomplish what he loves."

Has your addiction cost you? Think of that as a down payment on sobriety. And it's well worth the price. Sure, you've fallen. But that's just the beginning of your story. The best part is still waiting to be written. And the good news is that the pen is in your hand.

Recovery Step: You can turn your failure to victory if you are willing to turn your heart to God. Sure, you've fallen. We all have. It's time to get up.

A Higher Standard
December 23

The Old Testament prophet Amos preached to the Northern Kingdom of Israel. Jeroboam was king of Israel and Uzziah was king of Judah. Amos lived at a time of great prosperity in the land. But this prosperity led to complacency, and complacency led to chronic sin. And though surrounded by eight carnal nations, the behavior of God's children had plunged to depths even lower than those surrounding peoples.

Amos spoke truth to power.

"The people of Damascus have sinned again and again, and I will not let them go unpunished" (Amos 1:3).

Amos went on to proclaim the same word of judgment upon each of the neighboring countries. But the sins of others did not exonerate the mistakes of God's chosen people.

You cannot blame others for your struggles. If you are a follower of Christ, you are held to a higher level.

A documentary about Walt Disney is shown at each of the Disney theme parks. It contains these words from the entertainment giant: "Held to a higher standard."

Disney is held to a higher standard. Christians are held to a higher standard. You are held to a higher standard. And like Israel, when you fall, there is no excuse. There is hope, forgiveness, and a second chance – but no excuse.

Recovery Step: As a Christ-follower, you are held to a higher standard. You can live in freedom and recovery. To accept less is to invite catastrophe. But it doesn't have to be that way.

Regoaling
December 24

Regoaling. It's a new word.

Dr. Shane Lopez, a senior scientist at Gallup and author of the 2013 book, *Making Hope Happen*, wrote, "Hope doesn't relate to IQ or to income. It is an equal opportunity resource." Then he cited the source of most addiction – trauma.

In order to find recovery, Lopez contends, the addict must deal with her trauma. How does she do this? He writes, "Healing comes by *regoaling*."

To *regoal* means to let go of old dreams and create new ones.

That is the crux of recovery. When we drag our old lives into recovery, we often make the incorrect presumption that none of this will really change the trajectory of our lives. We can continue with our same relationships, careers, and dreams. Recovery will just make the old better.

But for many of us, recovery is the death of our old dreams. We don't die, but our dreams do. When we allow our old dreams to die, God gives birth to new dreams.

Paul was a living example of this. Years after he came to Christ and put his old ways aside, he testified, "Being confident of this, that he who began a good work in you will carry it on to completion until the day of Christ Jesus" (Philippians 1:6).

Recovery Step: As you look forward, and not back, ask God to breathe new dreams into your life. Begin the process of *regoaling*.

The Most Wonderful Day
December 25

Today is Christmas – the most wonderful day of the year. It is a day of celebration, worship, and new beginnings. But mostly, today is a day of hope.

Canadian author Suzanne Benner writes, "Jesus did not come to *give us hope* as much as he came to *be our hope*."

Paul described Jesus as "our hope" (1 Timothy 1:1) and "the blessed hope" (Titus 2:13).

If ever there was a time when the world needed hope, this is that time. And if ever there was a group who needed hope, we are that group – those of us who suffer from sexual brokenness and compulsive sexual activities.

John W. Kennedy, the news editor at Pentecostal Evangel News, cites a recent study of 487 men. This study, commissioned by New York University, found that 59 percent of American men view porn at least once a week.

Let that sink in – 59 percent.

Sadly, we know from research conducted by *Proven Men* and others, porn addiction is as rampant in the church as it is outside the church.

So what is the answer? It is the same answer that has treated the dilemma of man's heart for thousands of years. The answer is hope. And that hope is found in Jesus Christ, whose birth we celebrate today – the most wonderful day of the year.

Recovery Step: Celebrate the most wonderful day by giving your life to the most wonderful Savior who came to give you a most wonderful hope.

Babe Ruth
December 26

In 1926, Johnny Sylvester got kicked in the head by a horse. The wound got badly infected. Doctors told his parents the bad news. Johnny would die.

"I wish I could see Babe Ruth wallop a homer before I die," Johnny told his parents.

So they sent a telegram to the great slugger of the New York Yankees. And Babe Ruth sent an answer. He would hit a homer just for Johnny in the next game.

Johnny Sylvester instantly became one of the most famous boys in baseball history, as Babe Ruth did not just hit one homer that day; he hit three! It was an incredible gift to a young boy.

But let's get back to his injury. Were the doctors right? Did Johnny Sylvester die?

Yes, they were right. Johnny did die – at the age of 74.

Babe Ruth was a legend. He still is. Perhaps it was his inspiration that led Johnny Sylvester to become one of America's great business executives. We can learn from that. Inspire someone today. You never know when their last days will come. But God does.

Johnny Sylvester's story eventually ended like all of our stories end – in death. But even that can be a good thing, as John wrote, "Blessed are the dead who die in the Lord" (Revelation 14:13).

Do what the Babe did. Find someone who is hurting – perhaps in the midst of their addiction. Offer encouragement to them. Believe in them, and they just might believe in themselves.

Recovery Step: Offer encouragement to someone God brings into your life today.

Build a Canal
December 27

When dealing with critics, learn the lesson from the building of the Panama Canal. The builder of the canal was besieged with criticism. When asked how he was going to handle his critics, he said, "I'm going to build a canal."

Don't get sidetracked in your recovery if you know you're on the right track. When the critic says you'll never get well, you have only one reasonable response – get well.

If you are old enough to read this, you are old enough to know that every person who is attempting to achieve something worthwhile will meet the challenge of criticism. Washington, Lincoln, Kennedy, Reagan – they all faced a multitude of critics.

So did a particular Messiah you've probably heard of. No, criticism is no guarantee that you are off track. But a total lack of criticism probably is!

The Bible says of Jesus, "When they hurled their insults at him, he did not retaliate; when he suffered, he made no threats" (1 Peter 2:23).

There will be those who tell you that you aren't serious enough, committed enough, or good enough to overcome lust. And that's okay because what matters is not what others are saying, but what you are doing.

When the critic says you can't achieve recovery, there's only one way to silence him. Achieve recovery.

Recovery Step: You will never achieve recovery by listening to those who say you will never achieve recovery. So ignore the critic and get to work.

The Refuge of God
December 28

The Bible tells us the story of an amazing woman named Ruth. Her husband had died, so from that point on she faithfully cared for her mother-in-law. To do so, Ruth gladly left her homeland to live among people she did not know. This caught the eye of a wealthy man named Boaz, who blessed her greatly.

Boaz said to Ruth, "May the Lord repay you for what you have done. May you be richly rewarded by the Lord, the God of Israel, under whose wings you have come to take refuge" (Ruth 2:12).

For those who are willing to sacrifice their lives for the sake of others – as Ruth did – God offers a refuge of protection.

Josh Philpot, of Founders Church in Spring, Texas, wrote an article posted on *Desiring God.* In *Troubled Heart, Take Refuge in God*, Philpot wrote, "When I look back at my life, I realize that God's hand – his refuge – protected me from myself and the consequences of my sin."

God is in the business of protecting us from others – and from ourselves. So be a Ruth. There is someone in your life who needs help. They need *your* help. You have what they need – sobriety and recovery. So take the risk and get outside of yourself. Give of yourself to this person, while trusting in the protection and refuge of God for yourself.

Recovery Step: Let your recovery take you places you never expected to go. Like Ruth, commit to being a blessing to someone who needs you today.

The Blessing of Hard Times
December 29

Perhaps you feel abandoned and all alone. It's what the Bible calls the wilderness. But it doesn't have to be bad.

The minor prophet Hosea knew what it was to live life in the wilderness. And his God knew what it was to be there with him. "I took care of you in the wilderness, in that dry and thirsty land" (Hosea 13:5).

Writing for the Christian Broadcasting Network, William D. Black identified seven ways God uses tough times to shape our lives.

Tough times prove our identity in Christ.
Tribulation strengthens our faith.
Tribulation defines our sense of purpose.
The wilderness proves our obedience.
Hard times force us to lean on God.
Difficulties produce maturity.
Tough times hone our focus on what matters.

Your addiction has landed you in the wilderness of life. Or your spouse's addiction has done so. Perhaps you are in early recovery, but not sensing the benefits of sobriety – yet. That's okay. Stay at it. Remember, whenever you walk through the wilderness, you may walk in pain. You may walk in doubt. You may walk in frustration. But you will never walk alone.

Recovery Step: God loves you and is happy to walk with you – anywhere. Wilderness included.

Where Healing Begins
December 30

The final chapter of the final book of the Old Testament offers hope for the addict. "For you who revere my name, the sun of righteousness will rise with healing in its rays" (Malachi 4:2).

Every addict is in need of healing. The question is, where does that healing begin? Answers abound.

Elton John said, "Music has healing power."

Yoko Ono suggested, "Healing yourself is connected with healing others."

Hippocrates contended, "Healing is a matter of time."

Nicholas Kristoff weighed in, "The wilderness is healing."

And Dena Ornish argued, "Awareness is the first step in healing."

So who is right? I suppose that on some level, they all are. In most stories of healing and restoration, you find a little music, interpersonal connection, the passage of time, a period in the wilderness, and a sense of awareness.

But don't forget God. If you are in need of healing today – for your soul, from your habit, in a relationship – remember the ultimate source. Keep coming back to the one whose light provides "healing in its rays."

Recovery Step: All humans are broken and in need of healing. For you, that healing can begin today. You just need to know where to look. The next step is yours.

The Secret Sauce
December 31

Hope. It's the secret sauce of recovery – for both the addict and the spouse.

Paul prayed for the church, "May the God of hope fill you with all joy and peace as you trust in him, so that you may overflow with hope by the power of the Holy Spirit" (Romans 15:13).

Helen Keller knew a little about hope. She said, "Optimism is the faith that leads to achievement. Nothing can be done without hope and confidence."

Even academia has embraced the value of hope. Dr. John Maltby, a psychologist at Leicester University, tracked college students over three years and found that the more hopeful students went on to greater academic success. Maltby discovered that hope was even better at predicting academic achievement than intelligence, personality, or previous academic achievement. (*Journal in Personality*, 2010).

If you are suffering from porn or sex addiction today, there is hope. If you are married to such a person, there is hope for you, as well. And here's the good news – *hope is free*.

If Dr. Maltby's study had found that the key to success was intelligence, personality, or academic achievement, a lot of us would be in trouble. But he said the key is hope. More importantly, God says the key is hope.

So receive the benefit of Paul's prayer. "May the God of hope fill you with joy and peace as you trust in him" today.

Recovery Step: Embrace hope. It's the secret sauce to recovery.

BIBLICAL REFERENCES

Genesis 1:27 (July 17)
Genesis 1:31 (February 1)
Genesis 9:21-22 (July 18)
Genesis 12:1 (April 10)
Genesis 14:12 (March 1)
Genesis 23:2 (February 6)
Genesis 35:19-21 (May 12)

Exodus 3:14 (June 22)
Exodus 20:9 (February 8)
Exodus 34:12 (October 25)

Leviticus 4:2 (August 13)
Leviticus 26:13 (August 28)

Numbers 5:7 (August 9)
Numbers 13:32 (September 22)
Numbers 14:18 (October 2)

Deuteronomy 11:1 (July 6)
Deuteronomy 15:11 (March 16)
Deuteronomy 29:15 (August 4)
Deuteronomy 30:15 (October 22)
Deuteronomy 31:8 (November 1)

Joshua 1:2 (April 29)
Joshua 1:2 (August 15)
Joshua 3:16 (March 8)

Joshua 4:7 (August 17)
Joshua 6:2 (September 25)
Joshua 6:18 (March 26)
Joshua 7:21 (April 7)
Joshua 24:15 (July 14)

Judges 11:29-32 (May 25)
Judges 13:1 (July 1)
Judges 14:2-3 (March 15)
Judges 16:17 (September 9)

Ruth 2:12 (December 28)
Ruth 4:15 (December 2)

1 Samuel 2:26 (January 3)
1 Samuel 12:24 (May 18)
1 Samuel 13:7 (February 13)
1 Samuel 14:27 (February 10)
1 Samuel 17:47 (May 5)
1 Samuel 18:1, 3 (November 7)

2 Samuel 1:26 (January 23)
2 Samuel 9:1 (July 3)
2 Samuel 11:3 (August 1)
2 Samuel 12:24 (December 4)
2 Samuel 13:15 (February 12)
2 Samuel 14:13-14 (June 5)
2 Samuel 22:2 (September 29)
2 Samuel 24:14 (November 20)

1 Kings 3:9 (March 29)

1 Kings 14:3 (November 26)
1 Kings 19:10 (September 23)

2 Kings 2:15 (July 11)
2 Kings 4:7 (April 18)
2 Kings 5:10, 14 (February 19)
2 Kings 13:2 (November 10)

1 Chronicles 12:32 (January 16)
1 Chronicles 15:7 (April 12)

2 Chronicles 6:1 (February 28)
2 Chronicles 12:1 (November 28)
2 Chronicles 12:7 (July 30)
2 Chronicles 13:7 (June 19)
2 Chronicles 15:3 (June 26)
2 Chronicles 15:7 (July 8)
2 Chronicles 20:17 (September 5)

Ezra 3:10 (February 17)
Ezra 10:4 (January 17)

Nehemiah 2:18 (November 4)
Nehemiah 4:6 (April 20)
Nehemiah 9:2 (October 4)

Esther 2:17 (October 20)
Esther 4:16 (June 11)

Job 2:13 (April 4)
Job 6:24 (October 6)

Job 14:1-4 (December 11)
Job 42:12 (September 13)

Psalm 5:11 (May 30)
Psalm 6:6 (March 12)
Psalm 16:11 (October 17)
Psalm 19:1, 4 (May 8)
Psalm 23:4 (August 11)
Psalm 25:8 (November 20)
Psalm 25:11 (June 13)
Psalm 27:1 (March 19)
Psalm 27:10 (November 19)
Psalm 28:7 (September 26)
Psalm 32:2 (February 21)
Psalm 32:3 (April 9)
Psalm 32:8 (February 15)
Psalm 32:9 (October 30)
Psalm 65:3 (June 8)
Psalm 81:4-6 (December 1)
Psalm 82:5 (April 1)
Psalm 91:1-2 (May 21)
Psalm 94:11 (April 27)
Psalm 103:10-12 (November 8)
Psalm 103:13 (April 22)
Psalm 103:14 (May 1)
Psalm 118:5 (January 20)
Psalm 123:1 (August 5)
Psalm 138:8 (September 2)
Psalm 139:14 (October 14)

Proverbs 3:5-6 (June 20)

Proverbs 6:17 (February 5)
Proverbs 6:23 (April 15)
Proverbs 7:22 (September 30)
Proverbs 8:13 (March 21)
Proverbs 8:22 (December 12)
Proverbs 12:11 (June 15)
Proverbs 13:20 (January 14)
Proverbs 14:23 (January 9)
Proverbs 15:13 (May 17)
Proverbs 15:22 (February 22)
Proverbs 16:3 (October 12)
Proverbs 18:1 (May 16)
Proverbs 19:1 (December 6)
Proverbs 21:26 (May 24)
Proverbs 24:16 (October 11)
Proverbs 26:11 (December 15)
Proverbs 28:18 (May 19)

Ecclesiastes 1:14 (May 23)
Ecclesiastes 1:19 (January 10)
Ecclesiastes 4:9-10 (August 31)
Ecclesiastes 4:12 (April 2)
Ecclesiastes 5:10 (January 18)
Ecclesiastes 7:8 (November 18)
Ecclesiastes 7:20 (September 15)
Ecclesiastes 10:18 (August 6)
Ecclesiastes 11:4 (November 15)
Ecclesiastes 12:13-14 (January 25)

Song of Solomon 3:11 (October 28)
Song of Solomon 3:11 (December 16)

Isaiah 6:6-7 (July 12)
Isaiah 29:15 (September 14)
Isaiah 40:31 (September 11)
Isaiah 43:18 (September 16)
Isaiah 43:19 (April 26)
Isaiah 45:7 (May 10)
Isaiah 57:15 (December 13)
Isaiah 65:17 (November 24)

Jeremiah 8:4 (December 22)
Jeremiah 9:23 (June 2)
Jeremiah 29:11 (March 27)
Jeremiah 31:3 (January 7)
Jeremiah 33:6 (January 27)
Jeremiah 50:19 (August 24)

Lamentations 3:20-21 (March 2)
Lamentations 3:26 (October 10)

Ezekiel 18:4 (March 13)
Ezekiel 18:20 (January 11)
Ezekiel 33:7 (May 6)
Ezekiel 37:5 (July 20)

Daniel 6:16 (March 31)
Daniel 11:42 (July 25)

Hosea 3:1, 3 (May 27)
Hosea 10:12 (February 27)
Hosea 10:12 (March 24)

Hosea 13:5 (December 29)

Joel 2:12 (December 18)
Joel 2:25 (August 25)

Amos 1:3 (December 23)
Amos 3:3 (December 20)
Amos 4:12 (September 20)
Amos 9:14 (August 21)

Obadiah 15 (July 22)

Jonah 1:2, 3:1 (June 29)
Jonah 4:7-8 (October 16)

Micah 1:8 (June 24)

Nahum 1:7 (December 9)

Habakkuk 3:17-18 (March 6)

Zephaniah 1:17 (July 28)

Haggai 1:5 (August 22)
Haggai 1:6 (February 26)

Zechariah 5:3 (June 17)
Zechariah 9:12 (March 10)

Malachi 4:2 (December 30)

Matthew 4:1-2 (May 26)
Matthew 4:19 (May 22)
Matthew 5:1-2 (October 24)
Matthew 6:21 (May 7)
Matthew 7:5 (July 2)
Matthew 7:11 (January 15)
Matthew 7:12 (September 1)
Matthew 8:25 (August 2)
Matthew 11:28 (July 9)
Matthew 13:40 (September 21)
Matthew 14:29-31 (September 18)
Matthew 15:11 (April 11)
Matthew 16:18 (May 29)
Matthew 16:24 (March 17)
Matthew 17:1 (July 10)
Matthew 18:1 (July 27)
Matthew 22:37 (February 14)
Matthew 22:39 (October 7)
Matthew 24:33 (November 21)
Matthew 24:36-37 (March 22)
Matthew 24:44 (June 23)
Matthew 25:23 (September 17)
Matthew 25:25 (July 13)
Matthew 25:46 (July 15)
Matthew 26:6 (March 9)
Matthew 26:41 (September 27)

Mark 5:3 (August 18)
Mark 5:15 (February 2)
Mark 9:27 (November 2)
Mark 11:25 (January 22)

Mark 12:44 (March 18)
Mark 16:1 (August 3)
Mark 16:9 (October 8)

Luke 1:37 (October 15)
Luke 4:18-19 (March 5)
Luke 6:27 (November 17)
Luke 10:34 (April 17)
Luke 11:9 (December 19)
Luke 12:7 (April 19)
Luke 14:33 (August 7)
Luke 16:19 (August 16)
Luke 18:10-14 (March 30)
Luke 18:13 (June 6)
Luke 19:8 (October 19)
Luke 19:10 (September 4)
Luke 22:54-57 (November 14)

John 3:19 (July 31)
John 5:6 (March 3)
John 5:14 (April 25)
John 5:14 (May 4)
John 6:16-18 (November 27)
John 7:17 (July 5)
John 8:34 (September 24)
John 10:27 (August 23)
John 11:4 (February 3)
John 13:17 (March 28)
John 14:6 (May 31)
John 14:18 (April 8)
John 15:13 (September 6)

John 17:21 (September 28)
John 21:17 (April 14)

Acts 1:8 (October 9)
Acts 2:42 (January 1)
Acts 3:7 (June 18)
Acts 12:11 (July 26)
Acts 13:22 (April 13)
Acts 15:37-38 (August 26)

Romans 2:7 (November 12)
Romans 2:15 (December 7)
Romans 5:8 (April 16)
Romans 6:23 (October 29)
Romans 7:18 (April 23)
Romans 7:18 (May 2)
Romans 8:26 (June 27)
Romans 8:28 (December 8)
Romans 8:31 (November 16)
Romans 12:9 (January 28)
Romans 12:15 (November 13)
Romans 13:14 (January 4)
Romans 15:4 (August 20)
Romans 15:13 (December 31)

1 Corinthians 1:10 (June 30)
1 Corinthians 2:2 (August 29)
1 Corinthians 3:9 (November 6)
1 Corinthians 6:12 (April 24)
1 Corinthians 6:12 (May 3)
1 Corinthians 6:18 (January 29)

1 Corinthians 9:24-25 (August 8)
1 Corinthians 10:12 (January 5)
1 Corinthians 10:13 (January 19)
1 Corinthians 15:56 (February 20)

2 Corinthians 1:8 (August 19)
2 Corinthians 2:5-8 (September 7)
2 Corinthians 3:17 (November 11)
2 Corinthians 4:16 (December 21)
2 Corinthians 5:10 (August 27)
2 Corinthians 5:17 (November 29)
2 Corinthians 9:8 (April 30)
2 Corinthians 10:5 (October 31)
2 Corinthians 13:3 (October 18)

Galatians 5:1 (August 10)
Galatians 5:13 (January 30)
Galatians 5:16 (July 29)
Galatians 5:19 (November 23)
Galatians 5:22-23 (March 7)
Galatians 6:4 (January 12)
Galatians 6:8 (April 28)
Galatians 6:9 (August 12)

Ephesians 1:4 (November 30)
Ephesians 2:3 (June 3)
Ephesians 2:8 (January 8)
Ephesians 3:20 (May 28)
Ephesians 4:26 (March 14)
Ephesians 4:26 (August 30)
Ephesians 4:31 (September 19)

Ephesians 5:25 (September 8)

Philippians 1:6 (December 24)
Philippians 2:5 (June 28)
Philippians 3:10 (November 22)
Philippians 3:12 (June 14)
Philippians 3:13 (December 14)
Philippians 4:6 (July 23)
Philippians 4:8 (January 31)

Colossians 1:11 (July 7)
Colossians 1:13 (September 12)
Colossians 1:23 (September 3)
Colossians 3:1 (November 25)
Colossians 3:5 (January 2)
Colossians 3:13 (December 10)
Colossians 3:21 (November 9)
Colossians 3:23 (December 5)

1 Thessalonians 4:3 (May 20)
1 Thessalonians 4:17 (March 20)
1 Thessalonians 5:17 (June 1)

2 Thessalonians 1:11 (June 4)
2 Thessalonians 3:13 (February 25)

1 Timothy 1:1 (December 25)
1 Timothy 6:12 (October 27)

2 Timothy 2:5 (February 9)
2 Timothy 2:22 (April 5)

2 Timothy 4:11 (February 24)

Titus 1:16 (October 26)
Titus 2:12 (December 17)
Titus 2:13 (December 25)
Titus 3:4-5 (June 21)

Philemon 16 (July 19)

Hebrews 2:17 (February 16)
Hebrews 10:17 (June 25)
Hebrews 10:25 (January 21)
Hebrews 11:6 (February 23)
Hebrews 11:25 (May 11)
Hebrews 13:5 (March 25)
Hebrews 13:16 (August 14)

James 1:7 (October 5)
James 1:22 (February 4)
James 1:23-24 (November 3)
James 1:27 (July 4)
James 2:10 (June 16)
James 4:7 (January 24)
James 4:17 (July 16)
James 5:19-20 (January 26)

1 Peter 1:4 (June 9)
1 Peter 1:7 (September 10)
1 Peter 2:9 (May 15)
1 Peter 2:11 (February 18)
1 Peter 2:21 (December 3)

1 Peter 2:23 (December 27)
1 Peter 3:9 (October 21)
1 Peter 4:4 (October 1)
1 Peter 4:8 (May 13)
1 Peter 5:8 (March 23)
1 Peter 5:10 (January 13)
1 Peter 5:10 (July 24)

2 Peter 1:5-6 (April 6)
2 Peter 2:19 (November 5)
2 Peter 2:22 (February 7)

1 John 1:8 (May 14)
1 John 1:9 (March 11)
1 John 3:14 (July 21)
1 John 4:20 (June 10)
1 John 5:4 (May 9)
1 John 5:21 (October 23)

2 John 8 (January 6)

3 John 2 (March 4)

Jude 23 (April 3)
Jude 24 (October 3)

Revelation 2:4 (June 12)
Revelation 3:16 (June 7)
Revelation 3:20 (February 11)
Revelation 14:13 (December 26)
Revelation 20:12 (October 13)
Revelation 21:4 (April 21)

ABOUT THE AUTHOR

Mark Denison is a native Texan, raised in Houston. Though born into a supportive middle-class family, Mark was not raised in the Christian faith. He discovered Christ as a teenager, through the bus ministry of a local church. At the age of 15, Mark responded to God's call to ministry, and he began his formal training at Houston Baptist University, where he earned a Bachelor's Degree with a double major in Christianity and Speech. Mark would later earn Master's in Divinity and Doctor of Ministry degrees (M.Div., D.Min.) from Southwestern Baptist Theological Seminary in Ft. Worth.

While in college, Mark met Beth, whom he would marry shortly after graduation. Together, they planted Baybrook Baptist Church in the Houston area, and served there for 18 years. His other pastorates included First Baptist, Gainesville, Texas, and First Baptist, Conroe, Texas. While pastoring for 31 years, Mark also served as a chaplain to the Houston Rockets, chaplain to the Texas Senate and House of Representatives, and he served on the Board at HBU for 15 years – three years as chair – and wrote *The Daily Walk*. His other responsibilities included service on numerous denominational, educational, and institutional boards.

In 2014, Mark and Beth moved to Florida, where they began preparation to launch a national ministry, *There's Still Hope*. As a recovering addict himself, Mark knows the destruction sex and porn addiction can bring to a person, his family, and the church. Before launching this ministry in early 2018, Mark went back to school, earning a Master's Degree in Addiction Recovery from Liberty University.

Mark is a frequent writer for Covenant Eyes, a speaker at major events, and provides personal coaching and other resources to schools, churches, pastors, and other individuals. In addition to *The Daily Walk*, Mark has authored two other books on recovery, *Porn in the Pew* and *90-Day Guide to Recovery*. Mark and Beth are proud parents of one son, David, who is also involved in ministry.

For more information on Mark and his ministry, visit his website at TheresStillHope.org.

ABOUT *THERE'S STILL HOPE*

Mark and Beth Denison founded *There's Still Hope* to be a comprehensive Christ-centered sexual addiction recovery ministry. With a focus on addicts, spouses, churches, and pastors, TSH has quickly become a leading resource for those who struggle with sexually compulsive activities and for church leaders who want to provide help for their members. The ministry offers multiple recovery tools for those in need.

Mark is uniquely equipped to minister to those who struggle. A recovering addict himself, he has earned a Master's in Addiction Recovery, in addition to his three other degrees: B.A., M.Div., and D.Min. Beth is certified as a Spouse Recovery Coach through the ministry of Dr. Doug Weiss.

There's Still Hope offers one-day intensives for couples, personal coaching for addicts and spouses, and customized 90-day recovery plans, in addition to spouse recovery groups and one-year maintenance plans. The ministry also offers a 40-day plan to break free of pornography and a one-day program for churches called "Pancakes & Porn."

Churches may partner with TSH on many levels, providing them access to dozens of resources. For those seeking a daily connection with God and a relevant message on recovery, Mark writes *Recovery Minute* – a daily devotion, which is sent out by email every morning.

To sign up for *Recovery Minute* or to access any of the other resources from TSH, go to the ministry website at TheresStillHope.org.

ADDITIONAL RESOURCES

Twelve-Step Programs for Sex Addiction

Sexaholics Anonymous (www.sa.org)
Sex Addicts Anonymous (www.sexaa.org)
Sex and Love Addicts Anonymous (www.slaafws.org)
Sexual Recovery Anonymous (www.sexualrecovery.org)
Castimonia (www.castimonia.org)

Twelve-Step Programs for Spouses of Sex Addicts

S-ANON (www.sanon.org)
Co-Dependents of Sex Addicts (www.cosa.recovery.org)

Intensive Outpatient Sex Addiction Services

Hope Quest (www.hopequest.org)
Hope & Freedom Counseling Services (www.hopeandfreedom.com)
Sexual Recovery Institute (www.sexualrecovery.com)

Christ-Centered Workshops

Bethesda (www.bethesdaworkshops.org)
Faithful & True (www.faithfulandtrue.com)
Be Broken Ministries (www.bebroken.com)

www.ingramcontent.com/pod-product-compliance
Lightning Source LLC
Chambersburg PA
CBHW070733170426
43200CB00007B/514